MASTERS OF
SUCCESS

PROVEN TECHNIQUES FOR ACHIEVING
SUCCESS IN BUSINESS AND LIFE

IVAN R. MISNER, PH.D.

DON MORGAN, M.S.

EP
Entrepreneur.
Press

Editorial Director: Jere L. Calmes
Cover Design: Perlman & Peterson Design
Composition and Production: Eliot House Productions

This publication is designed to provide accurate and authoritative information in regard to
the subject matter covered. It is sold with the understanding that the publisher is not
engaged in rendering legal, accounting, or other professional services. If legal advice or
other expert assistance is required, the services of a competent professional person should
be sought.

—From a Declaration of Principles jointly adopted by a
Committee of the American Bar Association and
a Committee of Publishers and Associations

Library of Congress Cataloging-in-Publication
Masters of success/[edited by Ivan R. Misner and Don Morgan.
    p.   cm.
    ISBN 1-932156-79-8
    1. Success. I. Misner, Ivan R., 2956– II. Morgan, Don, 1946–
    BJ1611.M36 2004
    158.1—dc22   2003064310

Printed in Canada

11 10 09 08 07 06 05 04   10 9 8 7 6 5 4 3 2 1

Contents

Acknowledgements

Many contributors to this book showed us all how to turn humble beginnings into extraordinary finales. Each person who offered insight into the success process added inspiration and guidance to the finished story. Our book gained ground with each contribution, helping us to fill in the success mosaic.

We are also grateful to Gail Gilman and Mark Wright, whose editing added impact to the success stories from our contributing authors. We would particularly like to thank Jeff Morris and Karen Billipp, whose editorial skills made a manuscript into a book.

Our appreciation is also extended to LeAnne Harvey and Jere Calmes of Entrepreneur Press, whose foresight allowed this project to move forward from idea to finished product, and to Mike Drew, who introduced us to Entrepreneur.

We also wish to thank our wives and children for their ongoing support during the many months we were locked away in our offices writing this book.

Finally, we want to thank the many people whose stories are featured in this book and who courageously faced life's challenges with the optimistic understanding that the uncommon application of common knowledge will pave the way to extraordinary success.

—Ivan R. Misner and Don Morgan

Preface

There may be nothing more haunting than seeing severe disappointment, hurt, or misery in someone close to you. Such views are tormenting because as humans, we value success, good health, and self-satisfaction. It distresses us when we encounter abject lack of success in others, or ourselves, because we are wired to aim for the better things in life.

Success, or the lack of it, is a huge factor in our lives. We admire and sometimes even envy success in others. We dedicate a major portion of our lives to helping our children and those closest to us experience the "best of success." As a matter of fact, we seem so preoccupied with the success phenomena that its pursuit almost assumes a spiritual quality. Great thinkers and orators of our times and past have dedicated their energy to telling us how to be successful in both their writings and speeches. With all that's been written and said, you may wonder, "…another book on success?"

We learn most about life from others who go before us. The act of "learning at the feet of masters" is historically recorded in the world's great primers on religion such as the Bible, the Koran, and the Torah, and this method still works well! Rather than tell you what we, the authors, feel is your best route to success, we bring you real life stories about others who are becoming successful or, by all usual measures of success, have achieved some mastery of it. Many of these realistic stories are about normal people like you and me. Each person adds an integral piece to the jigsaw puzzle of success that guides us toward more of our own success. In addition, we've integrated these stories with many contributions from people who are well-known around the world and are arguably "masters" of success in their respective fields.

In the beginning of every chapter is an introduction to suggest a major life orientation to master during our lifetime. We assembled stories behind each of the chapter introductions to add credible encouragement for gaining mastery over what amounts to pretty simple things. Get passionate, set goals, be energetic and systematic, don't let adversity and risk stop you, build a reputation as a helping person, and use the right tools for the job at hand.

OK. We just gave the punch line away. But what seems simple is often the hardest to internalize. If success mastery is your goal, you must read on because these major orientations come from those who already are living successful lives.

Let's say that you will learn something about the architectural design for your successful life from this book about masters of success. Even more impressive would be for you to improve the blueprint and implementation of your exceptional success. Once this happens, let us know. Our goal for this book will have been successful. Our wish is for you to experience incredible and remarkable success.

Dive in, and may you gain huge inspiration from those who have gone before.

—Ivan R. Misner and Don Morgan

———•-•-•———

The best time to plant a tree . . . was 20 years ago.
The second best time is today.
—CHINESE PROVERB

Dedication

———•◦•———

Jean Paul Sartre once wrote, "One always dies too soon—or too late, and yet one's whole life is complete at that moment, with a line drawn neatly under it ready for the summing up."

This book is dedicated to the memory of Ron Hain, a contributing author to this book, business associate, and friend. The sum of his life can be measured by the many people he positively impacted throughout his lifetime. He will be missed.

—Ivan R. Misner

I am grateful for my wife and our children, who unknowingly encouraged me to work diligently on this project. My admiration for Annie Robinson Seales' dedicated focus on rebuilding her life after a horrific accident added further impetus to finishing the project. Our BNI staff helped keep the programs alive and moving forward while the mind and body was otherwise occupied. Ivan Misner receives my utmost thanks for being the catalyst bringing together this project to gel in a written monument for successful people throughout the world.

—Don Morgan

Success Comes from Within

All the resources we need are in the mind.

—THEODORE ROOSEVELT

We live, on average, about 75 years. That's some 657,000 hours—a substantial but finite resource of time that we can use to plan, pursue, achieve—and, with luck—enjoy a successful life. Time enough for anybody to achieve success, right?

Well, yes and no. We all know that some achieve success big-time, others in a more modest way, and many not at all—or so it would seem. For every name of world renown, there are thousands of successful people—friends, neighbors, relatives—who set their sights on something, plan their actions, then pursue and achieve their goals. We think of many people who are familiar to us as successful, and by the objective standard of setting and achieving goals, they certainly are. The others? We don't hear of any success in their lives—but we don't really know, do we?

We all use our allotted time differently. Those with natural talent, a generous and benign environment, and a certain fire in the belly tend to be the ones whose glowing stories we see in the mass media, especially when their success turns sour—but many of these succeed against long odds. The successful individual we know personally, who is not so well known to the world, we often don't think of as a "success"—she's just Norma, that nice lady who runs the nail parlor and has six terrific grandchildren whose mothers and dads all show up at Thanksgiving. And then there's Joe, the guy who spent five years in the pen and is now hammering nails, who is nobody's role model.

No matter what we call it, we all pursue success. We all have desires and strive to achieve them. Our desires may be different from anyone else's, and we may not consider achieving them to be "success." We look around and see people whose success we envy. What is Jake doing with his supply of hours that puts him so far ahead of me in money, friends, and influence? Why is he successful, and why am I not? Why is he flying his own Learjet while I'm rattling around in this two-year-old Jaguar? Why is she living in a new house and raising three perfect children while I'm still looking for a mate? Why is that guy's cardboard box so much bigger than mine, and where did he get that king-size shopping cart?

But without knowing all the facts, without being inside the mind of the other person, you can't say whether that person is more successful than you. Maybe he's worth $100 million but is unhappy because his goal was to become governor by the age of 40 and he's growing tired of the frenetic pursuit of power. And maybe you are not as wealthy as you wanted to be, but on the other hand you've made it through great personal difficulties and are pleased to have kept your finances afloat and your family intact.

Which of you is more successful? Fulfilling any personal desire is success, by any reasonable definition, and you've achieved some very important and satisfying goals.

The measure of your success is how well you use your productive time to achieve the goals that are important to *you*. Not how you stack up compared to everybody else—but how well you've used your own abilities and resources to achieve worthy goals, however humble, for yourself and the people who are important to you. Who knows? That would-be governor may be watching you and saying to himself, "I'm a miserable failure. When did I decide money was more important than enjoying my work? Why didn't I stay off the fast track and spend more time with my kids? Why can't I take it easy and enjoy life like George is doing?"

Dictionaries define success as the achievement of something desired, planned, or attempted. But in real life, success is a slippery concept, especially when you come to your own personal definition of it. Success is a relative thing and highly personal. Many an exhausted high achiever has reached a lofty goal only to discover that it was a false peak, that the true summit loomed much higher. Others have reached the highest heights only to find them barren and empty and then realized the only way down was . . . down. Yet many a modest achiever has trekked through a lifetime of rocky trails and boggy swamps to realize, after all, what a glorious and rewarding trip it has been. And the ex-addict who's stacking lumber? Every day on the job can be a victory.

So now that you know how ephemeral this notion of success is, how do you go about achieving it? If you're looking for a generic formula, you won't find it—there is none. Success depends on timing, circumstances, situations, and—most important—your own perception of what success is. Nor is there a mathematical standard for measuring when and how thoroughly you've achieved it. There are many ways to measure success, but in the final analysis, it's how you measure it for yourself that truly counts.

No formula for success? Then why are we writing a book about it? Because even though there's no magic recipe, there are recurring themes that appear consistently in stories about successful people. By reading about these people, you can gain an understanding of what different people did in different circumstances to achieve what they personally defined as success. And that understanding can guide you intuitively toward achieving the things you desire.

You'll read about successful people—some you know, others you've never heard of—who knew what they wanted to be from the time they were children and others who achieved success almost by surprise or accident. You'll discover how success has been achieved through inspiration and determination. You'll meet people who have overcome great misfortune and disability to succeed and others who seem to have been born with inevitable success coursing through their veins. You'll find definitions of success ranging from victory over personal weaknesses all the way to reaching the world's highest peak. Most important, you'll find that in the final analysis, success involves the *uncommon application of common knowledge.*

In the essays that make up the rest of this first chapter, you'll find evidence that the idea of success is even more complicated than these stories might imply. John Gray argues that success is not so much what you achieve as it is a way of viewing your achievements; Brian Tracy tells us that, because of the fundamental law of cause and effect, "you become what you think about most of the time."

As you read the stories and essays throughout this book, pay special attention not only to the names you recognize but also to those you don't. These are the people whose lives are most like yours and from whom you stand to gain the most insight. Think about how their goals, attitudes, actions, principles, and experiences could be applied to your life, your work, your dreams. Study whatever strikes a chord and resonates in your mind. Take what you can learn from each success story, mix it all together, apply it in liberal doses to your own situation, and give your story its own successful ending.

There is, after all, a formula for success—and it's yours to write.

———•◦•———

With more than 15 million copies of his bestselling book Men Are from Mars, Women Are from Venus *in print, John Gray, Ph.D., is a respected authority on relationships and finding satisfaction. Getting more of the tangible rewards in life is only part of the story, he explains; the rest exists at a different level.*

OUTER SUCCESS MAGNIFIES OUR FEELINGS

JOHN GRAY

Money, recognition, marriage, children, a great job, terrific clothes, winning a lottery, or any other form of outer success is like a magnifying glass that is turned on your inner feelings. If you are already peaceful, you will feel more peaceful. If you are already happy and loving, you will be happier and more loving. If you are already confident, you will be more confident.

On the other hand, to the degree that you are not happy, the joy, love, confidence, or peace in your life will diminish. Without your first achieving personal success, "having more" will just complicate your life and create more problems. If you are not happy first, getting rich will not make you any happier.

If you are already happy and you know that you are not dependent on more money to be happy, greater wealth can make you happier. There is nothing wrong with wanting more money. The quest for more money limits us only when we forget that the real source of happiness is within. The secret of getting what you want and wanting what you have is first to learn how to be happy, loving, confident, and peaceful regardless of outer conditioning. Then, as you achieve more worldly success, you can become happier. If you first learn to be happy with what you already have, material success will follow in an appropriate manner according to what you really want in life.

The Illusion of External Success

The inherent promise of all external success is an illusion. When we are unhappy, we think a new car, a better job, or a loving partner will make us happier. Yet with each acquisition, the opposite effect is achieved.

When we are unhappy, we commonly think "having more" will take away our inner pain. But it doesn't. There is never enough. As we continue to feel unhappy "because we don't have more," the illusion of outer success is reinforced. Increasingly, we believe that we can't be happy unless we have more. These are some common examples:

- "I can't be happy until I have made a million dollars."
- "I can't be happy until my bills are paid."
- "I can't be happy unless my wife changes."
- "I can't be happy unless my husband is more attentive."
- "I can't be happy unless I have a better job."
- "I can't be happy unless I lose weight."
- "I can't be happy unless I win."
- "I can't be happy unless I am respected or appreciated."
- "I can't be happy with so much stress in my life."
- "I can't be happy because there is too much to do."
- "I can't be happy because there is not enough to do."

Initially, getting what we want appears to work, but after a short period of happiness, we are unhappy once again. As before, we mistakenly believe that having more will make us happy and take away our pain. Unfortunately, each time we look to outer success for fulfillment, we feel more emptiness inside. Instead of feeling greater joy and peace in our lives, we feel more turmoil and dissatisfaction.

Without personal success, the more we get, the more unhappy we become. Why is it that the tabloids are full of unhappy stories about the rich and famous? For many celebrities, fame and money bring only misery, drug addiction, divorce, violence, betrayal, and depression.

Their lives exemplify that external success can bring fulfillment only if we are already in touch with our internal positive feelings. Outer success can be a heaven or a hell, depending on the degree of personal success we have already achieved.

Personal Success Comes from Within

Personal success comes from within and is achieved when you are able not only to be yourself but also to love yourself. It is feeling confident, happy, and powerful in the process of doing what you want to do. Personal success involves not just achieving goals but also feeling grateful and satisfied with what you have after you get it. Without personal success, no matter who you are or how much you have, it will never be enough to make you happy.

To achieve personal success, we must first recognize the futility of making material success our highest priority. What good is it to achieve a goal and then feel it is not enough? What good is it to get what you have always wanted and then not want it anymore? What good is it to have millions of dollars and then look in the mirror and feel unlovable? What good is it to sing your song and have others love it but hate it inside? To find true and lasting happiness, we must make a small but very significant shift in our thinking. We must make achieving personal success and not material success our number-one priority.

Experiencing Happiness

Lasting happiness comes from within. Getting what you want can only make you happy to the degree that you are already happy. Doing something well and learning something new can only make you more powerful to the degree that you are already feeling confident. Loving others can only be sustained to the degree that you already love yourself. Peace, harmony, and time to relax in your life can only be found to the degree that you are already relaxed and peaceful. The outer world can only bring us waves of love, joy, power, and peace when we are already feeling it inside.

When you are already happy, what you get in life allows you to feel it. It is like lying comfortably in a warm bath. If you lie really still, you won't notice the warmth after a while. If you move around a little and stir things up, you will begin to feel <u>waves of warmth again</u>. To feel the warmth, two conditions must be met: you must be in the warm water, and you must experience some movement.

In a similar manner, to experience waves of happiness in life, we must already be happy and then experience the waves generated by getting what we want. If we are already happy, it doesn't take enormous material success to generate delicious and delightful waves of joy.

If you are lying in a bath connected to your inner power and confidence, by just moving around you will experience waves of confidence. When you are lying in a bath of love and peace, your interactions will bring you waves of love and peace.

On the other hand, if you are feeling unhappy, unloving, insecure, or stressed, your daily interactions will bring you waves of unhappiness, disappointment, and distress. No matter how successful you are in getting what you want, it will bring only misery and stress.

The Real Cause of Unhappiness

When outer success leaves us feeling unhappy, we conclude that the cause of our unhappiness is in not having the next thing. It is easy to make this mistake. Most of the time, when we are unhappy, we are wanting something. We automatically conclude that we are unhappy because we don't have what we want. This conclusion is incorrect.

As you achieve more personal success, you discover that wanting more and not getting it does not cause unhappiness. Instead, wanting more creates positive and happy feelings like passion, confidence, determination, courage, excitement, enthusiasm, faith, appreciation, gratitude, love—the list goes on. Wanting more is not the cause of unhappiness. When you are already happy and confident inside, wanting more and engaging yourself in the process of getting more creates waves of joy, love, confidence, and peace.

Desire or wanting more is the nature of the soul, mind, heart, and senses. The soul is always willing to be more; the mind is always seeking to do more and know more; the heart is always longing to love more and have more; and the senses are always wanting to enjoy more. If we are true to ourselves, we will always want more.

It is natural to want more love in our relationships. It is good to want more success in our work. It is normal to enjoy the pleasures of the senses and to want more. Wanting more is our natural state. There is nothing wrong with desire. Abundance, growth, love, pleasure, and the movement toward more are the nature of life.

Wanting more and having less is not the cause of our unhappiness. Unhappiness is simply the lack of inner joy and has nothing to do with our external condition. The real cause of unhappiness is the absence of joy. Unhappiness is similar to darkness. Darkness is the absence of light. The way to remove darkness is simply to turn on the lights. Likewise, our unhappiness lessens as we learn to turn on the light within ourselves.

When we are connected to or are in touch with our true nature, we are automatically happy. Why? Because who we are is already happy. Our true nature is already loving, joyful, confident, and peaceful. To find happiness, we must begin an inner journey to recover and remember who we really are. By looking inside ourselves, we will discover that the joy, love, power, and peace we are looking for are already there. Those qualities are who we already are.

From *How to Get What You Want and Want What You Have* by John Gray, copyright ©1998 by Mars Productions Inc. Reprinted by permission of HarperCollins Publishers Inc.

———•◦•———

A leading authority on human potential and personal effectiveness, Brian Tracy is a regular consultant to the Million Dollar Round Table, IBM, McDonnell Douglas, and other multinational organizations. Tracy offers important concepts to consider when charting a course for success.

———•◦•———

THE LAW OF CAUSE AND EFFECT

BRIAN TRACY

Everything happens for a reason; for every effect there is a specific cause.

Aristotle asserted that we live in a world governed by law, not chance. He stated that everything happens for a reason, whether or not we know what it is. He said that every effect has a specific cause or causes. Every cause or action has an effect of some kind, whether we can see it and whether we like it or not.

This is the granddaddy law, the "iron law" of Western thought, of Western philosophy. The relentless search for truth, for the causal relationships among events, has led to the rise of the West in science, technology, medicine, philosophy, and even warfare for more than 2,000 years. Today this focus is driving the technological advances that are changing our world so dramatically.

This law says that achievement, wealth, happiness, prosperity, and business success are all the direct and indirect effects or results of specific causes or actions. This simply means that if you can be clear about the effect or result you want, you can probably achieve it. You can study others who have achieved the same goal, and by doing what they did, you can get the same results.

Success Is Not an Accident

Success is not a miracle, nor is it a matter of luck. Everything happens for a reason, good or bad, positive or negative. When you are absolutely clear about what you want, you only need to copy others who have achieved it before you, and you will eventually get the same results that they have.

This is referred to in the Bible as the law of sowing and reaping, which says, "Whatsoever a man soweth, that also shall he reap."

Sir Isaac Newton called it the third law of motion. He said, "For every action, there is an equal and opposite reaction."

For you and me, the most important expression of this universal law is: "Thoughts are causes and conditions are effects."

Put another way, "Thought is creative." Your thoughts are the primary creative forces in your life. You create your entire world by the way you think. All the people and situations in your life have only the meaning you give them by the way you think about them. And when you change your thinking, you change your life, sometimes in seconds!

The most important principle of personal or business success is simply this: You become what you think about most of the time.

This is the great discovery upon which all religions, philosophies, metaphysics, schools of thought, and theories of psychology are based. This principle is as applicable to individuals as it is to groups of individuals and organizations. Whatever you see or experience is the expression of the thinking of the people behind the phenomenon. Ralph Waldo Emerson recognized this when he wrote, "Every great organization is merely the lengthened shadow of a single man."

It is not what happens to you but how you think about what happens to you that determines how you feel and react. It is not the world *outside* you that dictates your circumstances or conditions; it is the world *inside* you that creates the conditions of your life.

Your Choice, Your Life

You are always free to choose. In the long run, no one forces you to think, feel, or behave the way you do. Rather, you choose your emotions and behaviors by the way you choose to think about the world around you and about what is happening to you.

Dr. Martin Seligman, of the University of Pennsylvania, calls this way of reacting your "explanatory style." It is the way that you interpret or explain things to yourself. It is the critical determinant of everything you are and everything you become.

The good news is that your explanatory style is learned. This means that it can be unlearned as well. Your way of explaining things to yourself is under your control. You can interpret your experiences in such a way that you feel happy and optimistic rather than angry or frustrated. You can decide to react in such a way that your responses are constructive and effective. You are always free to choose.

Your thoughts and feelings are continually changing. They are quickly affected by the events around you. For example, when you receive a piece of good news, your attitude immediately brightens and you feel more positive toward everyone and everything. If, on the other hand, you unexpectedly receive some bad news, you can immediately become upset, angry, and short-tempered, even if the news is inaccurate or untrue. It is the way you interpret the event to yourself that determines how you react.

How You Can Apply this Law Immediately

1. Examine the most important parts of your life—your family, your health, your work, your financial situation—and observe the cause-effect relationship between what you think, say, feel, and do and the results you are getting. Be honest with yourself.

2. Analyze how you really think about yourself in relationship to the kind of life you are living. Be absolutely honest. Consider how your thoughts in each area are causing, creating, and maintaining the situation around you. What changes could you make in your thinking to improve the quality of some part of your life?

From *The 100 Absolutely Unbreakable Laws of Business Success* by Brian Tracy, copyright ©2000, 2002, Berrett-Koehle Publishers. Used by permission of Brian Tracy.

Follow Your Passion

Let nothing dim the light that shines from within.

—MAYA ANGELOU

Not too long ago—a mere century or two back—people who had to make a living by their own labor faced a limited number of life choices: farming, factory work, selling, cleaning, or—for the educated—law, medicine, politics, or the clergy. Those few who, without inherited wealth, charted their own course were the rare exceptions—such people as Christopher Columbus, Jonathan Swift, Napoleon Bonaparte, Abe Lincoln, Mark

13

Twain, John D. Rockefeller, and Mahatma Gandhi. If you were female or a member of an ethnic minority, your choices were even more limited, almost to the point of being nonexistent.

The dawn of the 21st century finds the developed world supporting a dominant, healthy middle class, each member of which can partake of a smorgasbord of choices. The growth of technology, especially ready access to information, has paralleled the spread of democratic values around the world. Education is accessible to nearly all; information flows copiously at the touch of a key. Technology lets a few farmers grow the world's food, and it creates millions of new ways for the rest of us to be productive. The technology available to us at little or no cost lets us design a uniquely personal way to contribute value to society and be compensated for it and to travel anywhere on the globe to do so.

Freedom of choice presents new dilemmas. How do we choose the style of living and working that best suits us? Each of us has a unique set of native skills, learning styles, and personality traits. Instead of being shoehorned into a few traditional productivity roles, we can, at least in principle, combine these talents with our freedom and find work to do that we like. When we do so, we often discover an enthusiasm about our work that we can transform into passion.

And this is important, because passion, like innovation, is a success multiplier. The passion of the innovator advances the technology that frees us from the old job constraints and adds value to society. The passion with which we pursue our own success is directly related to the freedoms created by the millions of people who were successful before us.

Passion—the hunger, the drive, the love, the fire in the belly—is key in the achievements of any person engaged in any endeavor. Passion is fuel for success. If you don't have it, you need to keep looking for something to get passionate about. When you don't enjoy what you're doing, you work more slowly, less efficiently, less creatively, and people with more positive energy pass you by. Nothing great in life has ever been done without a little bit of passion.

Make a determined start to gaining more control over your life and maximizing your chances of success. Start doing what you feel most comfortable doing, what you are good at, what you can do to contribute the most to your community and society. Do the things that keep you engaged, that make your time fly by, that seem to get done automatically while you are enjoying yourself. It's a continuum: enthusiasm gets you moving, passion helps you gain mastery, and desire keeps you in the game. Before you know it, your enthusiasm, your passion, and your white-hot desire will lead you to success.

The contributors to this chapter demonstrate the role of passion in achieving success. Their stories illustrate the many roads to finding the passion that drives people to succeed. Some found that passion early and steered by this bright star; others found it almost by accident, simply by doing what felt right and letting that lead them wherever it would.

———•—•——

Demonstrate the enjoyment you derive from your activity, and others will wonder how you can work so hard at your task. The secret, your secret, is that for you, it's not work—it's just doing what you enjoy. Often we will be following one primary course only to discover one day that our real passion and energy lies in other directions. The examples are many, from the direct sales representative who takes on a major legal suit to the college student developing a career only to discover her lifelong passion in acting. Cynthia Greenawalt-Carvajal, a dynamic businesswoman and human-potential consultant in Florida, writes about a television star's success.

———•—•——

15

DEIDRE HALL: LIGHTING THE WAY TO SUCCESS

CYNTHIA GREENAWALT-CARVAJAL

For Deidre Hall, success comes in every color of the spectrum: as a wife, as a mother, as a sister, as a daughter, and, of course, as an actress. Many people know her as Dr. Marlena Evans, the popular daytime television character she has played on *Days of Our Lives* for close to 25 years. Although her work as Marlena has earned her three Emmy nominations as well as *Soap Opera Digest's* Outstanding Actress Award six times in its 16-year history, her career success is most powerfully affirmed by television's greatest off-stage award: longevity as an employed actress. Of the Screen Actors Guild's 90,000 members, only 2 percent actually make a living acting—and 25 years on television is rare indeed.

Hall attributes her success to one simple rule: Do what comes naturally. But the rule itself didn't come to her naturally. When she was in college in Florida, yes, performing was natural, and she loved doing it—from her radio show to modeling. But she didn't have a real career dream. "I was lost, searching," she recalls.

Her search took her to Los Angeles, where she moved in with friends and enrolled in school. As a way of supporting herself, she took television acting jobs, appearing in episodes of *Perry Mason, Night Gallery,* and other shows. "I worried when the acting made me miss classes," she says. " I kept telling myself, 'I'll do this acting thing until I finish college and get a career.'"

"Then one day I woke up: 'I *have* a career!'"

Overnight, Hall's focus shifted. "If this is my career," she told herself, "I had better learn and be respectful of this craft." She enrolled in acting classes: Shakespeare, speech, improv, anything that could advance her chosen career. She auditioned for and landed parts in more television shows.

There were setbacks, of course. "One time, my agent had arranged an audition for me and sent the producers an 8 by 10 glossy. I was so broke that my roommate and I would go out to eat and bring back a doggie bag for the next day's meal," Hall says. "On the morning of the audition, it was

100 degrees. I put on my hairpieces and false eyelashes, walked
pool, and climbed into my old Corvair. It wouldn't start. I sat
ing and crying, muttering, "I can't feed myself, can't care for
now I can't even get myself to an audition!"

"I went back to my apartment, feeling defeated. I was too embarrassed
to call my agent. That afternoon, he called. 'What did you do in the interview?' he asked. 'Nothing,' I replied. 'Well, you must have done something,'
he told me. 'You got the job!'"

As it turned out, the producers had auditioned about a hundred girls.
On the back of each 8 by 10 glossy they had written their impressions: too
thin, too tall, too blond, too thick an accent. In the end, the only photo-
graph with nothing written on the back was Hall's.

Hall is philosophical: "Just when you think you should give up, the
universe won't let you." Although luck is not something she recommends
as a career strategy, the experience gave her the reassurance to continue
and the strength to face life's obstacles.

Now Hall has gained recognition as one of the highest-paid actresses
in daytime television. If you ask her to give the secrets behind her success,
she will tell you several:

- "Don't fear failure. I never thought that I couldn't do it, and it didn't
  occur to me that it was hard. I just knew that there was always work
  to be found, and that I would always find work.
- "Be kind and respectful. I've lived my life knowing that if I was kind
  and respectful, others would be kind and respectful to me.
- "Work hard, with integrity. I knew that if I was willing to work hard
  and maintained my integrity, I would always have work.
- "Be easy to be around. It's about knowing what everyone wants
  from me to fulfill their objectives—producer, director, lighting
  technicians, cameramen. So many actors, so many people, come in
  whining, complaining, unprepared. But I learned that if I make the
  cameraman's job easier, he works harder for me."

Kindness and respect for others not only help explain her career success, they resonate throughout her personal life—especially as a mother.

"Catch your kids being good—and talk about them when they think you don't think they're listening," she advises.

She considers parents' belief in their children paramount in their success: "As my parents did with me, my husband and I want our boys to know that, though it won't be handed to you, God gave you the ability and the drive to do whatever you set out to do. I tell my sons, 'Yes, math is new, and math is tricky—*and* you can do it.'"

Whether encouraging her own child, making a co-worker's job easier, or saying "Good morning!" to a homeless person, Hall acknowledges the power of focusing kindness upon another human being. "The secret is what it does to *us*. It lights them up, but *you're* the one carrying around the light. And the more successful and powerful you are, the brighter the light can be," she concludes.

—•—

It doesn't matter whether you are considered normal or abnormal; there are plenty of options in the world where your success and talent can light up someone's life somewhere. If you do what gives you the most pleasure and satisfaction, you might just become good enough at it that others will notice and provide worldly rewards. You cannot succeed in the long run at something you dislike doing. Believing that nothing can take the place of determination, Erin Brockovich, whose success story became a hit movie, brought a small town to its feet and a huge company to its knees.

—•—

LIFE'S A STRUGGLE, BUT YOU CAN WIN

ERIN BROCKOVICH AND M. ELIOT

Forget what others may say or think about you. I see my future as bright, even with everything that has happened to me, both good and bad, because I have proven all the "experts" wrong. When I was a child suffering from undiagnosed dyslexia, everyone told me I'd be lucky if I graduated from 12th grade. I recently came across a copy of the *Lawrence Journal-World,* my hometown newspaper, where one of the reporters interviewed several of my teachers and childhood friends and quoted them as saying that they never would have expected this kind of success from me. I thought to myself, "You see, Erin, this goes right to the heart of what you believe."

The simple truth is, every person is *unique*, and success doesn't always mean uniformity, or *conformity*. Everyone's learning curve is different. The common factor among those who succeed is *consistency*, or the ability to utilize stick-to-itiveness. What is equally common is the fear factor among those who fail, who are afraid to see themselves for who and what they really are and accept it. For some who might be a little different, as I was, or a little rebellious, as I also was, it's even more difficult to go against the mainstream tide. Most won't or can't, and they therefore fail to develop their individuality, their talent, to celebrate what is unique about them. I call this the fear of individualism that is so pervasive in our society.

I was feeling a little sick the other day and stayed home, and while relaxing, I turned on a talk radio program. I can't believe what people are saying these days, how threatened they are by anybody who acts differently from others. "Why did he do this?" or "Why did she do that?" And no one is offering any solutions, which is not surprising to me. If we seek advice on why we *shouldn't* express ourselves as individuals, what can anybody possibly say to bring us out? This need to conform is killing our most creative minds. The solution? *Stop complaining or feeling sorry for yourself about what you don't have, and instead, ask yourself what you truly want!*

19

Rebellion is not a bad word. It's a *misunderstood* word, especially when it comes to young people. James Dean was a rebel. Amelia Earhart was a rebel. And so, by the way, was Thomas Edison. Ed Masry and my dad are two of the strongest rebels I've ever met. As far as I'm concerned, *rebel* is probably one of the nicer things I've been called in the last ten years!

Too often we confuse the concepts of success and failure with normal and abnormal. Who among us is normal, anyway? According to whom? And who cares what they think anyway?

Is the janitor who lives down the street and who makes very little money a failure because he doesn't make more money than his neighbor does? Some people have a narrower comfort zone than others. So what? As long as the janitor realizes it is less important to be the best janitor in the world than it is to be the best janitor *he can be*, he's not in any way what I would call a failure. And that's the whole point. As far as I was concerned, as long as I was being, or trying my hardest to be, the best Erin I could be, I could never be a failure, no matter what anybody else thought.

The reality of life is that you deal with your circumstances as they come to you. You do the best you can, you try to stay in a positive mindset, and, as another woman I admire greatly who has also faced life alone once said, you hang in there because "Tomorrow's another day." When things get difficult, you don't turn tail and run. If you do, you can't like yourself very much, and that to me is the only real failure.

I remember a long time ago when I was working for a company selling a shampoo line named Lanza. It's the type of job in which a lot of rejection is a normal part of the day. One day a senior rep, who was evaluating me, watched me lose a sale. Afterward, she took my pitch apart, almost word by word, and said to me, "You know what, Erin, I'm impressed by your ability to take criticism so well." "I don't see it as criticism," I said, "just another way to look at myself."

And that's really exactly how I felt. Rather than thinking, "OK, I just lost that sale, I must be a failure, I quit," instead I'd stop and ask myself if maybe I did something to offend somebody. Why didn't I get that sale? I'd want to know, so I'd ask the person who turned down the shampoo line to please help me help myself by telling me why. You'd be amazed how many people will take the time to explain the reasons for doing what they do and how often their actions have very little to do with you.

That's why, if you're out of touch with yourself, you're never going to succeed, because all the negatives that you experience every day you will carry on your own shoulders, as "your fault." Instead of doing that, you need to think things through. You must ask yourself, "What is it I'm trying to achieve? Why do I want to achieve it? How can I go about it?"

I've never been afraid to be different, to let someone else say I'm a failure. That just doesn't matter to me. I cannot do anything I don't believe in, that goes against my code of ethics. Therefore, anything in my life I've done I've chosen to do. Oh, sure, there have been times I've been frustrated, but I never let that stop me. I was frustrated not being able to finish school. Even though I couldn't learn the way other people did, I knew in my heart I had the ability to overcome my difficulties. In fact, when I tried again and stuck with it, eventually I was able to graduate from high school and go on to college, to get my associate's degree.

Do What You Like and You'll Succeed

What is the difference between talent and ability? _Motivation._ Better to try to be the best you that you can be than the best there is. _Passion_ is the key to solving this equation. Skill without talent is never going to win out over ability infused with passion. No matter what anyone else may say, think, or do, let your passion guide you in life. When it comes to career and achievement, stick with what you like, and you will be amazed at how good you already are at it. When I first began dealing with people as a salesperson, I discovered I had an ability to make them listen, and they often bought what I was selling. It was out of that first success that I realized I had an _ability_ to communicate with people, and whether I did well because I liked it or liked it because I did well, the bottom line was I liked it _and_ I did well. This is the combination you are looking for in order to succeed in whatever field of endeavor you choose to pursue.

Be Realistic about Your Situation and Yourself

Everyone can't be the leader of the team. We are all created differently, and while some of us have talents that are more obvious than others, we all have a level of attainment that we can reach. Remember, it is not the size of the dog in the fight, but the size of the fight in the dog.

Ego Is Our Greatest Stumbling Block

When we think we can get away with something, it is because we think we are smarter or better than everyone else. We may be; we may not be. These are not the deciding factors in any struggle. The willingness to try your best and fail will make your commitment that much stronger and your success that much more accessible.

From *Take It from Me: Life's a Struggle but You Can Win* by Erin Brockovich and M. Eliot, copyright ©2002. Used by permission of McGraw-Hill Companies.

———————

A man starts off his adult life doing what he feels is best for God, country, and family. Then, as he experiences life following the path he feels is chosen for him, he encounters and overcomes new challenges, is introduced to new people, and finds new directions for his life. Lucky is the man who can become enthusiastic about new directions, and even luckier are those around him who benefit as a result. Christopher Cousins is a networking marketing expert who discovered a success story growing in the Midwest.

———————

ROD JONES: 15,000 REASONS TO FOLLOW YOUR PASSION

CHRISTOPHER COUSINS

Whether by chance or by sheer determination, Rod Jones finds no walls between his life and his work. His work is his inspiration, and it is intimately tied, through his personal history, to the battlefields of Vietnam.

A member of the United States Marine Corps, Jones re-upped for a second combat tour in 1967. "Two of my four brothers were also in the military," he says. "By reenlisting, I was able to ensure they would not see combat. It made sense at the time, and I didn't want to spend the rest of my tour chipping paint stateside."

Two months into his second tour of duty, his life changed forever. During the Tet Offensive, while he was serving in a company that built temporary bridges, Jones's mobile crane hit a land mine. His left arm and leg were severely injured, and he needed immediate medical evacuation and multiple surgeries. Many months passed before he got back on his feet.

After a long recovery, Jones used his GI Bill benefits to earn a bachelor's degree in psychology and began working for Michigan Rehabilitation Services. Later, he completed a master's degree in rehabilitation. During an assignment with the Detroit Medical Center Rehabilitation Institute, Jones developed a comprehensive and successful service delivery system for people suffering from injuries like his.

Soon, he found that working within the state system cramped his creative thinking and problem-solving abilities. "I wanted to find another way to help people recover and function again," he recalls. "I answered a newspaper ad for a position at Work Skills Corporation."

In 1978, Work Skills supported a small program run by a group of concerned parents of disabled children. Here Jones found a true outlet for his creative energies. For the next 25 years he worked passionately to transform the small company into a successful venture without the red tape that clogs most service agencies.

As passionate as Jones is about helping people, he is equally skeptical about fundraising, the revenue mainstay for most nonprofit organizations. He was determined to make Work Skills a self-funding organization, and he applied his creative skills and energies to this task. The program grew from a grassroots collective of concerned parents into a full-scale business operation.

The result? A company that takes people with no opportunities for employment, teaches them useful work skills, and finds them jobs in the community. "We provide goods and services under contract to major businesses and industries," Jones explains. "Our contracts generate operating capital for the company while keeping fundraising and grants to an absolute minimum. Our relationship to major corporations gives people with barriers to employment the opportunity for real work experiences, especially in a manufacturing environment."

Operated by a dedicated group of business and industry volunteers, Work Skills now serves more than 15,000 people in Michigan who might otherwise have to rely on community handouts. People written off as unemployable gain self-esteem as productive citizens; the community gains a work force capable of accomplishing many of its important tasks.

Was it serendipity, or was it destiny, that Rod Jones hit that land mine all those years ago? Whatever the reasons, Jones's passion to help others like himself became the catalyst that transformed a small but effective community program into a powerful and beneficial organization providing valuable services to disabled individuals and to businesses in need of skilled workers.

Rod Jones thinks he has the best job of all: "I get to spend my time being the visionary."

Throughout life, those who quest for success often find more than one path open to them. Maturity brings the wisdom to change directions when opportunities to achieve a more lasting and meaningful success arise. Patrick M. Kelly, now a partner in Charge and Director of Litigation, western region with the international law firm Wilson, Elser, Moskowitz, Edleman & Dicker once played as a guitarist with the Beach Boys.

FOLLOW YOUR STRENGTHS, NOT YOUR BLISS

PATRICK M. KELLY

Speaking to those seeking happiness in life, the late philosopher and historian Joseph Campbell advised, "Follow your bliss." In other words, do for a living what you enjoy doing the most.

That's great advice for someone who, like Campbell, excelled at his passion. For most of us, the better advice is "Don't quit your day job."

The hard fact of life is that few bicycle enthusiasts can keep pace with Lance Armstrong, and not many tennis lovers can win playing doubles with the Williams sisters. Just one out of every 200 high school senior boys playing interscholastic baseball will someday be drafted by a major league team; for senior football players, the ratio going on to the National Football League is less than one in a thousand. That long shot is three times longer if the sport is basketball and the goal is the National Basketball Association.

My "bliss" was and still is music. I had some great years as a professional rock guitarist playing with such great groups as the Beach Boys. (I still sit in with the Beach Boys now and again.) The hard truth that I had to face was that my singing voice wasn't going to carry me into being a lead singer someday. I couldn't be the best at what I loved doing.

It's that desire to be *the best* at what we do that helped me set my path toward the law. While I might have been happy playing guitar as a sideman as a career, I wouldn't have felt *fulfilled, accomplished,* or *successful.* So I had to relegate my guitar playing to an avocation and undergo a frank self-assessment of my personal strengths. What could I truly excel at doing? In short, my definition of success was to excel, and that is the star I followed.

As the Dalai Lama reportedly has said, "Judge your success by what you had to give up in order to get it." I gave up something I truly loved in order to achieve a greater success. By *success* I mean not outward measurements, such as dollar signs or fame, but rather the inward yardstick of knowing that I was using my best abilities to their best advantage. I genuinely felt (and still feel) that my talents as a public speaker, advocate, and manager could take me to a higher pinnacle of achievement than could my skill on an electric guitar. I found myself steered from within toward the law, especially trial work and legal management.

There were, no doubt, easier paths available. It is said that the law is a jealous mistress, and it has been a demanding one in my case. All of us have to either accept the downside of success or choose not to reach for it in the first place. I might have spent a great deal more time at home with my family if I had taken a different road in my professional life, but then I would today be bitter for not having taken the challenge to excel in an area where my native abilities allowed me to excel.

We each face the same decision: safety or risk, easy or hard, stable or changing? I'm not at all critical of those who don't feel compelled to excel. Society couldn't survive with a populace of overachievers. I confess to a certain degree of envy for those whose main goal is an undemanding life. But the readers of this book have already cast their lots in favor of excellence. How, then, to achieve it?

I've known many truly successful people, from all walks of life. These are people who are, without any conceit, the best at what they do, and they derive great contentment from having employed and developed their talents to that degree. Not all are wealthy, famous, or even recognized by society as having attained something special. They have succeeded by applying their strongest abilities and best efforts toward their highest goals.

How do we recognize our own strongest abilities? I suggest a few simple questions, which, if answered honestly, should lead to the answer:

- What three accomplishments am I proudest of in my life?
- What three things have other people praised me for doing?
- What specific abilities allowed me to do all of these things?

My thesis is that there is a common thread, or sometimes a few common threads, to each person's foremost successes. They aren't always the obvious ones. Seemingly unrelated triumphs may spring from the same ability. Talents at math and at music come from the same facility for seeing relationships in abstract concepts. A great day on the ski slopes may be due to the same ability to anticipate obstacles as a great day in court. One who can motivate co-workers may also be a good writer, because both skills involve empathy—sensing another person's feelings and motives.

Recognizing our strengths is the first step. Putting those strengths to work is a lifelong journey. I liken it to a white-water rafting trip. The river places obstacles in our way—eddies, rocks, sandbars—any one of which can distract us from our progress toward success. Those who make it to the end of the rapids define their own course, steering when needed, paddling when needed, and learning from each mistake along the way.

Are you letting the river choose your course for you? With each minor alteration in direction, ask yourself, "Is this change leading me away from, instead of toward, the use of my best abilities? Is it letting my skills atrophy instead of exercising them?" If you answer "Yes," start paddling!

In my case, my "paddling" led me to, among other things, becoming the parent of two wonderful children, Patrick and Laura; senior partnership of an international law firm; presidency of the Los Angeles County Bar Association; membership on the Commission for Judicial Performance (which judges the judges); co-founding an award-winning periodical, the *Los Angeles Lawyer*; and co-authoring a major treatise, the *California Insurance Litigation Guide*. I followed my strengths—and I still get to sit in with the Beach Boys.

I suppose that's what Shakespeare had in mind in his advice to Laertes, "To thine own self be true." To excel, we must candidly distinguish what we do best from what we merely enjoy, then choose a course that will give opportunities to make the most of those abilities. We may be among the lucky few who find that their highest capabilities and their favorite pastimes coincide. If not, we'll still be on the path to high achievement and the satisfaction that it brings.

———•—

A new creation, a new business, a new venture begins with an idea. It used to be said that knowledge is power, but now we understand that applied knowledge is the real power. We all apply our knowledge daily, but we never have enough to achieve perfection—there are always rough spots. Masters of success understand that getting into and then out of the tough zones is where they learn the most. Only by constantly overcoming obstacles do we truly learn mastery. Writer Darrell Ross has had a checkered career history, from coaching hockey in the United Arab Emirates to building the largest referral marketing franchise in British Columbia.

———•—

CREATE A GLOBAL BUSINESS FROM A GOOD IDEA

DARRELL ROSS

There are many things in life that will catch your eye, but only a few that will catch your heart. . . . Pursue those.

—ANONYMOUS

We've all heard the story. Two out of three businesses fail in their first six years. The pain of a failed business is a miserable experience many of us understand too well. They say that next to the death of a loved one or the breakup of a marriage, losing a business is the most painful event in life.

Tom Matzen—entrepreneur, bestselling author, international business coach—tells us, "It doesn't have to happen this way. In my experience, starting and running a business doesn't have to have tragic consequences. In fact, properly done, a business can truly add more life to the entrepreneur and his family. Unfortunately, there are few entrepreneurs who have achieved success in their business careers and personal lives."

As a business coach, Matzen has helped more than 200 entrepreneurs get a good start on achieving their business dreams. He is also the president and CEO of Parmasters, the first year-round indoor golf training center franchise, founded in 1998 and named one of the "66 Hot New Franchises to Look for in 2003" by *Entrepreneur* magazine.

"It's sad, but very few golfers ever shoot par," notes Matzen. Parmasters is working to change that. We are training people to shoot PAR golf and we want our business to have PAR results. Running a business is just like shooting PAR golf."

For Matzen's business, PAR is an acronym:

P—Passion

A—Aim

R—Rough

Passion

> *Choose a job you love, and you will never*
> *have to work a day in your life.*
> — CONFUCIUS

"Even though my career is helping people build the business of their passion, I sometimes forget about the real importance of this principle," Matzen says. "Owning a business leads to the highest highs and the lowest lows. If you aren't in a business that you can be truly passionate about, it will soon become just a bad job with high economic risk.

"I believe life is meant to be lived and played full out. You can always find a way to make money around a passion. It just takes time and effort to plan your moves. The key is to know it can be done. Those who work their passion don't consider it *work*—it's just what they love doing, and their long 'work' days seem to fly by."

Aim

Start with the end in mind.

—STEPHEN COVEY

"In golf and in life, you usually get what you aim for. So start with a clear vision of what your business will look like when it's done," Matzen advises. "At Parmasters, we created a vision to be the ultimate franchise and change the way the world golfs. Our vision includes 720 golf training centers in North America and another 360 around the globe.

"Is this aggressive, bold, and far-reaching? Absolutely! Research tells us that only 50 percent of all franchises ever get beyond 50 sites. We believe that nothing dramatic ever happens for someone with small dreams. Make your goals bold and daring. Shoot for the stars, and you may at least hit the moon."

The Rough

It is the set of the sails, not the direction of the wind
that determines which way we will go.

—JIM ROHN

"Golfers know that some of their shots will land in the rough. It happens in golf, and it happens in life. Expect it, prepare for it, accept it, then do your best to improve your 'lie'—your position—whenever it happens," Matzen says.

"Parmasters got into the rough just after we invested two years and nearly $1 million developing our ultimate golf training system," he recalls. "We were ready to award our first golf training franchises. In four months, we had 44 franchises pending in five states! Then, suddenly, our biggest client launched a hostile takeover by co-opting one of our partners. We definitely were in the rough, not to mention shocked. Thanks to having prepared strong contracts, we defeated the takeover attempt, but our position was not good. We lost $600,000 in eminent franchise fees. Making our 'lie' even worse, the loss came at our lowest point of cash flow.

"It should have sunk us. When you land in the rough on the golf course, picking up your ball and going home is not rewarding. So, like a good golfer, we decided to do two things: 1) figure out what got us in the rough, and 2) find the best way out.

"Figuring out the problem didn't take long. Even though we knew his core values didn't match our own, we had knowingly brought in a 'shark' partner to provide skills that we lacked. How dumb was that? When he acted like a shark, we were actually surprised. And what did we learn? That's right: Never do business with a shark."

So how did Parmasters get out of the rough? "Our solution was simple," Matzen says. "It was like being off the fairway with a tree in your way and the only path to the green a high flop shot over the top of it; once you know your situation, the club to use becomes clear. We found a new partner, an investment banker who shared our core values and ethics.

"Not every shot and club will work out. But once you're clear about the path, your choice of club and shot is easier and offers a better potential outcome. And landing in the rough need not be scary. If you choose the right path and tools, it can lead to an even better outcome. As it turned out, our new partner brought us an expanded board of directors, several world-class advisors, and rapid expansion of our company over the following year."

In Matzen's terminology, it all comes down to PAR.

- *Passion.* Start your business or your project with a concept you are truly passionate about.
- *Aim.* Line up properly and take aim at your ultimate outcome.
- *Rough.* Be prepared to get out of the rough as often as necessary; accept it, adjust, and get back on track.

How's it going for Parmasters? "Currently, we have a good start on our 'round': 17 franchises awarded, 6 options, and another 30 in the works," reports Matzen. "Master franchises have been sold in the United States and

Canada, and there are options for master franchises in Japan, Taiwan, Ireland, and the Middle East. We are still on the 'front nine,' but it's looking good."

Matzen offers one final thought: "The reason you set a goal is for what it will make of you once you achieve it. Happy life, and may your strokes be few and straight up the middle."

———

A parent's major goal is to support the family, but this often brings interesting opportunities for other achievements, with the momentum of family activity fueling further success. Michelle Campbell of Michigan writes about a successful mom whose goal of helping her sons turned into a multi-million-dollar business.

———

ONE SHARP LADY DRIVING "TWO MEN AND A TRUCK"

MICHELLE L. CAMPBELL

Mary Ellen Sheets was one of three speakers during a local chamber of commerce luncheon. All three speakers were billed as successful local businesspeople, but something about Sheets was different.

The other two panel members said they had mentors who had helped them in their careers. All three offered to help members of the audience with problems at any time, and said they were willing to serve as mentors themselves.

After the luncheon, I decided I would call each of them to see if they would meet with me one day for lunch. Alas, speaker number one did not reply. Speaker number two was similarly mum. Mary Ellen Sheets was the only one who called me back—and she even left me her home number!

I wanted her advice on franchising so I could help a friend decide if she should franchise her homebased business. I also wanted to learn more about this successful woman.

When we connected and I explained my friend's scenario, Sheets told me she would send a book for my friend to read. She kept her word; a few days later it was in my mailbox.

Though I barely knew her, Sheets had already demonstrated two important success lessons. First, always call people back. Second, make good on your promises. So simple—yet so important.

A lot of entrepreneurs think success hinges on developing a good plan. I was amazed to find out how Sheets started her business.

She was a single parent of two teenage sons and a teenage daughter, worked as a computer analyst for the state of Michigan, and owned an old pickup truck. "My sons used it to move people for spending money in the early '80s," she says. "We put an ad in the local newspaper. The first line was "Two Men and a Truck"—although that was stretching it some."

After her sons graduated from high school, they went out of town to college. Sheets had $350 saved. She knew the old pickup wouldn't work for a real business, so she used that money to buy a (very) used moving truck.

"Can you picture a $350 truck?" asks Sheets. "I hired two men and started the 'real' company in May of 1985. I didn't know how to supervise the men, how to do bookkeeping, or anything about licensing, insurance, taxes. I didn't know anything—except to try to keep the customers happy."

At the end of the first year, Sheets had made $1,000. "I wrote 10 checks to local charities and gave the money away," she recalls. (I thought that was incredible.)

With her year of experience, her $350 truck, her two employees, her conspicuously absent business plan, and her profit diverted to local charities, Sheets did what I'm sure any rational person would do under similar circumstances. She left her good, secure job with the state of Michigan (which offered great benefits) and struck out into two highly regulated industries: franchising and trucking.

The laws regulating these industries are different in every state. Sheets was biting off such a big chunk, but—and this is the great thing—she had no clue. She was oblivious to the risks she was taking and the obstacles she would face.

She simply wanted her idea to work—and she knew that it had to work in order to put her children through college. She believed she would succeed as long as she cared about people. That is why the slogan for Two Men and a Truck® would be "Movers Who Care."

Mary Ellen Sheets "cared" her Two Men and a Truck into an operation of 100 franchises in 24 states with 2003 projected revenue of $100 million. (Since I work as a financial advisor with American Express Financial Advisors, I know that is a pretty great return on a $350 investment in 16 years.)

Sheets cares about the franchise owners along with her employees. She and her daughter, now president of the company, buy each employee birthday gifts. Seemingly small things like that make a huge difference in the success of a company.

She cares about her community as well, giving back by serving on the boards of the International Franchise Association, the Boy Scouts, Sparrow Hospital, Michigan Freedom Academy, Michigan Lawsuit Abuse Watch, and the Michigan Chamber of Commerce. She is also on the advisory board of Beaner's, a coffee shop franchise. She serves on the Michigan Truck Safety Commission as a state commissioner. She is "in training" for a local United Way committee. She also makes time to talk to many elementary, high school, and college classes, chambers of commerce, Rotary and Optimists clubs, and church groups.

Sheets works constantly to improve her business. "I would do anything to promote our company," she says. "I take every phone call. You never know, when meeting someone or speaking somewhere, what opportunity will follow from that meeting."

Success has not come without setbacks. When her daughter took over as president in 1994, Two Men and a Truck had 34 franchises. A handful of the franchisees banded together and said they were no longer going to pay royalties but were still going to use the name. Sheets spent years as well as hundreds of thousands of dollars in the courts and finally won every case. Some were finalized by negotiating a settlement. The company won some large judgments, but unfortunately some of the people who lost did not have the money to pay, so Two Men and a Truck ate the losses. It took years for the company to recover.

The real kicker in the whole debacle for Sheets: her former best friend ran one of the franchises that ended up in court. "I was so shocked and hurt. I learned that she'd told people she founded the company," she recalls.

Sheets has high ethical standards and truly cares about helping others succeed. So I asked her for advice on how to be successful. "Do something you like," she counsels. "You have your whole life ahead of you—but it's not a dress rehearsal! Do not waste your time in a job you do not enjoy. Work on your business every day. If you don't have any money that day, clean out your files. Call on some people. Each day do a little bit. One day you will look back and see you've really done a lot!

"Stay focused. If you wash windows, wash windows. Be the best window washer in town. Know that everyone is going to call you to come and wash their windows. They would be crazy not to call you!

"Don't listen to negative comments. If you have a gut feeling that you're headed in the right direction, you probably are. A lot of people made fun of me, a woman trucker, but I just kept going. I had the last laugh."

What about competitors? "Don't worry about your competition," says Sheets. "Who cares what they are doing or what they charge? Worry about your customers. Always give back to your community. It empowers you and your employees."

That $350 Sheets sank into her fledging business was, she reflects, "the only money I had ever saved in my life, and the only money I have ever invested in the business." In the hands of, say, a couple other business execs making empty mentoring promises during a chamber of commerce luncheon, I believe this mustard seed of an investment would have turned into little more than, well, two men and a truck. With the caring and daring Mary Ellen Sheets at the company's wheel, however, Two Men and a Truck grew into a powerful franchise concept—and showed me the way to success.

It's unusual to find a person who has overcome a physical challenge starting from a most unlikely situation, only later to meet the same challenge starting in far more difficult circumstances. Sim Chow Boon, a marketing expert in Singapore specializing in word-of-mouth referral marketing, was astounded to learn the story of a professional mountain climber in his own, very flat home country.

DAVID LIM: PASSION THAT CLIMBS

SIM CHOW BOON

Picture growing up in a very small country of some three million people where the tallest mountain is about 450 feet. Now, with this life experience, imagine tackling the ascent of mountains that are more than five miles straight up and where many lives have been lost. Finally, consider doing this deliberately, just because you want to. Now you have it, a person following his or her passionate interests.

When life surges through a man's veins, he has found the secret to being unstoppable. And when that same life is greeted with the insurmountable, the true test of faith, courage, and willpower begins. Such is the life of one David Lim.

Lim started climbing 12 years ago. Today, at 38, he is Singapore's most experienced mountaineer—no small accomplishment in a nation with only one hill to train on. In 1998, he led the first Singapore team to attempt Mount Everest. He broke a rib and was unable to make the summit, but as the leader, he ensured the success of the expedition by getting two team members to the top. Thousands cheered the team on their return home.

Not long after his return, Lim fell ill with what he thought was a stomach bug. Antibiotics had no effect, and he rapidly grew worse. Within a few days he could hardly taste his food, and simple tasks such as turning the ignition key in his car were becoming difficult. A few more days, and he could not breathe properly. He became almost totally paralyzed.

Doctors finally diagnosed his illness: Guillain-Barré syndrome, probably contracted in Kathmandu. GBS is a rare autoimmune disease in which the immune system goes haywire and attacks the myelin sheaths of the nerves. The resulting paralysis, although usually partial and temporary, can become permanent.

For months, Lim was confined to a hospital bed, hooked up to machines and tubes to help him breathe. Doubts about whether he would be able to return to a normal life plagued him, but visits from friends, family, and admiring strangers kept his spirits up and gave him the will to fight. His condition gradually improved, and after six months he was well enough to enter a rehabilitation center, where he worked to regain lost muscle strength. Two months later, he was home—on crutches.

But Lim was a man who refused to accept limitations, a man who had challenged mountains and won. Mere survival would not be enough; as he later wrote in his book *Mountain to Climb: The Quest for Everest and Beyond*, "People have to find a reason to live, without which life is just a nine-to-five living hell." His goal, his passion, was to resume climbing, and sheer determination drove him to work even harder to get back to the mountains he loved—which he did in 2000 with a Singaporean ascent of Aconcagua, the highest peak in the Andes at 22,841 feet.

His recovered energies are directed at more than propelling himself up mountains. He became Singapore's first professional mountaineer. He now runs the Central Singapore CDC Youth Adventure Programme, a tripartite program to build character in Singapore youth through mountain climbing and other activities, and from 1999 to 2000 he administered the CLIMB 2000 National Mountaineering Programme.

Lim's ordeal has left him with an inner strength. He knows that life is fully realized only when it is put at risk, for that is the only way one can learn what one is capable of. His own success is a testament to how courage, perseverance, and belief in oneself can conquer all mountains, whether real or metaphorical.

As Lim will tell you, his experience exemplifies three principles of success:

1. *Be passionate about what you do.* Bill Cosby once said, "Anyone can dabble, but once you've made that commitment, your blood has that certain thing in it, and it's very hard to stop you." For David Lim, a passion for climbing took him to the world's highest peak—and carried him through the lowest point of his life.

2. *Have a support group.* Surround yourself with like-minded people who share your passion, who believe in your ability to achieve your goals, who will help you when your dreams seem hopeless, who will have the courage to steer you back on track when you stray. The truest friends are those who respect you enough to tell you the truth, and whose advice you can respect and heed.

3. *Break your goal into small steps.* The river carries away the mountain grain by grain. Your plan should point the way to your goal, step by small step. The ascent and descent of Everest is divided into reaching a succession of camps along the way; each leg of the climb is mapped and planned to overcome the smallest known obstacles. Lim's recovery was a series of small steps—relearn how to breathe, then to eat, then to stand, then to walk—toward the distant goal of climbing mountains once again.

David Lim's life and accomplishments, both physical and spiritual, illustrate well these three principles of success—principles that can be applied equally well to any endeavor in your professional or personal life.

Social change that affects millions of lives can be catalyzed by the actions of one person; Rosa Parks's refusal to give up her seat on the bus led to the dismantling of Jim Crow laws throughout the South. There are still many wrongs to right in our imperfect society, and new generations of passionate activists seek ways to bring about constructive change. Writer and publisher Maxine E. Thompson, a southern Californian who uses her talents to support others seeking to succeed through the written word, has found a powerful role model to write about.

ROSIE MILLIGAN AND THE LITERARY EMPOWERMENT MOVEMENT

MAXINE E. THOMPSON

Harriet Tubman, an escaped slave who risked her life on the Underground Railroad helping other runaways escape north to freedom, was so spiritually guided that she knew when not to go down the wrong path because the slave catchers would be there. Proudly she boasted, "I never lost a passenger." Imagine. Without a compass, without a map, and with only God as her guide, she led more than 300 slaves to freedom.

Today an unsung hero, a modern Harriet Tubman, lives in our midst. Rosie Milligan, Ph.D., is a phenomenal and passionate African American leader in the literary community. She is leading many African American readers and writers out from under-representation through her publishing company, Milligan Books, and her bookstore, Express Yourself Books. History may record her work as paralleling what Harriet Tubman did for African American people in bondage.

The Underground Railroad was neither a train nor underground, but a network of secret trails and safe houses that led to freedom for enslaved blacks. Milligan believes that the modern "freedom train" for African Americans is the publishing of black authors for black readers. Published authorship gives ownership of the material to both the writer and the reader; ownership leads to freedom in learning about subjects that are important to one's own life. The stories, journals, and essays published about and by African Americans become the repositories of their culture.

African Americans are underrepresented in mainstream American publishing. Through Milligan's efforts, the voices of many black writers are being heard for the first time, telling Americans—especially African Americans—personal stories of the African Diaspora.

They tell the story of John Carlos, one of the two American 200-meter medalists in the 1968 Olympics who held up their fists as a silent protest against racism and were suspended from the team and thrown out of Olympic Village. Carlos's story was forgotten for more than 30 years until the publication of *Why? The Biography of John Carlos,* now being distributed by Milligan Books.

They tell the story of Cathy Harris, the black woman who exposed racial harassment within the ranks of the U.S. Customs Service and caused the laws to be changed. Milligan published her book, *Flying While Black: A Whistleblower's Story.*

They tell what it was like to be a black doctor from the 1950s to the 1980s, in two novels by James A. Mays, M.D., *Mercy Is King* and *Trapped.*

They reveal the astonishing talents of young black writers: 11-year-old Leah Grier, whose *Healing: One Child's Journey* tells of grieving and surviving the death of her father; 8-year-old Marquise Cormier, who recounts his fight against being placed in "special education" classes in *I Am Not a Problem Child!*; 12-year-old poet Rae Shaw Conner's hauntingly creative voice in *Keep It Real: Poetry from a Young Heart.*

Where does Rosie Milligan's passion come from? She's the daughter of a Mississippi landowner and farmer. "I left Mississippi and came west to plant a new kind of crop," she says. "I learned from my father, Simon, the importance of owning your own. There's something special about having your own. It gives you a sense of pride, confidence, and purpose."

Milligan Books is the fastest-growing female-owned African American publishing house in the country. That's because it's fulfilling an important need. "This is a new form of reparations," she says of her visionary publishing. "As published authors, we take charge of our creativity, and we pay ourselves through making a living from our talents. We are no longer waiting for the mainstream to validate our voices."

Milligan is known for her willingness to take risks, to walk nontraditional paths, and visit areas out of the mainstream. Writers of controversial political stories, unpopular genres such as historical fiction, and black poetry come to Milligan Books from all parts of this country, as well as from Africa. She has published more than 100 African American authors and has unselfishly helped others set up their own publishing companies and bookstores. Having found her niche, Milligan is happy to share her passion, to see other publishers carry her vision forward.

Her success is attributable in part to her networking skills—her ability to communicate with bookstore owners, distributors, radio talk show hosts, newspaper editors, and talented book editors—and to her unflagging energy. Does she ever grow tired? "Tired? What's that?" Milligan responds. "I cannot fix my mouth to say the word when I think of all the real hard work that our forefathers had to do so that we could have these opportunities that we can now partake of. No, I am no ways tired. We have real work to do. Who will tell our stories? You cannot tell them from the grave."

Now widely acknowledged as the "mother of the literary empowerment movement," Milligan is proud to a major force behind a powerful social revolution, a tidal wave of literary economic empowerment that will likely surpass the Harlem renaissance of the 1920s and '30s. This time, the writers will own the rights to their intellectual property, and the benefits will flow to the next generation.

The passion she brings to her life's work is expressed in her motto: "Erase no, step over can't, and move forward with life."

Our earliest passions can linger with us for a long time, maybe even forever. Despite incredible success in one area, some of our best contributions to our community find origins in our earliest desires. You don't leave behind old passions; instead, you build on them and find new outlets for their expression.
Talk-show host and actress Oprah Winfrey stays connected to her early passions and now uses her success to spotlight what she still carries with her.

OPRAH WINFREY: YOU ARE RESPONSIBLE FOR YOUR LIFE

JANET LOWE

School clearly played a major role in Oprah Winfrey's life, as her own words show.

If you grow up a bully and that works, that's what you do. If you're the class clown and that works, that's what you do. I was always the smartest kid in class and that worked for me—by third grade I had it figured out. So I was the one who would read the assignment early and turn the paper in ahead of time. That makes everyone else hate you, but that's what worked for me.

The door to freedom is education.

To those of us to whom much is given, we are compelled to do all that we can to save our young people. For to save ourselves, we must educate ourselves.

Oprah's teachers have been special to her.

For every one of us that succeeds, it's because there's somebody there to show you the way out. The light doesn't necessarily have to be in your family; for me it was teachers and school.

She aspired to become a fourth-grade teacher, largely because Oprah admired her own fourth-grade teacher, Mrs. Duncan.

If I wasn't doing this, I'd be teaching fourth grade. I'd be the same person I always wanted to be, the greatest fourth-grade teacher, and win the Teacher of the Year Award. But I'll settle for 23 Emmys and the opportunity to speak to millions of people each day and, hopefully, teach some of them.

One of her teachers in Milwaukee recognized her potential and placed her in Upward Bound, a program that prepared talented low-income students for college. After that, Oprah rode the bus to Nicolet High School in Fox Point, a Milwaukee suburb. Although the experience revealed to Oprah how poor her family was, she still appreciated the attention of the teacher, Gene Abrams.

About a group of young women in Chicago whom she has mentored, Oprah said:

When we talk about goals and they say they want Cadillacs, I say, "If you cannot talk [correctly], if you cannot read or do math, if you become pregnant, if you drop out of school, you will never have a Cadillac, I guarantee it! And if you get Ds or Fs on your report card, you're out of this group. Don't tell me you want to do great things with your life if all you carry to school is a radio."

Oprah left Tennessee State University in her senior year to accept a full-time job on television but later returned, completed a class project, and earned her degree in speech and drama. That year she delivered the commencement address.

From *Oprah Winfrey Speaks*, copyright ©1998 by Janet Lowe. Used by permission of John Wiley & Sons, Inc.

———•———

Persistence and System

There are no secrets to success. It is the result of preparation, hard work, and learning from failure.

—COLIN POWELL

In most success stories, persistence is a recurring theme. People who achieve what they set out to achieve are usually seen to be steadfast in pursuit of their goals, unwilling to let difficulties stand in their way. Dogged determination is the cornerstone of many successes. This is why the harder people work, the luckier they seem to be.

But persistence alone does not guarantee success. The successful pursuit of a goal also requires following a system or plan. It's more than just hanging on when everybody else has let go; it's persistence with purpose.

Success is often the result of the *uncommon application of common knowledge.* When you hear successful people talk about the "secret" of their success, you rarely hear any real secrets. What you do hear about is their unwavering adherence to some system or approach they believe in and follow with intensity and determination—an uncommon focus on something that less successful people simply take for granted or pay lip service to. Successful people focus on the goal and work through or around everything else. In sports, this is called keeping your eye on the ball.

Even when the ideas are easy to understand, they often don't get implemented because people think the execution is too difficult. After author Ivan Misner presented a keynote speech in Sweden a while back, an audience member approached him and said, "Everything you said makes so much sense. Much of it was about things that I've heard were important to do, but I never did them because they seemed too simple. I thought there had to be more to it than that. So I wasted valuable time looking for some secret." Then she added, "I don't understand why people often find it easy to make things so difficult. Myself included."

It's been said that success comes in "cans" and failure comes in "can'ts." You probably know people who are masters of the "yeah, but" approach, who find it easy to make things difficult. They seek out a success model, then spend their time dismissing it because "it's too simple" or because "we're different." They rationalize that "it might have worked in that situation, but this situation [or product, service, business, industry, city, state, country] is different." This is nothing more than their way of avoiding doing what they don't want to do. It's an excuse for nonperformance, and for some, that's better than results: it's failure, justified in advance.

The road to success has detours to failure. Nearly every successful person has encountered failure at least once, and usually multiple times. It is, however, these failures that lead to success. Masters of success are those who learn from their mistakes but don't dwell on them, who pick themselves up, resolve to avoid making the same error again, and keep moving toward their goal. They succeed because they consider each mistake an opportunity to learn—not an excuse to quit. They succeed because that is the only important thing. And success hides a multitude of blunders.

Success comes to those who have not only passion and vision but also persistence and a commitment to performing the fundamentals and who keep working and learning until they can perform them flawlessly. In the end, success is not about being different or having secret knowledge. In the end, everybody knows what the goal is and how to achieve it. This is common knowledge, and it's been around for a long, long time. Success is about knowing these things and having the will to go after them without giving up, making excuses, or getting sidetracked. It's about the *uncommon application of common knowledge.*

Mastering a new skill or learning a new concept can take a while. We make mistakes, take some tumbles, endure some fumbles. The idea is to persist through our mistakes, learn from them, then apply those lessons as we move ahead. Who better than Harvey Mackay to teach us about success in business? Once a top-level tennis player, Harvey Mackay is one of America's most popular and entertaining business speakers.

SUCCESS IS GETTING UP MORE THAN YOU FALL DOWN

HARVEY MACKAY

I'm constantly asked what I think is the secret of success. Well, it's a lot of things, but at the top of my list are two beliefs.

1. You need to be a hungry fighter.
2. A hungry fighter never quits.

I've learned over the years that success is largely hanging on after others have let go.

When you study the truly successful people, you'll see that they have made plenty of mistakes, but when they were knocked down, they kept getting up . . . and up . . . and up. Like the Energizer Bunny keeps going . . . and going . . . and going.

Abraham Lincoln failed in business, lost numerous elections and his sweetheart, and had a nervous breakdown. But he never quit. He kept on trying and became, according to many, our greatest president. Consider some other examples.

- Dr. Seuss's first children's book was rejected by 23 publishers.
- Michael Jordan was cut from his high school basketball team.
- Henry Ford failed and went broke five times before he finally succeeded.
- Franklin D. Roosevelt was struck down by polio, but he never quit.
- Helen Keller, totally deaf and blind, graduated cum laude from Radcliffe College and went on to become a famous author and lecturer.
- Adam Clark labored 40 years writing his commentary on the Holy Scriptures.
- The *History of the Decline and Fall of the Roman Empire* took Edward Gibbon 26 painstaking years to complete.
- Ernest Hemingway is said to have revised *The Old Man and the Sea* 80 times before submitting the manuscript for publication.
- It took Noah Webster 36 years to compile *Webster's Dictionary*.
- The University of Bern rejected Albert Einstein's Ph.D. dissertation, saying it was irrelevant and fanciful.
- Johnny Unitas was cut by the Pittsburgh Steelers, but he kept his dream alive by working construction and playing amateur football while staying in contact with every NFL team. The Baltimore Colts finally responded, and he became one of the greatest quarterbacks ever to play the game.

- Richard Hooker worked seven years on the humorous war novel, *MASH*, only to have it rejected by 21 publishers.
- Charles Goodyear spent every last dollar over five years filled with experiments to try to develop a rubber life preserver before he succeeded.

I love the story about the high school basketball coach who was attempting to motivate his players to persevere through a difficult season. Halfway through the season he stood before the team and said, "Did Michael Jordan ever quit?" The team responded, "No!" He yelled, "What about the Wright brothers? Did they ever give up?" "No!" hollered back the team. "Did Muhammad Ali ever quit?" Again the team yelled, "No!" "Did Elmer McAllister ever quit?"

There was a long silence. Finally, one player was bold enough to ask, "Who's Elmer McAllister? We've never heard of him." The coach snapped back, "Of course you've never heard of him—he quit!"

As you can see, it's important never to give up. I remember a young jockey who lost his first race, his second, his third, his first 10, his first 20, then it became 200, and 250. Finally, Eddie Arcaro won his first race and went on to become one of the all-time great jockeys.

Even Babe Ruth, considered by sports historians the greatest baseball player of all time, failed on many occasions. He struck out 1,330 times.

Sir Winston Churchill, a person who never quit in a lifetime of defeats and setbacks, delivered the shortest and most eloquent commencement address ever given. Although he had taken three years to get through eighth grade because of his trouble learning English grammar, Churchill, much later in life, was asked to address the graduates of Oxford University. As he approached the podium with his trademark cigar, cane, and top hat, he shouted, "Never give up!" Several seconds passed before he rose to his toes and repeated, "Never, never give up." Then he sat down.

Silver-spoon scions and '60s hippies always looked down on the success system that wiser generations knew simply as "the work ethic." Have we, too, forgotten that hard workers from humble beginnings can achieve extraordinary results? Ivan Misner worked his unique marketing company up from scratch to a large operation spanning the globe.

SUCCESS IS NOT AN ENTITLEMENT

IVAN MISNER, PH.D.

Everyone wants some degree of success. We might want it in different forms, but I've never met anyone who didn't want to be successful at something important. This is good. I believe everyone is entitled to pursue success.

But success itself is not an entitlement.

Success is determined largely by our hard work and our choices. I know many people who work hard but make bad choices. It's amazing how many of them think they deserve to be more successful because they feel they've worked very hard for it. On the other hand, I don't know many, if any, successful people who made good choices but didn't work hard.

Working hard is only the first part of success. Making good choices is the second part. It takes both to achieve success.

I knew someone who was constantly lamenting her "bad luck." She wasn't happy with the various jobs that she had over the years, and her personal life was a shambles; she was almost 30, hadn't completed college, and constantly had money problems. She often blamed situations or other people for the various predicaments she was in. However, the glaringly obvious truth was that, although she worked fairly hard, she continually made horrible choices. One day she would complain about money, and the next day she'd buy something totally extravagant and completely unnecessary. The next week she'd complain about not being able to get a good job while showing up to work an hour late for personal reasons (which happened regularly).

From time to time, she talked to me about her issues, and I'd point out the choices she'd made that led to the problem at hand. Each time she'd pay lip service to acknowledging the connection, but the truth is she never took ownership of the real problem—her choices. She once lamented, "Why me? Why me? I deserve better!" I didn't offer my opinion on this question, but what I wanted to tell her was, "Everyone feels like she 'deserves better' at some point in her life. Get over it, stop complaining, and start doing something about it. Work hard *and* make better choices!"

I've worked with thousands of people who have experienced some degree of success in their lives. One of the recurring themes I've seen is that successful people plan their work and work their plan. They think through their options, make the best decisions they can with the information they have, then work hard to carry out their choices.

As the CEO of an international business, I know that my choices can affect hundreds of employees, franchise owners, and associates, as well as tens of thousands of clients around the world. Years ago, I was talking to a friend about some tough decisions I had to make and my concerns about them. He gave me some great advice: "Not every decision you make has to be a good one. Just make sure that you make more good ones than bad ones—and when you make a bad one, minimize the impact by fixing it quickly."

Wow! This is great advice. It squarely hits the point about working hard and making good choices. Not all the choices you make have to be on the mark, just enough of them to produce the results you want. Some of my biggest lessons in business have come not from my successes but from my losses—neither of which had much to do with luck but with the choices or commitments I had made.

Not long ago, I was talking to someone I've known for years about the growth of my business and some other personal goals I've recently met. He said, "Man, you're lucky! It must be nice."

"Yeah, I'm lucky," I responded. "Let me tell you the secret of my 'luck.' First, I went to college for ten years. During that time, I started my own business, and for the next two decades I worked *really long* hours. Along the way, I mortgaged my house a couple of times for the business, and I wrote six books. And if you apply that kind of effort to whatever you do, you can be just as lucky."

He laughed and said, "OK! OK! I get it!"

Did he really get it? I don't think so because he hasn't changed his behavior or started making different choices.

For most of my three decades of hard work, I didn't feel very lucky or incredibly successful. It took time, effort, and decent choices before I felt a modicum of success. The problem is that many people want to go from point A to point Z and bypass all the challenges in between. They work hard, so they "deserve" the success they want.

Success is not an entitlement. It's not a right or a claim that we should have. Yes, people have the right to *pursue* success, but that's it. Success is most often earned, not handed over because you are entitled. If being successful were that easy, everyone would have the success he thinks he deserves. I think I was in my thirties before I truly understood and internalized that idea.

I've been trying to instill this wisdom in my 9-year-old son by teaching him the "mantra of success." The other day I asked him, "Trey, what's the secret to success?"

He said, in a young boy's slightly bored, singsong tone, "The secret to success without hard work and good choices is still a secret, Dad. Can I go out and play now?"

Okay, maybe nine is a little young to start the training.

But maybe not.

———•··•———

Everyone knows it, and no one likes it: Practice makes perfect. Whatever the endeavor, practicing the fundamentals in a correct and committed manner is crucial to achieving anything worthy of being called success. Enthusiasm gets us going, but our commitment to prepare to succeed separates those of us who win from those of us who only wish. Vince Lombardi Jr., lawyer, author of Coaching for Teamwork: Winning Concepts for Business in the 21st Century, *and son of one of the all-time great football coaches, understands success firsthand.*

WHAT IT TAKES TO BE NUMBER ONE

VINCE LOMBARDI JR.

"The successful man is himself," my father used to say. "To be successful, you've got to be honest with yourself."

People have an unerring nose for dishonesty, fraud, pretense, and posturing. You can't fake it. When faced with a crisis, a leader must draw on resources from within to meet the challenge. This is tough to do if you don't know your inner strengths. So it is vitally important that you determine your principles, who you are, what you stand for, and what your strengths and weaknesses are—in other words, self-knowledge.

That means that you have to discover and work with your own model. You can't be Vince Lombardi, nor should you try. You should be you.

As my father said, "In all my years of coaching, I have never been successful using somebody else's plays."

Total Commitment

I would say that the quality of each man's life is the full measure of that man's personal commitment to excellence and to victory—whether it be football, whether it be business, whether it be politics or government.

53

Closely related to the habit of sacrifice is the habit of *total commitment*. The difference is really a matter of shading. Sacrifice implies an awareness of what you're giving up, whereas total commitment implies a lack of awareness about anything except the task at hand. Total commitment means no loafing, idling, standing around, goofing off, or phoning in sick.

The essence of commitment is the act of making a decision. The Latin root for *decision* means to cut away from, as an incision during surgery. When you commit to something, you are cutting away all other possibilities, all other options. When you commit to something, you are cutting away all the rationalizations, all the excuses.

Coach Lombardi expected 100 percent effort, 100 percent of the time. No excuses, no rationalizations. He confessed that it was hard to define a 100 percent effort, beyond a simple statement: "It was all there was. There was nothing left." He said, with conviction, that he knew that kind of effort when he saw it. Upon arriving in Green Bay, Wisconsin, he felt that perhaps half of the Packers gave 100 percent most of the time. To win a championship, he told them, they all had to give 100 percent, 100 percent of the time.

> *I'd rather have a player with 50 percent ability and 100 percent desire because the guy with 100 percent desire is going to play every day, so you can make a system to fit what he can do. The other guy— the guy with 100 percent ability and 50 percent desire—can screw up your whole system because one day he'll be out there waltzing around.*

Intensity, singleness of purpose, total commitment: these were qualities that I believe had the most to do with the Packers' success. And no one worked harder, no one wanted to win and succeed more, than my father did.

From *What It Takes to Be Number One* by Vince Lombardi Jr., copyright ©2001. Used by permission of McGraw-Hill Companies.

Careful study of a self-made businessperson or elite athlete reveals important qualities: hard work, ingenuity, persistence, energy—and knowing when to advance or retreat. These are tenacious people who firmly adhere to their principles, their methods, and their belief in doing something until they get it right every time. Shelli Howlett is a self-made businessperson having built her franchise operation throughout the greater Dallas-Fort Worth area and beyond.

NAKED ON THE EDGE OF TOWN

SHELLI HOWLETT

The year was 1979; the place was Tehran International Airport; the man standing with his wife and two young children was Nosrat Bakhshian, an Iranian businessman about to board a flight for the United States. The government had imposed martial law in all cities of the Persian Gulf state that day and, after arriving at the airport the morning of January 16, Nosrat had learned that Shah Reza Pahlavi had fled and the country was about to be engulfed by an Islamic revolution.

The news confirmed the decision Bakhshian, a Jew and supporter of the monarchy, had made and the action he was about to take. If he stayed, he and his young family risked discrimination at best and death by mob at worst. Still, leaving Iran was a gut-wrenching move.

Eighteen years earlier, he had started a small commercial printing company and, despite many setbacks, had built it into an enterprise employing 40 people—substantial in the Iran of that day—and wielding assets of several million dollars. He drove a Mercedes, lived comfortably if not lavishly in a recently built 4,000-square-foot private home, and owned a business with a clientele of blue-chip multinational companies.

55

Bakhshian had achieved his successes, despite difficulties, because of a specific set of personal qualities. He was hardworking, logging years of 80-hour weeks at the printing business. Only recently had he begun to ease up and look forward to retirement as he and his wife achieved a level of security.

He was optimistic, discounting his fellow Iranian Jews' fears of a Holocaust-like persecution under the coming Islamic regime. "That won't happen," he stated when concerns were raised in the period before the revolution. "There may be a few riots. Then this will go away."

He was remarkably resourceful, having started his enterprise in 1961 when printing equipment and supplies were in such short supply in Iran that he sometimes had to resort to bribery to obtain them. He was persistent, having weathered the bankruptcy of his original partners, which forced him to start over with a crushing burden of debt and ruinous interest rates of 15 to 20 percent.

Bakhshian summed up his attitude toward such adversities for his three sons: "If I drop you at the edge of town naked with no identification or money, in six months you'll have a job and own some property." It was a standard he strove to live up to, and did.

Now, he was about to need all these qualities and more as he abandoned his thriving business, his comfortable life, and all but a fraction of his personal wealth in a desperate flight to save the lives of his family. The revolution he feared took place, followed by the establishment of a radical fundamentalist Islamic government that would make it impossible for someone like him to live in Iran. When he boarded the plane for John F. Kennedy Airport in New York, it was the last time he would see Iran. He was leaving behind the comfort, prestige, and security he had spent his life building, as well as the culture he knew and loved.

But Bakhshian accommodated this punishing loss with the same courage and strength he had used to build his former life. Before long, he had settled in the Dallas–Fort Worth area and started a new company, SixB Labels, that in time grew to become a substantial enterprise.

In Texas, another of Bakhshian's qualities, perhaps his most striking trait, came to the fore. He had an unusual ability to connect with people, to understand their needs and address them without demanding to know what was in it for him. One asset he brought to this field was a gift for languages. He spoke Persian and French fluently and had some facility with other languages, from English to Russian. This ability had helped him land lucrative printing contracts in Iran with multinationals such as AT&T.

With his unusual background, Bakhshian cut an exotic figure in the Texas printing scene. Yet he quickly understood he would have to approach business in America differently if he were truly to stand out. Rather than being one of a handful of technically skilled commercial printers, as he was in Iran, he would be one of thousands of well-equipped competitors struggling for sales. Without the resources to purchase a large quantity of sophisticated equipment, he would be unable to go after the mainstream commercial printing business that had sustained him in Iran. His older sons, Fari and Farzin—who had been earning degrees in printing technology at the Rochester Institute of Technology in Rochester, New York when Bakhshian, younger son Bobby, and the rest of the family came to America—helped him develop a plan to specialize in label printing, a less competitive field requiring considerable technical expertise.

Bakhshian worked hard as always and, despite everything, remained optimistic. Only a couple of years after they started SixB Labels with a single printing press, he announced it was time to buy another.

"Why?" asked Farzin, pointing out that their single press was then busy only 40 percent of the time at best.

Nosrat Bakhshian explained: "When you're building a business and have gotten some customers, if that press breaks down, you're going to lose those customers." With a second press, even if it often sat unused, they would be able to make deadlines and fulfill commitments in the event of mechanical problems.

"Don't worry," he continued. "The business will come. But you have to prepare for it." He then proceeded to order a second press, stipulating as always the latest, most advanced, most costly technology available. Before long, his optimism was vindicated as enough orders came pouring in to keep both presses busy.

Bakhshian's wisdom and generosity had a powerful influence on many people. Naturally, his own family was most affected. Farzin, Fari, and

Bobby have institutionalized their father's networking proclivities by setting up a series of structured networking events for people in the printing and allied industries. They invite printers, designers, and other specialists to regular meetings and give them color-coded badges. The gatherings feature speakers from a variety of fields, so attendees can network and get a variety of viewpoints rather than a one-note sales pitch from the sponsoring company. Like their father, they promote the industry rather than seeking only personal gain.

It is a measure of the respect that his sons hold for him that, after Bakhshian's untimely death in 1991 at age 68, none of them took over the president's title that he vacated. "My business card to this day still says 'Vice President,'" says Fari. Farzin carries the title of Sales Manager, and Bobby is Director of Marketing. All of them exhibit many of the traits Bakhshian would have wanted in his descendants, including his tenacity, his compassion, his ability to communicate and connect, and especially his resourcefulness.

One thing they aren't likely to have to do is to start practically from nothing, naked on the edge of town. Nosrat Bakhshian already did that for them.

———•-•-•———

Hard work alone isn't enough to gain an edge. We have to apply our native talents—a good brain, perhaps a unique physical ability—with diligence, intelligence, and excellence. A common man who creatively combines these assets may not only achieve success—he might help win a war. Bill Auxier knows such a man—his grandfather. Inspired by the success of his Grandpa Earl, Bill, a successful business and family man in Michigan, is director of marketing for a surgical instrument company and co-owner of a sign company with his wife, Elise. When asked about his "crowning success," his priorities become apparent. "My crowning success is, along with my long-time wife and business partner, Elise, raising my two children."

GRANDPA EARL

BILL AUXIER

Some men are destined to be famous. Others are destined to be the men behind the famous men, working just as hard but content to make their mark behind the scenes. My grandfather is one of those less-known men. Most people don't even know he exists, but the world would never have been the same without him.

Earl Bartholomew entered the world on the first day of the new century: January 1, 1901. His parents ran a feed store in rural Oklahoma, and every day was a struggle to make ends meet. They managed to put bread on the table, but not much else. Earl and his two siblings did their best to help out, and from the beginning, Earl's talents as a craftsman shone through. He was good at putting things together and would often contribute to his family by building furniture for their home. He filled the empty house with chairs, tables, and even a sofa.

Growing up poor did not inhibit Earl; in fact, it did just the opposite. He became quite determined to escape the poverty his family knew. His escape route was a combination of hard work, personal pride, curiosity, and intelligence.

Earl graduated from high school as class valedictorian. He enrolled in the University of Oklahoma, where his hard work and determination to succeed paid off. He was especially good at math—perhaps too good. At the end of the semester, one of his math instructors confessed a ploy he had used. On several occasions, feeling unprepared to answer Earl's eager questions, the professor "forgot" to bring his briefcase. He would ask Earl to go to his home and retrieve it. By the time Earl returned, class was over.

Earl graduated with honors and earned three degrees: bachelor of arts, bachelor of science, and master of science. When presented with the opportunity to teach thermodynamics at the Harvard School of Mechanical Engineering, he jumped at it. Earl and his new wife, Juanita, packed their bags and moved to Boston. In reflection, Earl said that some of his fondest memories came from the time he spent at Harvard. While there, he solidly established himself as a leading expert in the field of thermodynamics. However, Earl's career at Harvard was short-lived. Industry beckoned, and Earl could not resist.

In 1926, Earl became an integral part of the research team at Ethyl Gasoline Corporation. Ethyl's mission can be summed up in the wording on a plaque once exhibited in the lobby of the Detroit research laboratory: "The problems of engines, fuels, and lubricants are inseparable."

With the coming of World War II, Earl's responsibilities increased. In his role as head of the research laboratory, he spent a great deal of time developing products to help the war effort. Many of his projects were top secret; one was considered so important that the patent applications were placed under a cloak of secrecy until the war was over.

Ethyl Corporation, as it was then known, was the birthplace of tetraethyl lead, the fuel additive that raised the octane rating of aviation fuel and improved engine performance. During the war, the demand for tetraethyl lead exceeded supply; rationing became mandatory, and military aviation fuel received top priority. Even though American aviation fuel had an octane rating only slightly higher than that of German fuel, it was often the difference between life and death. It enabled U.S. fighter pilots to outmaneuver the Germans in dogfights and gain control of the airspace over Europe.

On another front, General George Patton, fighting Field Marshall Erwin Rommel's forces in the deserts of North Africa, ran into problems with the diesel engines of his tanks: after being shut down, they would not restart. Patton traveled to Earl's laboratory in Detroit seeking a solution. For Earl, it was a simple challenge. With a few modifications, he formulated a new diesel fuel that could withstand the rigors of the North African desert with no ill effects on the machinery. This improvement helped the Allies prevail across North Africa and, eventually, all the way to Berlin.

Earl Bartholomew earned great respect within his professional circle and was recognized with the Society of Automotive Engineers' Harry L. Horning Memorial Award for lifetime achievement. His innovations won him several patents, and today his name is synonymous with excellence among his peers. Yet most people have no idea who he was, and his contributions to winning the war never gained him the national recognition that others received for similar accomplishments. But none of that mattered to Grandpa Earl. He was simply doing his job.

What made him so successful? How did this man, who started from such humble beginnings, play such a significant part in helping his country win the war? Curiosity, hard work, the pursuit of excellence, personal pride, single-mindedness, thinking outside the box, a strong work ethic, and intelligence all played a role. Earl used his brain as a carpenter uses a hammer, to put together the parts of a yet-to-be-discovered structure.

Above all, Earl knew to keep going after others gave up. Whether it was finding that one last compound in the beaker during a chemistry exam, formulating aviation fuel with a slightly higher octane, or puzzling out how to keep diesel fuel from destroying tank engines, Earl Bartholomew understood that success came from taking that extra step.

How can you double the size of your business—twice in six years? First, evaluate your current direction, assess the competition, and think "outside the box." This process will often reveal a new path to growth. Next, work like hell for many long hours to implement that new vision. Mike Garrison and Richard Osmann discovered that success lives very nearby— in the same town. Mike, co-founder and partner in the Referral Institute, teaches businesspeople how to succeed through word-of-mouth referrals. Richard, president of Provanedge Inc., a process engineering company, gained a taste of success firsthand as summa cum laude while finishing his doctorate of education.

QUIET VISION: THE TAUBMAN WAY TO SUCCESS

MIKE GARRISON AND RICHARD OSMANN, ED.D.

Watching his father help 500 European Jews escape the Nazis during World War II—by claiming them as cousins—might have made a formative impression on the character of young Nicholas Taubman. Or maybe it was the selfless example of his mother giving his father her wedding ring back, to sell for his down payment on three failing auto parts stores in Roanoke, Virginia.

Taubman, as private as he is successful, doesn't discuss what made him into the man who would one day take over his father's auto parts business and turn it into a $2.5 billion-a-year retail titan. The self-effacing Taubman knows the difference between a celebrity CEO and a solid business leader. He has always endeavored to be the latter, going about his life with quiet dignity, shunning the spotlight while attending to his company, his community, and his family.

Not exactly the stuff of movies or exposés. No glitz. No glamour. An observer could just about nod off at this point in the story (a possibility that might bring a smile to Taubman's face).

Then the lightbulb goes on. With 32,000 employees (the company calls them "team members") and more than 2,400 stores in 38 states, Advance Auto Parts didn't get where it is today without somebody at the reins possessed of some moxie. Who is this guy?

The son of Jewish immigrants Grace and Arthur Taubman, Nick Taubman made a nationwide business from his father's small group of stores due in no small measure to his deliberately unglamorous lifestyle and incredible work ethic. Although retired now, Taubman worked six- and seven-day weeks for the 30-plus years he ran the company after his father's retirement.

With a schedule like that, was Taubman a maniacal, controlling workaholic? Hardly. Friends and associates call him "unassuming" and "low-profile"—as well as "focused" and "resourceful." They also usually call him "Mr. Taubman," not only out of respect for his stellar accomplishments, but also because of the respect he has shown to those who work in the Advance Auto Parts "family."

Taubman had the humility and insight to pursue success by surrounding himself with skilled and knowledgeable leaders, providing the company with a team of top talent to move it toward his vision. He would probably note that many people had a hand in the company's good fortune. He'd be much less likely to trumpet something just as obvious—that he knew how to pick the right people and let them do their job.

His strategic vision and unbloated ego enabled him to mold the company to the realities of the marketplace. He quickly recognized that the firm could grow much larger by targeting a narrower niche of customers.

This epiphany came as he visited one of the company's stores, then known as Advance Stores, in North Carolina in the early 1970s. The comfortably sleepy regional retailer had expanded its product mix haphazardly over the years, selling an undifferentiated array of household goods and auto parts. "Everything I'm looking at I can buy [somewhere else] with more service, more variety, and cheaper," Taubman realized, as he recalled during a 2002 interview with the *Roanoke Times*.

If Advance had continued to offer a little of this and a little of that, it would have been just another variety merchandise store. Taubman saw that battling the "sell-it-all" big-box stores would be a bad bet. Getting hammered in the retail version of trench warfare was not his idea of a good time.

So he coaxed his company out of its rut and turned it toward more profitable territory. Changing the name Advance Stores to Advance Auto Parts, Taubman and his team enforced a laserlike product focus and moved quickly to dominate the auto parts aftermarket. It was quite a change: new focus, new stores, new strategy. All of which meant new suppliers and new products for the sales staff to learn.

Taubman built on his vision, imagining a nimble niche business that would not only provide auto parts for consumers faster than his competitors, but would also deliver auto parts to repair shops—an unusual crossover move in the industry at the time. "I decided . . . that we were going to be a large company," he said in the 2002 *Roanoke Times* article. "Size matters."

Taubman and his Advance Auto Parts team were dedicated to seeing the transformation process through to its conclusion. "There were far more failures than successes," he admitted.

Taubman could take risks because his personal ego was not on the line. By separating himself from his business success, he was able to make the hard decisions necessary for the company to grow.

One of those hard decisions was eventually to take Advance Auto Parts public. Taubman recognized that going public would open the company to a wider variety of experts who could shape its future. "When you're a privately held company," he said in a 1985 *Washington Post* interview, "the president is only accountable to God and the creditors."

Communicating his vision to top executives—and investors—was critical so everyone would be pulling and building in the same direction. The results were nothing shy of magnificent: the company doubled in size every three years from the late 1980s to the mid-1990s.

What didn't grow was Taubman's own opinion of himself, nor his willingness to indulge in public accolades. He remained the same private, noncelebrity business leader who shunned headlines in favor of bottom lines.

Taubman led by example, demonstrating even in his transition to retirement that the culture of mutual respect, hard work, and strategic focus he created could sustain itself profitably after his departure. His quiet vision remains as a living hallmark of his successful leadership at Advance Auto Parts.

———•◦•———

Effort and system are essential to getting good results and, in the end, winning. Following a system means learning and developing the skills related to each fundamental component of that system: repeatedly practicing musical scales to play the piano, exercising and drilling to play football, honing networking skills to build a business. Your results will be commensurate with the time and energy you put in to learn the components of your system. Author Ivan Misner is fond of saying, "The secret to success without a little bit of hard work is still a secret."

———•••———

THE FUNDAMENTALS OF SUCCESS

IVAN MISNER, PH.D.

I learned an important lesson about the fundamentals of success many years ago while playing high school football in southern California. We had a fairly good team in my junior year. Most of the team members were juniors, so the following year the team had mostly seniors, and we had some pretty high expectations for the season. Something like this can make people a bit overconfident, and that's exactly how we were at the beginning of my senior year.

When the season started, we experienced that brutal rite of passage known by all football teams as Hell Week. It's called that for a very good reason: the conditioning that a team is put through is pure hell.

During Hell Week, the team does very little other than drills and conditioning exercises: isometric exercises, wind sprints (you know, those short-distance sprints as fast as you can possibly run), hitting bags, tackling dummies, running in place and hitting the ground on command, more wind sprints, running up and down stadium steps, hitting the sled (while the fattest coaches known to man are standing on them yelling at you)—and did I mention wind sprints? Lots and lots of wind sprints! We were doing so many drills, we never even saw a football (except those that were thrown at the backsides of the slower players).

We knew we were going to be a good team, and we felt we didn't need to go through all this nonsense. We wanted to play ball, not run around the field hitting bags and doing wind sprints. So we staged a little rebellion. We pulled Coach aside after a practice and told him, "We don't want to do wind sprints anymore. We want to play ball!"

Now, I don't know if you know any high school football coaches, but I must confess that I don't believe they are the most self-actualized guys you'll ever meet. Most of them aren't really in touch with their more sensitive side, and in my experience, they don't react well when confronted by their players. They generally have two answers for anything they don't like. The first is, "No!" The second is, "What part of 'No!' didn't you understand?"

Imagine our surprise when he said, "OK, I'll make you a deal. If you get here an hour early tomorrow morning for a little bus ride, I'll let you drop the conditioning program, if you want."

It took us about two seconds to say, "Road trip and no wind sprints? We're there, Coach!"

Next morning, Coach showed up with a big yellow bus and drove the 40 of us off into the unknown—which turned out to be Cal State University, Fullerton. This was in the mid-'70s, and we knew that the Fullerton stadium was one of the practice fields for the Los Angeles Rams. When we realized we were going to see a Rams practice, we were stoked!

Sure enough, the Rams were there when we arrived. However, we soon discovered that it was a closed practice. No one was allowed in the stadium except the players, coaches, and trainers—no press, no spectators, and certainly no rowdy boys from a high school football team. The fences were covered with green mesh, and there were security guards at every gate.

Coach walked over and said something to a guard. The guard called over one of the assistant coaches, and Coach chatted with him for a few minutes. Then he turned and hollered at us, "Come on, boys, we're going in!"

As we entered the stadium, we were in awe. It's one thing to be in a football stadium looking down at the field, but it's something else entirely to be on the field looking up. Even though it was the same size as our field back home, it felt gigantic. And as if that weren't enough, the Rams started to come onto the field.

If you've never seen professional football players up close and personal, let me tell you—these men are huge! When they are suited up in full regalia, they are absolutely gigantic. Let's see if I can give you some perspective: imagine a railroad car wearing a football helmet. These guys had one eye in the middle of their heads and hair on their teeth. They were frightening to stand next to.

We watched as our heroes stepped onto the field. There was number 74, the leader of the Fearsome Foursome, Merlin Olsen. Here was future Hall-of-Famer Jack Youngblood, and over there was All-Pro Isiah Robertson. We were starstruck. These guys were our idols. We watched in total awe as they lumbered out onto the grass, and for the next two hours—did wind sprints!

Yes, that's right—wind sprints. They were out there tackling dummies, hitting bags, running in place, attacking the sled (with really fat coaches on top, yelling at them)—and did I mention wind sprints? Lots and lots of wind sprints.

Watching all this, we were amazed to see that not only were they doing the same conditioning exercises, they were doing these exercises *in the exact same order we were doing them!* It turned out that the Rams' assistant coach had been the college roommate of one of our coaches and had given him the Rams' conditioning book. We watched for two hours as the coaches ran the Rams through the same kind of program we were being drilled on.

When the practice was over, our coach took us out to the parking lot. "Boys," he said, "we're going to drive back to our campus now. Along the way I want you to think about what we've seen here today. I don't want a lot of chatter. I want you guys to really think about what you saw. When we get home, I'll have a few words to say, and then you guys can decide what you want to do."

Now, I don't know if you've ever been on a school bus with 40 high school football boys, but let me tell you, it's not pretty. The bus driver cringes in a wire cage, and every 20 minutes or so he throws back a chunk of raw meat to keep the animals quiet. But this occasion was different; I've never before or since seen a football team stay so quiet for so long. During the 45-minute ride back to our school, we thought long and hard about what we had witnessed.

"When we arrived, Coach marched us off the bus and stood us in a big semicircle in the parking lot. No one spoke. He looked at us. Then he said:

Boys, it doesn't matter if you're talking about Pop Warner football, high school football, college football, professional football, or life. If you do not learn to execute the fundamentals flawlessly, you will never be a champion on or off the field. It doesn't matter if you are talking about football, school, or work. When you leave this school and go on to college, you must learn the fundamentals and do the drills that will make you successful in your continuing education. When you go on to your professions and careers, you will see that there are fundamentals that you must learn in order to be a champion in your profession. Only those of you who are willing to develop the physical and mental conditioning necessary to execute these fundamentals will ever succeed in football or in life. This is something you must choose. I can't choose it for you.

"I'll never forget what he said next—this football coach from a small, lower-middle-class, southern California high school:

I can't push a noodle. I can't make you do these things. You have to want to do these things in order to succeed. Your decision today will determine the kind of team this is going to be and the kind of person you will grow into. I'm simply your coach. You are the ones who must have the desire to execute the fundamentals, day in and day out. So talk with each other and make a decision. I'll be in my office when you choose.

"And he walked away."

It took us about ten seconds to vote, and to this day I can hardly believe that I, along with 39 other young men, *enthusiastically* voted to do—wind sprints.

We had a great season. But more important, we learned a supremely important life lesson: Success comes to those who execute the fundamentals flawlessly. It comes to those who work hard on the right things. It comes to those who drill and learn and drill some more.

It comes to those of us who, day in and day out, are willing to do the wind sprints necessary to succeed.

Start with a need, a desire, and then a simple idea, and you have the nucleus of a successful venture. Make the right choices—especially the choice to move ahead—then create a system to deliver the product or service repeatedly over the years, and perhaps you, too, will create an international sales training franchise. Sam Schwartz is a businessman in the Washington, DC, area who is determined to find the same level of success as David Sandler.

DAVID SANDLER: SYSTEMATIC CHANGE

SAM SCHWARTZ

When faced with adversity, people often have two choices: give up, or reinvent themselves and move on. In the late 1960s, David H. Sandler founded a business that became the Sandler Sales Institute, an international firm providing training programs to businesses and sales professionals. Today, his Sandler System improves tens of thousands of businesses and professional lives in the United States and abroad. All because he was abruptly fired one day in 1967.

Back then, 36-year-old Sandler lived the proverbial American dream—a healthy family in Baltimore, a beautiful home, presidency of a family snack-food business, even a boat and a country club membership. But one Friday afternoon, a proxy fight ended with David Sandler out of a job. For the first time in his adult life, there was no paycheck. And while losing the boat and country club was a disappointment, the threat to his family's security was downright frightening.

So now he had to find a job. Fast. Through the classified ads, he found a part-time sales position that would pay the bills and keep him busy until he could rebuild his business. It wasn't the kind of job he really wanted; it was just a way to keep his head above water and his family fed. But that part-time, temporary job would evolve into a long, successful career. It seemed professional sales was his niche.

As he progressed through his new career, he discovered a disturbing trend that he couldn't ignore. The general public's image of a salesperson was unflattering at best: loud, pushy, and eager to trick them into buying things they didn't need. Unacceptable! For years, the Xerox and Dale Carnegie sales approaches had been considered the cutting edge for tackling this tough issue. But Sandler believed that to truly change this distasteful reputation, salespeople needed a different kind of attitude and behavior change. So against the odds, this lone salesperson jumped into the fray with a whole new approach.

Determined to bring integrity to the profession, Sandler developed a simple yet profound approach to successful professional selling—the seven-step Sandler System. He believed that "if you don't have a selling system of your own when you are face-to-face with a prospect, you will likely lose control of the sales call; prospects have a system of their own. The prospects' system never says, 'Sold,' it says, 'Salesperson loses.'"

The seven-step process is a refreshing, time-proven system. It's not a quick-fix technique; each precise step builds on the last. Sandler used an analogy to illustrate this point. In a submarine with seven compartments, people can't move from one compartment to the next without mastering the first and closing the door behind them. In his book, *You Can't Teach a Kid to Ride a Bike at a Seminar: The Sandler Sales Institute's Seven-Step System for Successful Selling*, co-authored with John P. Hayes, Ph.D., Sandler says, "Techniques are important, but salespeople who learn to deliver their techniques with the appropriate attitude and behavior get to the bank most often." And they get there with their dignity intact.

What makes the Sandler System work so well? First, it takes two kinds of people: the people who want to change the way they sell and live and the people who are steadfastly determined to teach, train, and help others grow. Then it takes time. Clients don't master a new attitude by spending a nine-to-five in a crowded seminar room. Rather, the Sandler System's training philosophy is based on gradual, incremental growth and development reinforced over time. It allows clients to learn a new skill and put it to use under pressure in the field.

To build this unique approach to the sales process, Sandler studied books such as *I'm OK, You're OK*, by Thomas A. Harris, and *Games People Play: The Psychology of Human Relationships*, by Eric Berne. Unlike his predecessors, Sandler relied on psychology. The cornerstone of the Sandler System is a basic understanding of people and the human condition. After all, isn't that what selling is all about?

Choosing to focus on the human dynamic, Sandler applied transactional analysis, a theory developed by Berne and described in *Games People Play*, to the selling world. Stated in its simplest form, the Child ego state wants to buy, the Parent ego state gives the permission, and the Adult ego state makes the decision. It made sense. And at the time, no one had tied this useful theory to professional sales.

With a solid theory firmly in mind, Sandler formed Sandler Systems Inc. In 1983, he began selling franchises and providing training and support to franchisees. He made his first sales on the strengths of the innovative selling system and his persuasive personality. As the program began to prove itself, entrepreneurs bought franchises because of the unmistakable success of earlier franchisees.

The keys to so many successful franchises lay in Sandler's respect for his employees and franchisees. He motivated them to make his plans theirs. A master of commitment, he believed in "up-front contracts" that committed employees to specific tasks. Their goals clear, they were willing to move mountains to deliver results without any more follow-up from him than an occasional progress talk. "Most salespeople need managers who allow them to be on 'goal time,' not 'clock time,'" he often preached. With this approach, the level of supervision found in the typical organization just wasn't necessary.

Unwilling to overshadow his franchisees, he said, "I do not want to be the lead man out in front. I want the Sandler franchisees to be out in front." To make his point, he used an analogy of a golfer and caddies. The Sandler franchisees would never be his caddies; they had to be perceived as having strength and potency in the marketplace. For years he turned down

71

their requests to write a book, jump into the speaking circuit, or appear on television shows. But he finally wrote *You Can't Teach a Kid to Ride a Bike at a Seminar*—published in the United States and abroad—to share his story and the Sandler System.

True to his philosophy, he had the first 50,000 copies printed exclusively for the franchisees. Instead of the traditional hardcover book jacket with the author on the back, Sandler franchisees were able to feature their own pictures and biographies instead. His point? To make the public equate the Sandler Sales Institute with a strong group of dedicated people, not one man.

David Sandler left a profound mark on the professional sales community. Tens of thousands of clients have benefited from the Sandler System training and the lasting improvement in not just their level of professional success but their personal lives as well. After his death in 1995, the entrepreneurial team of employees and franchisees around the world continued to carry his legacy forward and fuel the creative engine that produced innovative programs. By 2003, there were franchises throughout the United States and Canada as well as in Athens, Greece; Birmingham, England; and Dublin, Ireland. More are in the works.

So what made David Sandler choose to reinvent himself and not give up? Why did his ideas take off and grow? Supporting his family was certainly a primary concern. And they were a vital source of support and motivation. The rest came from a philosophy of success. First came plain hard work and balance. With limitless energy, Sandler believed in running hard for three weeks and taking the fourth week off. Then he kept his focus on success, even in the face of failure. He often said, "Being broke is a condition . . . being poor is a state of mind." How could a philosophy like this leave room for anything but reinvention?

The early loss of his family business was not a failure; it was a wake-up call. He vowed never to be in that condition again. So equipped with vision, fortitude, and integrity, one salesman succeeded in establishing an exceptional approach to sales that rivaled the giants of the day.

To paraphrase Ralph Waldo Emerson, "Build a better mouse-trap and the world will beat a path to your door." The world will find you much faster, however, when you create—or follow—a successful system to masterfully market that mousetrap. A successful system means that all the parts are integrated and designed to reinforce productivity and forward movement by the other parts. Apply the notion of success systems to your efforts and you will help transform the art of success into the science of success. Ed Craine and Charles Legalos are business partners working as organizational consultants in the San Francisco Bay area.

A MARKETING SUCCESS SYSTEM

CHARLES LEGALOS, PH.D. AND EDWARD CRAINE, MBA

One of the crucial factors in keeping any business growing is the ability to bring in new business. Of course, that's often easier said than done. Most average businesses struggle to bring in a good stream of relatively steady new business. But some businesses manage to bring in a steady stream of high-quality new business. Could there be a system to their success? More important, would your business improve if you adopted that system? We were determined to find out.

When we originally set out to find out why some people are more successful than others in generating new business, we were specifically interested in three axioms of business development lore:

1. *The 80/20 Rule.* That is, 80 percent of the results in an organization come from 20 percent of the people.
2. *Give again.* In other words, give back. Plow resources into your business. Give to your community. Give to your network members. If you want to get business, you have to give business.

3. *It's not what you know, it's who you know.* Your contacts make a difference in business development activities.

Much of what is said and written about these axioms is anecdotal. We wanted see if we could quantify some of these ideas. Our initial research focused on members of a large business referral organization called Business Network International (BNI). Its members meet weekly in chapters where the sole purpose is to obtain more business through referrals found by other members. Chapters typically have from 15 to 35 members. Members record the number of referrals they give and receive as well as the dollar value resulting from closed transactions of referrals received. This organization is very structured and has a broad geographic and social distribution among its membership. Its policy is to admit only one person per business category in each group or chapter. As a result, we were able to include a large cross section of businesses in our study.

The first area we measured was the members' perceptions regarding one another on a "helpfulness" scale. We asked each member to record who in the group they can give referrals to on a consistent basis. Next, they were asked to record who in the group they can get referrals from on a consistent basis. This measure was not based on actual referrals given and received but only on each member's perception of the others' ability to give qualified referrals. From this data we compiled a PowerGrid™, or matrix of the members' perceptions of ability to give and receive business referrals with each person within the group. A person was considered "helpful" if he or she was seen by those reporting as being able to give them referrals on a consistent basis. Next, we measured the members' reported closed business in dollars received from BNI referrals to see if there was any correlation between helpfulness and money earned.

Although our research is preliminary, the early results are compelling and sometimes surprising. Our data revealed that 20 percent of members reported earnings substantially higher than the other 80 percent! The 80/20 rule does seem to apply, lending validity to our first axiom. More important, these high achievers shared several characteristics.

First, the high earners were seen as the most helpful. More people identified the high earners as being able to give referrals versus receive referrals. This classified them as "Givers" on our PowerGrid chart. Because the high earners were also identified most often as Givers, it reinforced the organization's philosophy and our second axiom that in order to get business you need to give business: "Givers gain."

Second, most of the high earners also had more reciprocal relationships, or what we call Critical Contacts™. These are relationships where two parties believe they can, and do, naturally refer business to each other consistently. What makes this relationship particularly referral-friendly is that, regardless of the business each is in, they serve primarily the same target market. Members in the high-earning group typically had five to seven of these reciprocal arrangements, while the low-earning members had only one or two critical contacts. Based on these preliminary results, we are becoming more certain that our third axiom is also true—it's not what you know, it's who you know that really gives the edge to business.

The third characteristic we've found that high achievers share is that they have the most accurate assessment of their ability to give or receive referrals. By looking at our PowerGrid chart, we were able to compare each member's perception of who he or she can give referrals to with what other members think this individual can offer each of them. We do the same for each individual's perception about being able to receive a referral from each other member, comparing it to whether each member can give a referral to this individual. For example, say John and Jane were in the same BNI group. If John thought he could receive referrals from Jane and Jane thought she could give referrals to John, they would be in agreement. On the other hand, if Jane thought she couldn't give John referrals, they would not be. The more a member's perceptions are in accordance with others' views of him or her, the more successful that member will be. More important, the more accurately you can define your relationships like this in the group, the more likely you are to be in the 20 percent of high achievers.

Our work with corporate and individual clients reinforces and extends our findings. For example, when we consulted with a Fortune 500 company, we found that the most productive salespeople had unknowingly developed several Critical Contacts. Those with the most success seemed to have about seven. This is consistent with our study.

Therefore, in order to achieve maximum success in bringing in new business, our emphasis has been on developing seven contacts for each salesperson. By following this principle and focusing on a small number of Critical Contacts, several of our small-business clients dramatically increased their income as well.

Based on our early research findings and our clients' results, we were able to conclude that there are two keys to achieving great results from your business development program. We recommend two strategies:

1. *Create a team of Critical Contacts that will form the basis of your network.* To create your team, identify seven other businesses that sell to your target market but do not compete with you. Approach these people with the suggestion of teaming up to help each other expand your respective businesses.

2. *Become a Giver to those individuals in your referral network.* As we stated earlier, in order to receive, you need to give. Find or create a forum where you meet regularly so you can get to know and help each other. You need to understand your team members' goals, accomplishments, and problems. Learn how to sell or refer them to your other contacts and to train them how to sell and refer to you.

When you give a good referral, both your client and your Critical Contact partner will be grateful and feel the need to reciprocate. Your clients will think of you as the go-to person whenever they need a contact or piece of information. This will give you the opportunity to become the preferred hub through which your clients and their referrals travel to meet their needs. Your clients will naturally gravitate toward you and your team when they need a product or service, including your own. Your team members will expand their businesses and have more referrals for you. Done properly, and given enough time to work, developing your Critical Contact team and becoming a Giver will cause your business to explode!

Success often is not very glamorous. It usually comes from a lot of tedious effort aimed at improving one's activity. Following a system of beliefs helps us focus that effort and set priorities. When we stick to our system of beliefs and apply its principles throughout our organization, we demonstrate integrity—an essential hallmark of success. Dan Rawls, a successful young business owner in Tennessee, writes of a successful man who infused his business with his personal beliefs.

———•◦•———

A SECRET RECIPE FOR SUCCESS

DAN RAWLS

S. Truett Cathy has only one secret.

In this era when business success stories often have dramatic trajectories—from big-splash start-up through megamerger followed by megaflameout—the tale of Cathy's slow, plodding march toward fortune draws barely a glance from headline writers. The bright lights illuminating sexy scandals, accounting shenanigans, and aim-for-the-stars bravado leave Cathy's company blissfully in the shadows.

Cathy started with a simple vision. Into this vision he invested four years of research.

He experimented. He tested. He needed the result to be complicated so no one could easily replicate his creation. And he needed it to be good. Really good.

At last, he had it. He wrote it down, folded the piece of paper, and put it in his pocket. It was his recipe for success.

To this day, Cathy refuses to divulge the details of what he wrote.

His secret was not the diagram of an amazing computer chip. Nor was it a map of the human genome. It was—are you sitting down?—the recipe for a chicken sandwich.

That's right. A chicken sandwich. But in 1946 it happened to be the first sandwich of its kind to be sold in a restaurant. That restaurant—Cathy's first, the Dwarf Grill (a tiny diner near Atlanta, Georgia)—was the egg out of which his Chick-fil-A® quick-service restaurant chain would peck its way to a billion-dollar-a-year business with more than a 1,000 locations spread throughout 36 states and the District of Columbia.

While Cathy keeps his sandwich recipe under wraps, this founder and CEO of Chick-fil-A is happy to discuss his company's success secret. "You have to re-earn your reputation every day," he says.

Well, almost every day. Chick-fil-A is never open on Sunday.

"Our decision to close on Sunday was our way of honoring God and directing our attention to things more important than our business," notes Cathy in *Eat More Chikin, Inspire More People.* "If it took seven days a week to make a living with a restaurant, then we needed to be in some other line of work. Through the years I have never wavered from that position."

Cathy's view of success might differ from many other business leaders'. Going against the grain by closing his establishments on the most restaurant-going day of the week makes perfect sense in light of his priorities.

"When I was asked how I would like to be remembered when I leave here," explains Cathy, "my first response was that I want to be remembered as having kept my priorities in order." Numbers one and two on his priority list: God and others.

For Cathy, success is all about giving, not receiving. Giving to God, to his family, to his employees and countless young people.

"Success is a continual thing," he observes. Cathy says he wants to have "not only a successful business, but also a successful family and a successful relationship with my staff and the people who trusted me by offering me bank loans as I built our business."

Few people in such high-profile positions profess their religious convictions. Those willing to espouse their belief in biblical principles as a blueprint for success are even more rare. Cathy does both.

"If you want to construct a successful life, you have to consider what is important to you and what you are striving for," he says. "Being a Christian, I feel it is very important to have a good relationship with the Lord. I see no conflict between biblical principles and good business practices."

Cathy built his views right into his company's mission. Chick-fil-A's official statement of corporate purpose says, "We exist to glorify God by being a faithful steward of all that is entrusted to us and to have a positive influence on all who come in contact with Chick-fil-A."

Cathy's devotion to these principles explains his similarly steadfast commitment to others. As Chick-fil-A's Web site explains, "That's why we invest in scholarships, character-building programs for kids, foster homes, and other community services. Come to think of it, it's also not a bad motive for striving to serve a really, really good sandwich."

Although his special emphasis on relationships with family, employees, customers, and his many foster children grows out of Cathy's beliefs, he has the business savvy to understand that taking care of people also helps his long-term success. Happy employees, after all, do a better job of serving customers. Customers who are treated well become repeat customers.

"The concentration in most companies is put on the dollar value rather than the people, but if you take care of the people, you will generate the profit that you are looking for. Just don't concentrate on it," he urges. "Money is all right as long as you keep it in your hand and not your heart."

One of his favorite Bible teachings puts his view of success in perspective: A good name is more to be desired than great riches.

"I enjoy things that success brings to you, but material things are a minor part of it," Cathy explains. "I have a wife who has been very dedicated, and we've been married 55 years. We have three wonderful children who are happily married, we have 12 natural grandchildren and more than 145 adopted grandchildren. So who could want more?"

Cathy cares for his foster grandchildren through an organization he and wife, Jeannette, started in 1984: the WinShape Foundation. The name comes from the goal of "shaping winners." The WinShape Foster Homes provide love, care, and discipline to children in Georgia, Tennessee, Alabama, and Brazil.

"I tell young people that success is a choice that you make in life," says Cathy. "I think it's easier to succeed than fail. I am not saying that success is easy. What I am saying is that it is easier to pay the price of success than the price you have to pay for failure."

Cathy knows something about paying the price. A fire destroyed his first restaurant. Although the disaster could easily have deterred his climb to the pinnacle of success, his commitment and beliefs kept him focused.

"Business is like a roller coaster," he observes. "There are many ups and downs. It's how you handle the difficult situations that makes the difference."

Cathy outlines his three keys to success—"and these are pretty simple," he says. "You've got to want to. You've got to develop the skills and the know-how. You've got to do it."

Chick-fil-A has found three more keys to success through its popular trio of "Eat Mor Chikin" cows. The amusing mascots "have become more than characters in an advertisement," muses Cathy. "They're real. Wherever I go I carry a bunch of our plush cow toys. They always make people happy."

They're no doubt popular with his many foster grandchildren, too. "When I work with young people, I ask them what they want to be when they grow up," says Cathy. "One boy said, 'When I grow up, I want to be just like you.' I picked him up and said, 'This is the highest compliment I have ever received.'"

Making people happy is S. Truett Cathy's real secret to success. It's a secret he is happy to share.

———•••———

Achieving success is a never-ending process that runs through all areas of our lives. It requires us to focus on a long-term goal while simultaneously attending to all of life's details. It demands that we excel at each task and make the best possible choices along the way. And it invites us to seek a stabilizing force that can keep us balanced as our interests mature and shift between our career, our family, and our community. Dan Georgevich has built one of the most successful marketing franchises in the Midwest by focusing on small details and watching the goal.

THE VOICE OF SUCCESS

DAN GEORGEVICH

Morning rush hour in Detroit: a seething mass of motorists jockeying for position on a crazy quilt of congested interstates. Bumper-to-bumper traffic, honking horns, high stress. Doesn't look like any fun. Hey, wait a minute. Why is that guy in the pickup truck laughing? And that lady over there in the BMW? Why the big smiles on the faces of everyone in that minivan? There must be more than meets the eye to morning in Motown.

It's what meets the ear, not the eye, that brings all that mirth to the mugs of Detroit's morning commuters: the voice of Dick Purtan. Host of the *Morning Show* on Detroit's WOMC Oldies FM 104.3, Purtan and his team entertain listeners throughout Michigan, Ohio, and Ontario with comedic commentary on current events and public figures.

It's a format Purtan has perfected over the 40 years he's been behind the mike, bringing him a long list of local and national awards—and on the flip side, the reason he was dumped from a Baltimore station in 1968 after only five weeks on the air. "They thought I was too wild for the town," says Purtan, who started his career as a country-and-western DJ on a Syracuse, New York, station for $1 per hour while he attended graduate school at Syracuse University.

His break came on the day he drove broadcasting legend David Susskind to the airport after a speech at the university. Susskind put Purtan in touch with his friend Ben Richmond, who owned several radio stations around the country. Richmond hired Purtan for a slot on his station in Jacksonville, Florida, and the rest, as they say, is history.

Purtan's time-tested resume and trophy collection sure make him look like he's hit the pinnacle of success. His official kudos include the Radio and Records Industry Achievement Award, the National Association of Broadcasters Marconi Award, *Billboard* magazine's Major Market Air Personality of the Year—twice—and a nomination for induction into the Radio Hall of Fame in Chicago. He's been profiled on ABC, CBS, NBC, and CNN, and featured in *People, Newsweek, Time,* and *US* magazines. The New York Museum of Radio and Television Broadcasting archives contain excerpts of his show. He even had a role in Eddie Murphy's *Beverly Hills Cop II.*

Asking Detroit's most popular and long-standing radio personality why he's been so successful can be a little frustrating, though. He'll tell you at first that he doesn't know—which can lead to a little head-scratching by an uninitiated interviewer. C'mon, you're famous, doing fine in the dough department, and you enjoy broad respect in your profession. What gives?

"I've seen people go for the money instead of what they enjoyed," says Purtan. "When you do that, relationships fall apart because all you do is wheel and deal. The truth is, if you commit yourself to doing a good job every day, you're gonna make money. You can't go for the money and expect that things will turn out. Living your life a day at a time and working hard makes for a happy family and teaches your kids realistic ethics for every part of their lives. Going for the money may work in the short run, but it doesn't work in the long run."

His real success, he says, is in providing a solid personal foundation for his six daughters, three of whom have followed him into the broadcasting industry. Daughter Jennifer is an executive vice president with ABC Radio;

Jackie is a writer and performer on Purtan's show; and Joanne worked as a health reporter and women's advocate on Detroit's Channel 7 TV.

"You don't realize how important the family aspect is until you're older," Purtan says. "When you're young, you spend much of your time working your job and thinking about your job, but it changes when you get older. I now believe that the ultimate success is doing a great job of balancing work and personal life, setting a strong example for your children, and giving as much as you can to the community."

This master of the airwaves also has a personal hero, whom he credits with no small part of his success. He even gets to live with her. It's his wife, Gail. As if her commonsense approach to raising their daughters weren't inspiration enough, Gail has waged a six-year fight against ovarian cancer. Dick Purtan himself is tumor-free after being diagnosed with prostate cancer a decade ago.

Dick and Gail together transformed their private struggles for life into public crusades for improved cancer research funding and treatment in Michigan. Their philanthropic contributions through the Gail Purtan Ovarian Cancer Research Fund at the Karmanos Cancer Institute, as well as the Purtan Family Ovarian Cancer Research Foundation, have raised more than $1 million for ongoing research efforts in Detroit and around the country. The couple's tireless support was lauded with the fifth annual McCarty Cancer Foundation Humanitarian Award in March 2003.

Radio has been the perfect forum for the Purtans' philanthropic endeavors. In addition to the foundations he and Gail started for cancer research, Dick's radio show has been pivotal in raising more than $5 million for the Salvation Army's Bed and Bread Truck program over the past 15 years. He also sits on the board of Children's Hospital of Michigan and has raised more than $300,000 for charity from the sale of his *Best of Purtan* CDs and cassettes.

"When Gail was diagnosed, I realized a lot of things," Purtan says. "Every day becomes important—and I don't mean professionally. You realize you only go around once, unless you are Shirley MacLaine. You learn to live with things, make adjustments, and you have to constantly sort things out. I used to think dealing with cancer or other fatal diseases was something you could prepare for, but I don't think so anymore. You have to learn to live patiently.

"I love what I do," he says with enthusiasm. "And that's the ultimate. My goal throughout my career was to do the best I can every day, and parlay that into weeks and months and years in a job I love. This isn't a job, it's just fun."

His positive attitude illuminates a career—and a life—that has demonstrated remarkable staying power. Throughout his career, Purtan focused on one professional goal: to be on the radio long-term. "I think setting specific goals can be a dangerous thing," he explains. "If you don't make it, you look upon yourself as a loser. I never wanted to put myself in such a critical position, so I kept my goal general. Most radio personalities don't last. I don't really know why I've broken the mold and been around all these years. That's a question for my audience."

Back out there on the highway, rush hour is winding down—but the smiles Dick Purtan brought to so many faces no doubt lasted well into the workday. Learning to face life patiently, from a traffic tie-up to a personal crisis, is a lesson his listeners love learning anew every morning.

———•———

How long do you have to work at something to succeed? As long as it takes. (Or until you decide to move in another direction.) Setbacks will happen. Accept them. Turn bumps in the road into lessons and new opportunities, then get on with the next step of your journey. As one of the world's leading experts on personal development and success, Anthony Robbins shares some of his ideas on the pathway to success.

———•———

THE PATHWAY TO SUCCESS

ANTHONY ROBBINS

Success truly is the result of good judgment. Good judgment is the result of experience, and experience is often the result of bad judgment! Those seemingly bad or painful experiences are sometimes the most important. When people succeed, they tend to party; when they fail, they tend to ponder, and they begin to make new distinctions that will enhance the quality of their lives. We must commit to learning from our mistakes, rather than beating ourselves up, or we're destined to make the same mistakes again in the future.

As important as personal experience is, think how invaluable it is to have a role model as well—someone who's navigated the rapids before you and has a good map for you to follow. You can have a role model for your finances, a model for your relationships, a model for your health, a model for your profession, or a model for any aspect of your life you're learning to master. They can save you years of pain and keep you from going over the falls.

There will be times when you're on the river solo and you'll have to make some important decision on your own. The good news is that if you're willing to learn from your experience, then even times you might think were difficult become great because they provide valuable information—*key distinctions*—you will use to make better decisions in the future. In fact, any extremely successful person you meet will tell you—if they're honest with you—that the reason they're more successful is that they've made more poor decisions than you have. People in my seminars often ask me, "How long do you think it will take for me to really master this particular skill?" And my immediate response is, "How long do you want it to take?" If you take action ten times a day (and have the proportionate "learning experiences") while other people act on a new skill once a month, you'll have ten months of experience in a day, you will soon master the skill, and will, ironically, probably be considered "talented and lucky."

I became an excellent public speaker because, rather than once a week, I booked myself to speak *three times a day* to anyone who would listen. While others in my organization had 48 speaking engagements a year, I would have a similar number within *two weeks.* Within a month, I'd have two years of experience. And within a year, I'd have a decade's worth of growth. My associates talked about how "lucky" I was to have been born with such an "innate" talent. I tried to tell them what I'm telling you now: mastery takes as long as you want it to take. By the way, were all of my speeches great? Far from it! But I did make sure that I learned from every experience and that I somehow improved until very soon I could enter a room of any size and be able to reach people from virtually all walks of life.

No matter how prepared you are, there's one thing that I can absolutely guarantee: if you're on the river of life, it's likely you're going to hit a few rocks. That's not being negative; that's being accurate. The key is that when you do run aground, instead of beating yourself up for being such a "failure," remember that *there are no failures in life.* There are only results. If you didn't get the results you wanted, learn from this experience so that you have references about how to make better decisions in the future.

We will either find a way, or make one.

—HANNIBAL

One of the most important decisions you can make to ensure your long-term happiness is to decide *to use whatever life gives you in the moment.* The truth of the matter is that there's nothing you can't accomplish if:

1. You clearly decide what it is that you're absolutely committed to achieving.
2. You are willing to take massive action.
3. You notice what's working or not.
4. You continue to change your approach until you achieve what you want, using whatever life gives you along the way.

Anyone who's succeeded on a large scale has taken these four steps and followed what I call the Ultimate Success Formula. One of my favorite Ultimate Success Stories is that of Soichiro Honda, founder of the corporation that bears his name. Like all companies, no matter how large, Honda Corporation began with a decision and a passionate desire to produce a result.

In 1938, while he was still in school, Honda took everything he owned and invested it in a little workshop where he began to develop his concept of a piston ring. He wanted to sell his work to Toyota Corporation, so he labored day and night, up to his elbows in grease, sleeping in the machine shop, always believing he could produce the result. He even pawned his wife's jewelry to stay in business. But when he finally completed the piston rings and presented them to Toyota, he was told they didn't meet Toyota's standards. He was sent back to school for two years, where he heard the derisive laughter of his instructors and fellow students as they talked about how absurd his designs were.

But rather than focusing on the pain of the experience, he decided to continue to focus on his goal. Finally, after two more years, Toyota gave Solchiro Honda the contract he'd dreamed of. His passion and belief paid off because he had known what he wanted, taken action, noticed what was working, and kept changing his approach until he got what he wanted. Then a new problem arose.

The Japanese government was gearing up for war, and they refused to give him the concrete that was necessary to build his factory. Did he quit there? No. Did he focus on how unfair this was? Did it mean to him that his dream had died? Absolutely not. Again he decided to utilize the experience and developed another strategy. He and his team invented a process for creating their own concrete and then built their factory. During the war, it was bombed twice, destroying major portions of the manufacturing facility. Honda's response? He immediately rallied his team, and they picked up the extra gasoline cans that the U.S. fighters had discarded. He called them "gifts from President Truman" because they provided him with the raw materials he needed for his manufacturing process—materials that were unavailable at the time in Japan. Finally, after he survived all of this, an earthquake leveled his factory. Honda decided to sell his piston operation to Toyota.

Here is a man who clearly made strong decisions to succeed. He had a passion for and belief in what he was doing. He had a great strategy. He took massive action. He kept changing his approach, but still he'd not produced the results that he was committed to. Yet he decided to persevere.

After the war, a tremendous gasoline shortage hit Japan, and Honda couldn't even drive his car to get food for his family. Finally, in desperation, he attached a small motor to his bicycle. The next thing he knew, his neighbors were asking if he could make one of his "motorized bikes" for them. One after another, they jumped on the bandwagon until he *ran out* of motors. He decided to build a plant that would manufacture motors for his new invention, but unfortunately he didn't have the capital.

As before, he made the decision to find a way no matter what! His solution was to appeal to the 18,000 bicycle shop owners in Japan by writing them each a personal letter. He told them how they could play a role in revitalizing Japan through the mobility that his invention could provide and convinced 5,000 of them to advance the capital he needed. Still, his motorbike sold to only the most hard-core bicycle fans because it was too big and bulky. So he made one final adjustment and created a much lighter, scaled-down version of his motorbike. He christened it the Super Cub, and it became an "overnight" success, earning him the Emperor's award. Later, he began to export his motorbikes to the baby boomers of Europe and the United States, following up in the '70s with the cars that have become so popular.

Today, the Honda Corporation employs more than 100,000 people in both the United States and Japan and is one of the biggest carmaking empires in Japan, outselling all but Toyota in the United States. It succeeds because one man understood the power of a truly committed decision that is acted upon, no matter what the conditions, on a continuous basis.

 ### *The Crystal Ball Cracked . . .*

The following are actual rejection notices received for these famous—and incredibly successful—books.

- *Animal Farm*, by George Orwell: "It is impossible to sell animal stories in the USA."

- *The Diary of Anne Frank*, by Anne Frank: "The girl doesn't, it seems to me, have a special perception or feeling which would lift that book above the 'curiosity' level."
- *Lord of the Flies*, by William Golding: "It does not seem to us that you have been wholly successful in working out an admittedly promising idea."
- *Lady Chatterly's Lover*, by D. H. Lawrence: "For your own good do not publish this book."
- *Lust for Life*, by Irving Stone: "A long, dull novel about an artist."

Honda certainly knew that sometimes when you make a decision and take action, in the short term it may look like it's not working. *In order to succeed, you must have a long-term focus.* Most of the challenges that we have in our personal lives—from indulging constantly in overeating, drinking, or smoking to feeling overwhelmed and giving up on our dreams—come from a short-term focus. Success and failure are not overnight experiences. It's all the small decisions along the way that cause people to fail. It's failure to follow up. It's failure to take action. It's failure to persist. It's failure to manage our mental and emotional states. It's failure to control what we focus on. Conversely, success is the result of making small decisions: deciding to hold yourself to a higher standard, deciding to contribute, deciding to feed your mind rather than allowing the environment to control you—these small decisions create the life experience we call success. No individual or organization that has become successful has done so with short-term focus.

From *Awaken the Giant Within* by Anthony Robbins, copyright © 1991. Used by permission of Anthony Robbins.

Goals and Vision

If you can dream it, you can do it.

—WALT DISNEY

When we study the lives of successful people, we find that typically they are goal-setters. They understand that what they accomplish is within their control if they focus on the goal. Everyone wants to achieve or attain certain things; successful people know how to turn those wants into achievable or attainable goals.

We all set conscious goals, of course. Sometimes the goal is just to get through the day and go home and have supper, something that can usually be achieved by following a familiar and timeworn plan. But short-term goals are not what we mean when we talk about being goal-oriented. Successful people set goals well into the future: graduate from medical school, start a business, make a million dollars. Setting long-term goals pulls them into behaviors aimed at achieving the goals. The influence of setting a goal stretches all the way from the future back into everyday life. Goals define a person's lifestyle.

Conscious goals can turn into unconscious goals. We may become so deeply committed to a long-term goal that it takes over our everyday life and we stop thinking about it; when this happens, our goal becomes our autopilot. Conversely, unconscious goals can become conscious goals when we recognize a need to adjust them and then begin to plan accordingly. If circumstances change—new interests arise, old habits become destructive, disease or calamity intervenes—unconscious goals may have to be consciously changed.

The community we grow up in usually shapes our early conscious and unconscious goals. We strive to obey the law, be good to others, grow up, get married, and prosper. We also let these norms limit our choices: when someone says, "You can't do that!" we often pay heed. Success is possible when we learn to set imaginative and ambitious goals that drive us to live according to our highest ideals.

Athletes, businesspeople, and leaders in all endeavors recognize the power of deliberate goal-setting. Writing down long-term goals, subgoals, and intermediate objectives is a big step toward recognizing that they are achievable. The goal-setter can visualize achieving them as a kind of journey, and the power of imagining this journey creates a self-fulfilling prophecy. Once established and maintained with sufficient effort over time, a goal imagined becomes real.

Do the thing, and it shall be yours.

The way to success is not always plainly marked; goals are often hidden in the mist. Achievement can mean choosing new directions until goals become clear. Starting confused and with only a vague yearning, Tom Hopkins came to achieve extraordinary success as a sales leader, and later as a premier sales trainer helping more than three million people learn the secrets of success.

THE MOST NECESSARY SKILL OF ALL

TOM HOPKINS

For years I've been asked: How did you get it all together and do all you've done?

I don't believe people ask in idle curiosity. I think they have the same reason that compelled me when I was 21 to ask much the same question of an extremely successful corporate executive: a sincere desire to learn how to make my own dreams come true.

The average human being has the ability to achieve almost anything. Lack of basic capability is rarely the problem—we all have great reserves of untapped power. The problem is almost always in finding out what you want. Before we go any further, let me define how I'm using the word *want* here. I'm not talking about mere wishes now; I'm talking about wants that gnaw at you.

Maybe you think you don't have any gnawing wants. If you think that, you're wrong. You have the wants. But they're bottled up where you can't get at them. Your early experiences and training poured them in and pounded the cork home. And there they sit, building pressure for their next destructive burst of envy and vindictiveness. They may leak out as blind resistance to change, stubborn refusal to put out extra effort, and instant insistence that all your problems are caused by others. Instead of trying to bottle your true wants, learn to understand them. From such understanding springs the knowledge of how to use this vital force to power your drive for greater things. Your drive has to come from this source: there is no other that works for long.

It's often the fear of failure that makes us bottle up our wants. But failure isn't the worst possible result. Not trying is. If you try, you can succeed; if you won't try, you have already failed. Do you suffer from this fear? Then decide in advance that you've failed—and after that go out and give it the best try you're capable of.

Lots of us are willing to risk failure, but we still don't exert ourselves. We don't see any reason to. Why? Because we wouldn't do anything very exciting or satisfying with success if we could win it. If that's your problem, you need to give it a lot of attention. Finding the answer will take deep thinking. Widen your horizons, seek out new friends and activities, and search for unthought-of rewards that will make success worth its price to you. The pivot point here is finding what will motivate your own unique personality. Many of us are so blinded by what society and other people think we should want that we can't hear our own cries for help. Getting in touch with your true self must be your first priority.

If you really want something, that want will make a difference in your life. You'll work to satisfy that want. You'll sacrifice pleasures for it. You'll even be willing to change and grow for it. In fact, you'll deliberately change yourself and grow so that you can have what you really want. But you won't do any of these things for mere wishes. That's why you must put what you think you want on paper. Then look at your goals, written there in black and white, and commit to them. You're not done yet. It's no good to write pages of goals down somewhere and then go on about your old routine as though nothing had happened.

Every day, look at each goal. Think whether you're doing what has to be done, whether you're paying the price that has to be paid. It doesn't matter at this point whether or not you already possess all the abilities and resources you must have if you're to achieve your goal—those you can pick up along the way. But you won't start without having the desire. The first step is to commit to the goal *in writing.* The great majority of people never once in their lives will take this simple first step on the journey to achievement. For this reason alone, they'll never take the last step that brings them what they wish for. Apathy stifles more careers than inability ever does.

In recent years, we've heard quite a bit about people who can't find themselves. Confusion about identity keeps millions of people operating far below their potential and helps pay the rent for the nation's psychoanalysts. Some people really need professional help in this area. Most of us would do better to bury the past and concentrate on getting in touch with what we really want from the future.

Because you can't unleash your creativity or accelerate your growth until you commit yourself to a goal, any positive goal is better than no goal at all. You'll probably make many false starts before you discover the course that'll keep you happily involved for the rest of your life. That's wonderful. All the time that you're committed to written goals, you're growing rapidly. You're experiencing much. Striving on the field, you're learning a ton for every pound the apathetic person learns sitting in the bleachers of life. Every moment that you're playing the great game of living to the fullest, you're charging toward an understanding of your best potential, of what your finest destiny is. Allowing ourselves to bury our lives in apathy is the greatest crime—and we commit it by not committing ourselves to goals that are real to us.

You can achieve almost any goal that you have the courage to set—but sometimes it takes a painful experience to light the way.

That was so in my case. When I was 17 years old, I broke my father's heart. He had saved enough from a very average income to send me to college to become an attorney; 90 days later I was home telling him that I had quit college—and for the first time I saw him cry. With tears in his eyes he said, "Son, I'm always going to love you even though you'll never amount to anything."

That was my first motivational speech.

When I walked out of that room, I was burning with something not everyone has the chance to feel. I didn't just want to succeed—I had to succeed.

But I couldn't see how to do it. I became a bridge deck specialist and carried steel up construction ramps for 18 months—and all the time my father's words were eating at me. I had a wage job that led nowhere except to old age.

I went into sales—and the wages stopped. I earned nothing because that's what I knew about my profession. Then, just as I was going under for the third time in sales, a man came by and sold me on the Edwards training seminar. I went, I learned the closes and techniques, I lost no time putting them to work. Soon after that, I started tasting the sweet fruits of success for the first time.

Some time later, I told the management of the company where I worked that my goal was to meet personally with Mr. Edwards. They arranged it for me. When the day came, I told him, "Mr. Edwards, my goal is to someday take your place and someday be able to train people as well as you trained me."

That all came to pass because I set goals to make it happen. Committing to the goal was the essential element. You can't rise unless you set goals that make you stretch.

Start with short-term goals. My first goal in sales—beyond making enough to eat and cover my back—was to buy a new car. Autos make great starting goals but, unfortunately, they often become the end goal. There's more to life than rolling around in an expensive car. A lot of average salespeople set average goals, achieve them, and then fade into a state of suspended animation. Like a bear in winter, they go to ground and live off their fat. The true champion keeps setting new goals whenever he achieves old ones. Achieved goals are like yesterday's newspapers: useful only for lining bird cages.

From *How to Master the Art of Selling* by Tom Hopkins, copyright ©1982, Warner Books. Used by permission of Tom Hopkins.

Often we are the biggest barriers to our own success. Why do some highly talented people never reach their full potential? Psychologists have long understood the power of the sub-conscious. Living between two worlds of athletics and psychology, Don Morgan offers insights into the relationship between conscious and subconscious goal-setting.

SUBCONSCIOUS AND *SMART* CONSCIOUS GOALS

DON MORGAN

Long-term life goals become embedded in our psyche, where they are taken over by our subconscious. Once installed in our subconscious, the goal, or some variation of it, gets converted to our reality over time. It's as if there were a little group of goal analysts working within our subconscious who systematically look for opportunities to position us closer to our defined destination. When told about the goal, these little analysts work for us nonstop, systematically finding opportunities to pull us closer to that end point. Usually working best when we are sleeping, the analysts find the right answer and put it in our consciousness for use the next morning.

Sometimes forgetful or occupied with other achievement activities, these goal analysts need to be reminded of the important tasks. Writing down our goal or hanging a picture that symbolizes it on the wall is a tangible reminder that helps our subconscious analysts get back to work on the most important project. These little analysts act like a life autopilot, taking care of small daily course corrections along our journey.

With all performance activities, experience makes the task easier. With time and practice, goal-setting becomes part of our normal life. The first step to achieving a new goal is to visualize a new future condition. Since we are not able to predict the future exactly, the vision will be a little hazy around the edges. But through focusing on a glimpse of a desired future, we are able to identify a number of time-limited goals to pursue that—when achieved—will allow that vision to emerge as our reality. Because many of us think best in pictures, we should learn to specify our goal as a picture. A picture helps our subconscious, and the other real members of our success team, to guide us forward.

"SMART" goals are the best goals. These are the ones you create through a deliberate and conscious process. Your goal needs to be Specific, Measurable, Achievable, Realistic, and completed within a specified Time—or SMART.

The mind is better able to picture the goal if you are highly *specific* in your written description of it. To evaluate progress along the way, and to know when you arrive, your goal must be *measurable*. Keep a positive outlook about getting to your goal by making it *achievable*. You will develop increased self-confidence and positive self-esteem if your goals are *realistic*. Finally, your goal must be completed by a specified *time*. No one benefits by working toward a destination that never arrives.

Implement SMART goals and you won't have to look for success—it will find you. Be ready. You will face many obstacles along the way, the toughest one perhaps being the *Y* factor: *you* may become the biggest obstacle to your own success. The famous *Pogo* cartoon says it best: "We have met the enemy and he is us!" Self-doubt lives in the place where we store fear of failure and avoidance of self-responsibility.

It works this way: If I declare that my goal is X, then I am committing in public, or at least to myself, that I will arrive at that declared destination. If I don't arrive at the goal, a neon failure sign flashes in my brain, signaling my emotions and my soul to feel miserable because I failed.

Goal-setting lives in that place where we openly accept responsibility for our outcomes.

Hundreds of millions of people define and achieve new goals every minute of every day. Every invention, every building, our Constitution, our Bill of Rights, a corporate document detailing a billion-dollar business structure, and so much more began when someone visualized an altered future. Focusing on the vision illuminates the goals that must be achieved.

Conscious goal-setting works better than most people realize or imagine. When the mind visualizes the idea, the rest is possible once you apply the right ingredients, including a clearly defined vision, goal, plan, and effort. A goal-setting process gets you on track to living your future life right now. A self-fulfilling prophecy takes over, and by doing the thing, you make it yours.

Achieving your passionate goals will consume most of your attention and energy, and you will have little time left over for the rest of your life. Passion, desire, hard work, and focused resources dedicated to a specific goal will help you master that event. But they can also become your downfall. Other areas of your life may suffer. Recognize the importance of seeking a balance between the many facets of your life. Not only will this balance give you a better perspective on your special projects, will give you a needed rest or pause from your frenzied activity.

———•·•———

Failure is not obligatory for those with physical or emotional challenges. Disabled people succeed by concentrating on reaching one small goal after another. From them we learn the most important lesson of taking the next step, and the next, and the next. Bobbi Kahler's disability became the force behind her success as a trainer, author, and consultant.

———•·•———

NEVER LET OTHERS DETERMINE YOUR LIMITATIONS

BOBBI KAHLER

When I was six, the small, rural school that I attended in Illinois decided to bring in a speech pathologist to evaluate my speech and to tell us what everyone already knew: no one could understand a word I said. I was to receive special attention—but I didn't feel special.

Evaluation day came, and I, to the best of my ability, completed the tests. I said the alphabet, recited the Pledge of Allegiance, and sang "The Star-Spangled Banner." The speech pathologist's range of expressions— from bewilderment and astonishment to alarm—told me I was not doing well. I got even more nervous, which made my speech even worse. I walked home from school feeling devastated.

I was so upset by the time I reached home that I couldn't even make myself understood to my mother. I had to resort to writing notes and using hand gestures to tell her about the experience. Suddenly the phone rang. It was *him*.

As the speech expert gave my mom his report, I heard only her side of the conversation: "Oh, that is troubling . . . . Yes, that is quite alarming . . . . We are aware that there are some problems . . . ." After about 15 minutes, my mom said, "That is truly incredible, because, you see, when Bobbi left for school today, she was a girl." Apparently, he was referring to me as "your son, Bobbi," although I had worn a dress that day and had my hair in two pigtails. The fact that he couldn't even remember I was a girl didn't contribute to my self-esteem.

When the call was over, my mother gave me the gist of it. There were 18 sounds I couldn't say. I stuttered. I slurred. The expert said the problems were catastrophic and nothing could be done. He said I was destined to suffer a lifelong disability.

I stood in the middle of our kitchen, staring down at our blue tile floor. In my six-year-old mind, I was a hopeless failure.

My mom walked over to where I was standing and knelt down in front of me. She placed her hands on my shoulders and gave me a tiny shake so that I would raise my eyes. Quietly but firmly, she said, "We are not going to listen to him. Never let someone else tell you what you can or cannot do."

That sentence is the best advice I've ever received. You can guess how different my life might have been if my mom had agreed with the speech pathologist, shaken her head, and given up. Instead, she taught me to use *adversity as fuel*. The obstacles we face can be our greatest opportunities for growth. Not a day goes by when I don't remember with gratitude what my mother said that day in the kitchen.

It took me several years to overcome the barriers to clear speech. I was a freshman in high school before I could feel that people weren't staring in horror at me when I spoke. During high school, I forced myself to compete in speech and debate because I thought it would help me become a better speaker and overcome the fear I had of talking to people. It was excruciating. I was embarrassed and very clumsy. I practiced every day so I could pronounce everything right. Finally I got better and even was able to win some tournaments. Even when I won, however, I didn't consider myself a good speaker because I had to work so hard at it. I think I was always afraid that I hadn't cured the problem but was just hiding it. There was always this small but loud inner voice shouting my inadequacies.

I believe that the way we approach an obstacle is simply in our state of mind. Will the obstacle defeat us? Will we rise above it? Believing in the outcome *determines the outcome.* My problem was that despite my high school achievements as a debater and my later success in college, I had stopped believing in myself. Sure, I wasn't letting other people limit my success—I didn't need to. I was doing it all on my own!

Because my parents didn't believe in college, I put myself through school by working in a law firm. After graduation, I stayed on with the firm and conducted their training and development programs. It wasn't long before I became restless and ventured out to start my own training and development business. Still I suffered from self-doubt and constantly questioned myself: Do I deserve success? Who am *I* to be successful?

It was a chance meeting with Roger Anthony, speaking at a conference, that turned me around. I told him I admired his work and wanted to be a speaker. I had been responsible for developing and delivering training programs for years but had never thought of myself as a speaker (I guess I thought I was using shadow puppets). He said, "It sounds like you already are, but you just haven't accepted that yet in your own mind." Of course, he was right. We've heard it said before that you have to "name it to claim it." I think it should be, "Once you name it, you have to claim it." Shortly thereafter, I contacted the National Speakers Association and applied for membership. To my delight, I was accepted as a professional member. And with that acceptance came a whole new way of thinking about myself.

I have been speaking and training professionally for more than ten years in the fields of law and business. I am the director of training and development for a marketing franchise company (Business Network International) in Oregon and southwest Washington and a licensed trainer for the Certified Networker Program®. I have trained hundreds of professionals and entrepreneurs in the art of power language and effective networking. I am the author of the book *Bring Your Business into Focus* and am working on my next book, *Yes, I Can Do That! The Entrepreneur's Guide to Pursuing Your Passion,* which has been endorsed by Barry Spilchuk, co-author of *A Cup of Chicken Soup for the Soul.*

The irony of my chosen career has never escaped me. I've gone from a small girl whose speech could barely be understood to a woman who speaks for a living. And even though the process took many years, much practice, and even more patience, I never believed that I wouldn't one day be able to speak as well as anyone else. I'm not saying that it wasn't frustrating—it was. But I never thought of giving up and sinking into the pit of despair. I knew it was something I would overcome one step at a time. The lessons I learned so many years ago in my mother's kitchen still apply, and I've never since allowed someone else to determine my limitations. The road to success depends on *you!*

———•·•———

David Lega is 29 years old. He speaks to us with the wisdom of an old man, but he reflects a child's curiosity toward life. This is the story of one who at an early age faced his own limitations and who now shows us all that the impossible exists only in the human mind. Gunnar Selheden, a marketing expert and businessman in Sweden, tells this story as a signal to those of us who think we may face challenges. Gunnar, along with his wife and family, enjoy taking time to gain a broader perspective through a combination of sailing, business, and family life.

— •◦• —

"IF I CAN DO IT, SO CAN YOU!"

GUNNAR SELHEDEN

David Lega was born in 1973—fully paralyzed. His doctors thought for several months that he would never be able to communicate with the world in any way. But little David was a fighter and was determined to prove the doctors wrong. His parents saw him move his head for the first time when he was six months old, and when he was two-and-a-half he was able to sit up without any support. At the age of six, he managed to sit up all by himself for the first time by rocking back and forth.

Today David Lega leads an active life in a modern apartment in central Göteborg on the Swedish west coast. His arms are still paralyzed, but he has achieved about 30 percent mobility in his legs.

Lega is one of the lucky ones. He belongs to the first generation of disabled Swedish children who were given correct medication and training from day one. Among the first to be integrated into a regular school, he had teachers who gave him both support and demands. "I have always been surrounded by people who have dared to demand something of me, but who also commended me for what I achieved," says Lega. "Receiving credit for your progress is good for your self-confidence. It leads to higher self-esteem, and it makes you want to keep progressing. There are few people who have failed as many times as I have. But each time I got a little closer to success."

When Lega was a child, his father used to put him on a chair and push him over so that he finally learned the reflex of lifting his head before hitting the floor. Dinner was not served until he managed to get up in his

103

chair by himself—regardless of how long it took! In school, his teacher made it clear to him that his writing was lousy, even though she knew it would take him 40 minutes to rewrite the page with the pen in his mouth. Despite his frustration, Lega was determined to improve, and it was those requirements for his performance, rather than a simple acceptance of his limitations, that drove him to give his very best and continue to develop.

As an alternative to physiotherapy, Lega got into sports at the age of six. Bocce was the right thing for a young boy who had just learned to sit up by himself. An airgun mounted on a supporting rod became his next interest, giving him thousands of hours of balance training. He pulled the trigger with his tongue. Every new thing he tried and succeeded in doing gave him the courage to move on to the next challenge.

From Buoyancy Aid to the World Championships

During the summer of 1986, the world championship for disabled swimmers was held in Göteborg. Among the 30 spectators were 12-year-old David Lega and some of his disabled friends. After completing his race, the English swimmer Peter Hull joined the children and showed them all his medals. "I looked at Peter's body with no arms or legs and heard him say, 'If I can do it, so can you!'" remembers Lega. "When you look at someone who is ten times worse off than yourself and see him do ten times better than yourself, there are no excuses left. The expression 'That's easy for you to say!' just doesn't apply. That moment with Peter Hull marked the start of my 16-year career as a swimmer."

At that time, Lega still needed his buoyancy aid, so he spent the next six months learning how to swim, treating this task with the same dedication he had shown for every new challenge in the past. "During this period I set countless personal records, and every time it filled me with the same joy—I had beaten myself!" he recalls. "People who always compete against others will face too many defeats. That's often what kills the enthusiasm in a young student, athlete, or entrepreneur. But when you look to your own development—today I made a somewhat better product presentation than last week!—this will lead to good business further down the road."

David Lega spent 16 years training to compete as a disabled swimmer and was with the Swedish national team between 1993 and 2000. Today, he is able to look back on a large number of medals from European and world championships from the late '90s. He still holds the world record for seven distances (S1 classification). During the International Paralympic Games in Atlanta, he was given the Whang Youn Dai Award (Triumph of the Human Spirit) for the best male performance.

"I have been given so much by so many," says Lega. "Now it's time for me to give something back. The race I did in Sydney in 2000 was the race of my life. Deep inside I knew that this was the peak of my career, and it was time to move on. The driving force in everything I do is knowing that I can develop. If I can't keep developing, I lose my motivation."

The Wheel of Life

Lega has created his own philosophy of life and a model for reaching new goals. The essence of his philosophy is that every part of our lives is a spoke in our individual wheel of life. "I think it is important for people to develop themselves in areas other than their primary area of performance," he says. "If you do so, you'll lead a better life and reach farther. Focus on finding the areas that are important to you."

Here is his personal list of spokes:
- Sports—both training and competition
- Education and university
- Work—having a strategy for getting the job you want
- Family and friends
- Organizations
- Hobby and leisure time
- Handicap development

Lawyer and Lecturer

David Lega's career in sports may be over, but he continues to motivate and encourage those around him, sharing his philosophies through popular lectures worldwide. He is a member of the International Paralympic Committee and gives lectures and seminars for athletes about to join the

Swedish Olympic team. Always the competitor, he sees the lectures he gives as the competition and the evaluations he receives as the results. To be nominated Best Lecturer in 2001 and 2002 is a medal as good as any.

"I have a personal assistant with me 24 hours a day, and this allows me to focus on being a productive part of society," says Lega. "I can put on my trousers in the morning, but it would take me about 15 minutes to do it. This is time that I would rather spend serving other people, companies, and society."

Since 2001, he has run the David Lega Foundation, which has grown into a major aid program for disabled children in Albania. And, as if he weren't busy enough, Lega will graduate as a lawyer from the University of Göteborg later this spring. His goal is not to work as a lawyer but to be an inspiration to people in a similar situation who dream of getting a good education.

Lega's disability has forced him to face his limitations, but in doing so he has discovered more possibilities than he could have ever imagined. Along the way, he has redefined his definition of success. "When I was six years old, it was to be able to sit up by myself," he says. "When I was an active swimmer, it was to have a gold medal around my neck. In both situations I had done something that I wasn't able to do before—that's success! There are a million things I will never be able to do, so I've focused on what I can be really good at. Everyone can excel at something—they've just got to figure out what it is!"

SPORTS FACTS ABOUT DAVID LEGA

- Has broken the world record in swimming 14 times (S1 classification)
- Holds the current Swedish record at 11 distances (S1 classification)
- Elected member of the International Paralympic Committee, 2000
- One gold, three silver, and one bronze medal at the European Championships in Germany, 1999
- Three gold and two silver medals at the World Championships in New Zealand, 1998
- One gold and three silver medals at the European Championships in Spain, 1997

- Winner of the Whang Youn Dai Award (Triumph of the Human Spirit) in Atlanta, 1996

OTHER ACHIEVEMENTS
- Voted into the Swedish Science Council's Ethics Committee, 2002
- Awarded the Royal Swedish Medal, size 8 with blue ribbon, 2001
- Voted into the Swedish Athletes Academy, 2000

When did you last try to motivate someone? You may have discovered how ingenious people can be when they don't want to do what you want them to do. Dr. Wayne Dyer, often called the "father of motivation," has created bestselling books and audiocassettes on this topic and has appeared on thousands of television and radio shows.

SECRETS FOR SUCCESS AND INNER PEACE

DR. WAYNE W. DYER

Treat Yourself As If You Already Are What You'd Like to Be

Whatever it is that you envision for yourself—no matter how lofty or impossible it may seem to you right now—I encourage you to begin acting as if what you would like to become is already your reality. This is a wonderful way to set into motion the forces that will collaborate with you to make your dreams come true. To activate the creative forces that lie dormant in your life, you must go to the unseen world, the world beyond your form. Here is where what doesn't exist for you in your world of form will be created. You might think of it in this way: In form, you receive *in-form*ation. When you move to spirit, you receive *in-spir*ation. It is this world of inspiration that will guide you to access anything that you would like to have in your life.

What It Means to Become Inspired

Some of the most significant advice I've ever read was written more than 2,000 years ago by an ancient teacher named Patanjali. He instructed his devotees to become inspired. You may recall that the word *inspire* originates from the words *in* and *spirit*. Patanjali suggested that inspiration involves a mind that transcends all limitations, thoughts that break all their bonds, and a consciousness that expands in every direction. Here is how you can become inspired.

Place your thoughts on what it is you'd like to become—an artist, a musician, a computer programmer, a dentist, or whatever. In your thoughts, begin to picture yourself having the skills to do these things. No doubts. Only a knowing. Then begin acting as if these things were already your reality. As an artist, your vision allows you to draw, to visit art museums, to talk with famous artists, and to immerse yourself in the art world. In other words, you begin to *act* as an artist in all aspects of your life. In this way, you're getting out in front of yourself and taking charge of your own destiny at the same time that you're cultivating inspiration.

The more you see yourself as what you'd like to become, the more inspired you are. The dormant forces that Patanjali described come alive, and you discover that you're a greater person than you ever dreamed yourself to be. Imagine that—dormant forces that were dead or nonexistent, springing into being and collaborating with you as a result of your becoming inspired and acting as if what you want is already here!

By having the courage to declare yourself as already being where you want to be, you will almost force yourself to act in a new, exciting, and spiritual fashion. You can also apply this principle to areas other than your chosen vocation. If you're living a life of scarcity, and all of the nice things that many people have are not coming your way, perhaps it's time to change your thinking and act as if what you enjoy having is already here.

Visualize the beautiful automobile that's your dream car and paste a picture of it on your bedroom door, as well as on the refrigerator. While you're at it, paste it on the dashboard of the car you're now driving! Visit a showroom, sit in your car, and note the beautiful new-car aroma. Run your hands over the seats, and grip the steering wheel. Walk all around your car, appreciating the lines of it. Take your car for a test-drive, and visualize that you're entitled to drive this car, that you're inspired by its beauty, and that it's going to find a way into your life. In some way, somehow, this is your car. Talk to others about your love for this car. Read about it. Bring up a picture on your computer screen, and leave it there to view each time you're near that computer.

All of this may seem silly to you, but when you become inspired and act as if what you want is already here, you'll activate those dormant forces that will collaborate to make this your reality.

Extending Inspiration Everywhere

Treating yourself in the manner described above can become a habitual way of life. This doesn't involve deception, arrogance, or hurting others. This is a silent agreement between you and God in which you discreetly work in harmony with the forces of the universe to make your dreams become a reality. This involves a knowing on your part that success and inner peace are your birthright; that you are a child of God; and as such, you're entitled to a life of joy, love, and happiness.

In your relationships with your lovers, co-workers, and family, act as if what you would like to materialize in these relationships is already here. If you want a sense of harmony in the workplace, maintain a clear vision and expectation of this harmony. Then you're out in front of your day, seeing 5 o'clock arriving peacefully for everyone when it's still 7:30 in the morning. Each time you have an encounter with someone, your 5 o'clock vision pops into your head, and you act in a peaceful, harmonious way so as not to nullify what you know is coming. Furthermore, you act toward everyone else as if they, too, are all that they are capable of becoming.

These kinds of expectations lead you to say, "I'm sure you'll have everything ready this afternoon," rather than, "You're always late with everything, and I wish you would get on the ball." When you treat others in this way, they also fulfill the destiny that you've reminded them is there for them.

In your family, particularly with your children, it's important always to have this little thought in mind: Catch them doing things right.

From *Ten Secrets for Success and Inner Peace* by Dr. Wayne W. Dyer, copyright ©2001. Used by permission of Hay House Inc., Carlsbad, CA.

———•◦•———

You can start out with a vision, but vision has a way of evolving. If it's founded on firm principle, vision becomes clearer with time. As it comes into focus, it shapes both the visionary and the organization. For 18 years, Amy Turley-Brown has worked alongside a man whose long-term vision has reached out to 16 market-driven economies across the globe—so far.

———•◦•———

BNI: SUCCESS BY ACCIDENT, DESIGN, AND VISION

AMY TURLEY-BROWN

"You might say that BNI was born because I needed it," says the founder of Business Network International, now the world's largest and most recognized referral organization. "Banks are funny about home mortgage loans. Mine felt I should pay them every month."

In the mid-1980s, Ivan Misner, Ph.D., president of AIM Consulting, was providing management services to an eclectic mixture of organizations, from the California Driving Schools and Wells Fargo to the U.S. Navy. Business was good, so in 1984 Misner bought a new home for his growing family—whereupon his largest client ran into financial trouble and chose not to renew his contract.

"I knew I had to act immediately or lose my home and my business," he says. "I thought of two options: public speaking and referrals.

"I was already making some money giving speeches here and there, and I knew I could do more of that. But referrals seemed to offer more promise. I had an idea that if I could build a strong, wide-reaching network of contacts, I could keep my consulting company afloat.

"After a little field research," he says, "I came up with the idea of a networking group that would meet once a week and, in a highly structured way, swap referrals over breakfast before going off to work. Membership would be limited to one per profession, and each member would have to show up regularly or lose his spot to a competitor. The result would be a strong and stable group that would be the core of an extended network involving every member's friends, business associates, clients, vendors, even competitors."

Such a group, Misner realized, would have to be based on trust and mutual benefit. "That's when our core philosophy came to me: 'Givers gain,'" he says.

"It's an old, old idea. Ever heard the saying 'What goes around comes around'? It's like that, but not in the usual cynical sense. More like the Golden Rule: 'Do unto others . . .'

"'Givers gain' means that the good you do comes back to help you in ways you can't foresee."

Based on this philosophy, group members are encouraged to think first of what they can do for others—services they can perform, valuable information they can provide, problems they can solve—with no expectation of getting anything in return.

"You gain the satisfaction of doing good for other people," Misner points out. "You get a reputation as a generous and helpful person. You become known far and wide as someone who has valuable information and expertise, someone who can solve problems, someone who has the best products or services. Someone, in short, whom people like and will come to.

"Good works performed in a spirit of true generosity will eventually accrue to the benefit of the giver. In a business setting, this means your company will prosper."

Several of Misner's business friends agreed to try his idea, and they held their first official meeting in January 1985.

Word began to spread among area merchants that BNI, as the group called itself, was a good place to drum up more business. The one-per-profession rule also meant that the first group quickly reached its limit. Business owners clamored to join, but the chapter was full. The organization wanted to grow, but expanding the group meant compromising an essential structural component. The only remedy, Misner realized, was to help others open new chapters.

Soon the wisdom of this approach became apparent. New chapters began to spring up all over southern California. Each new group extended the networking potential of the others; businesses in different chapters could refer prospects to one another without competing, and a broader selection of services and products became available for referral within each local group.

It wasn't long before Misner recognized that he would need a central organization to operate this widely scattered and loosely networked array of referral groups, chapters, and regions. To set the stage for growth beyond southern California, he decided to license areas that could form the basis of future franchises throughout the United States and overseas.

An early target was the San Francisco Bay Area. "We got inquiries and interest, but I didn't meet anybody I considered prepared to establish and operate a new region," Misner recalls. This turned out to be a limiting factor. I began to understand that the key to solving the growth problem was not to target geographic areas but to train new directors to open up their own regions.

"Our first new region turned out to be not San Francisco but Arizona. Naturally, it was by referral. However, it wasn't the original contact who ended up running the region, but one woman who attended the original meeting."

Similar meetings began to occur across the country as BNI gained national recognition. Growth accelerated, and by 1989 Misner faced a dilemma: He could no longer run both his consulting company and BNI. He would have to choose one or the other. "Referral networking was more challenging and more fun, and was showing all the signs of becoming a terrific success. It was a no-brainer," he says. "I sold AIM Consulting and devoted myself full-time to the new venture."

As with any business, growth brought new problems to solve. Name recognition would be crucial as a marketing tool. When Misner's application to trademark the company's original name, "The Network" was denied, he used the opportunity to choose a new name that would reflect the true worldwide potential of the organization: Business Network International, also known as BNI.

Misner licensed new BNI regions in Arizona, Montana, Hawaii, and Connecticut. In 1991, New York became the first state to franchise. By the mid-1990s, the Bay Area had joined up and, with the opening of Canada and the United Kingdom, BNI went international.

"I was amazed at how fast the word spread," Misner says. "Steve Lawson in Canada told his brother Martin in Great Britain about BNI, which led to new chapters there. When I went to London, I met Graham Southwell, who was moving to New Zealand. I put Graham in touch with our Australian director, who helped him open up in New Zealand.

"Funny things happen. One Californian I know learned about BNI during a visit to a chapter in Singapore. He was so impressed that when he returned home he looked for a chapter to join in southern California."

Misner wrote several books on networking that garnered BNI a great deal of exposure. "The media don't want to interview people about business," he explains, "but they'll interview anyone who's written a book."

Now almost 20 years old, BNI has become truly global, with more than 3,000 chapters spread across more than 16 countries in North America, Europe, and the Pacific Rim. Since 1985, BNI has generated more than 12 million referrals valued at more than $4 billion (U.S.) in business for its members. To what does Misner attribute this phenomenal growth?

"First, BNI was based on a healthy organizational philosophy and mission," he says. "The guiding principle is simple: Givers gain. The mission is to help members increase their business through a structured, positive, professional, word-of-mouth marketing program that enables the development of long-term, meaningful relationships with high-quality business professionals.

"Ask around. You'll discover that many members, directors, and staff can readily tell you exactly what I just told you. It's essential to have a vision and to stay dedicated and focused on it.

"Of course, our vision has evolved; it has grown as the organization has grown and surpassed its original conception. And it will keep evolving, because we're still growing."

Another key, according to Misner, is training. "The training and education of our extended team is absolutely integral to our operation," he notes. "We've trained hundreds of directors and thousands of members on both how to run a chapter and how to build their business through word-of-mouth marketing.

"Finally, a secret ingredient: surround yourself with caring people who understand and value integrity and good character. But I guess that's not really a secret, is it?"

In the early days, when his "business" was still AIM Consulting, Misner quickly found himself deriving more satisfaction from his "hobby," running BNI. But he didn't think it would become a full-time job. "I wish I could say I saw it all from the beginning—that I envisioned this great international enterprise, a network of hundreds of chapters stretching around the globe. But I can't say that," he admits.

"I didn't invent referrals, and I didn't invent networking. I found a way to make them more powerful, and one thing led to another. But the truth is, I was just looking for a way to pay the mortgage while doing what I liked."

Necessity truly is the mother of invention.

As a successful racing sailboat skipper, Don Morgan under-stands the technology for plotting one's exact location any-where on the globe using the Global Positioning System (GPS). Having practiced as a psychotherapist for 20 years, Morgan has taught innumerable clients how to evolve a new life direction through reliance on selected general principles found within the social sciences.

GOAL-SETTING PROCESS (GSP)

DON MORGAN

There are several tricks to the art of goal-setting that, once learned, enable individuals to achieve loftier goals and significantly improve their lives. For two decades, I counseled dissatisfied people. Many had con-flicting goals similar to those associated with "empty-nest syndrome"; oth-ers presented more serious threats, such as drug or alcohol addiction, which became my specialization. My ultimate task was to help these clients identify (1) what they didn't like in their lives, (2) what they wanted out of life, and then (3) how to begin achieving the new stuff they wanted. Taking away all the psycho-mumbo-jumbo technical aspects, my basic job fol-lowed a simple-to-understand but hard-to-implement program that is rel-evant to achieving success in any aspect of life.

The first trick is to take stock of where your life is going. Look at your current direction. Are your subconscious goals pulling you along the right path? Theoretically, an individual could be totally satisfied with every-thing in all areas of his or her life. Realistically, most of us can find room for improvement. An honest self-appraisal will turn up something that is no longer satisfying. When you find it, you are at a fork in the road of your life.

These turning points, well known to psychological professionals, can elicit an emotional response ranging from vague dissatisfaction to severe panic, depression, and even suicide. This is when the old goals no longer satisfy and new ones have yet to emerge. Empty-nest syndrome is a good example of this phenomenon. One day, the family's primary child caregiver wakes up to find the babies grown up and living on their own. The old child-rearing goals become irrelevant, and the replacement goals haven't emerged. The emotional results are disabling; the solution is to establish new goals quickly.

In this first step, the point is to discover the direction you are being pulled by your old, often subconscious goals, and then what's wrong with the direction.

The second task is to identify and vocalize your thoughts for creating a new, consciously planned life. Leaving aside the seriously self-destructive or addictive behavior, some clients in my practice want safer recreational activities; others need more interaction with their friends; others want time to integrate their inner beliefs and value system with the feelings for a family or loved ones; and still others need the stability of a career.

Through discovery, I help clients realize what they are missing and how to specify a new direction. This immediately brings on a small crisis: clients may begin to sense that setting deliberate goals means being responsible for achieving them.

Thus, the third objective is to take ownership and control over defining and then implementing your own new directions. Declaring a new life direction, through a SMART goal-setting process, implies a heightened sense of responsibility for actually achieving that life. The phrase "I don't know what I really want to do" is a smoke screen for "I don't know if I want to take responsibility for that part of my life."

The self-fulfilling prophecy is real. Defining and then beginning to live a new life makes it much more likely that you can achieve this goal. The mosaic world we inhabit offers an amazing array of sociocultural things, people, places, and events, options available to us all. Although your cultural context has a huge bearing on the type of success you may be allowed to wish to pursue, achieving success requires a deliberate process of getting control over all aspects of your life.

In our practice, my colleagues and I taught our clients to break the process into manageable pieces to make it easier to plot out their life journeys. Every individual, regardless of nationality or background, experiences life through seven life areas that transcend all cultures. Being aware of these life areas adds clarity and understanding to a deliberate goal-setting program. Everything we do as human beings can be viewed within these seven all-encompassing areas.

Health

Our health is a dominant factor in our lives. It's been said in many ways that without your health, all the riches in the world are worth nothing. Health is more than the absence of disease or infirmity; it includes physical, emotional, social, and psychological well-being. Even a vague sense of ongoing dissatisfaction is not fully healthy. Successful people are aware that health is related to our physical, emotional, and mental abilities, each of which impinges on our success. Our bodies may be in top shape, but if our minds and souls are hesitant, we will lose in highly competitive athletic, business, or life situations.

Family

The family is the nucleus of our understanding about the world and our place in it. We grow up within the family and are driven to perpetuate ourselves through our own offspring. Family can be the ultimate support group that gives us the required emotional energy to tackle our life challenges. Lack of a supportive family has a strong influence on our goals and ultimate life direction. This basic building block of society shapes many of the early goals that become embedded in our psyche and influence our behavior through our early years. We derive much of our life understanding and involvements in the other six life areas through the family.

Spirituality

Our core beliefs about our purpose, the meaning of life, and the way to interact with others are formed through this area. These inner beliefs guide our attitudes, which in turn direct our life choices about goals to pursue. If our spiritual beliefs adhere to a strong, established system (such as a religion) for making choices in life, then much of our life becomes preordained: we follow the dictates of our belief system. If our spiritual belief is not strongly tied to an existing religious system, then we will invent some other set of core beliefs to help guide our choices through life.

Career

Your career is more than a job. It is your occupation, your way of earning a living, and the way you contribute to society. The jobs you obtain throughout life may change, but how you contribute to society usually shows a common thread throughout all the jobs. This common thread is your career. Your jobs might include being an at-home parent, or they might be in the trades or professional services. The personal satisfaction you receive from each of the jobs within your career is for you to measure. Remuneration from your career is one way of measuring success, but in itself, money may not be a fully satisfying measurement of success over the term of your life.

Recreation

The pursuit of sports and hobbies has been recorded throughout history. Their actual function is to give a balance, or a restful pause, to the other serious areas of our lives. Engaging in recreational pursuits enhances and strengthens other life areas. Through medical research, we know that regular exercise is crucial to physical and socio-emotional health. Participation in organized team sports is a way to enhance one's career opportunities and form friendships. A huge industry exists to support our recreational activities, as this life area plays an important and critical part in the success of our lives.

Intimacy

Intimacy with another or a few others is the sticky glue that bonds people together. Intimacy helps to maintain stability in society and contributes to our self-confidence and self-esteem. People with low self-confidence don't perform at high levels. Those with low self-esteem don't feel worthy of making strong social contributions. Through intimate and familiar relationships with a few others, we increase our sense of self-esteem, allowing us to move forward and achieve goals, which reinforces our self-confidence, and an upward spiral of success is created.

Community

The community is where we find our friends and associates, the individuals we consider part of our network. Our friendship networks help to formulate and modify our inner beliefs. Our friends also introduce us to other recreational and career pursuits. In some instances, a few friends become part of our inner intimate circle. Friendships are formed through our recreational pursuits and our active participation in the other six life areas. Friends organized and supported in a personal network will facilitate our success as we seek to help one another achieve goals.

Many experts on success talk about living a balanced life by allocating time to career, hobbies, family, and community. At times, we might focus more exclusively in one or two areas as we develop mastery over them. But to maintain continual progress toward success, we have to take time-outs to regain balance and get a broader perspective. Life is a complex interplay of partially played-out subconscious goals bumping into new, emerging ones. Some are embedded in the subconscious, and others are deliberately designed through conscious and deliberate thought. Mastering success in one area requires a decreased attention to other areas for as long as that takes. Once we become successful in that area, our dissatisfaction with other areas may emerge as a new success path for our future. It sounds a little confusing, and it is.

However, the power of setting goals is well established. All we have to do is briefly review the recent history of inventions, human performance records, and new concepts. Conscious and deliberate goal-setting process, GSP, is not to be taken lightly if your purpose is to achieve success. Identify a general desired direction, define a future goal, and then create the plan to get there.

What's next? Just do it.

Success builds on itself. We learn from early experiences and use them as stepping-stones to the next-higher tasks. All things we learn or come across can be used in our later pursuits, not least of which are the people we encounter along our route. Jerry Schwartz and Dotty White are marketing consultants in Baltimore, Maryland, with more than 1,600 business clients. Looking to the extraordinary success of Brian Tracy, the authors rediscover the importance of paying attention to those you meet along the way.

TREKKING TOWARD SUCCESS WITH BRIAN TRACY

JERRY SCHWARTZ AND DOTTY WHITE

Imagine being surrounded by sand. You scan the horizon in all directions and see only the peaks and valleys of sand dunes shifting in the desert wind. Grains of sand bite into your cheeks, invade your eyes, clog your nose.

You are crossing a desert, and the trip has become so much harder than you had anticipated. Every step holds a new obstacle.

How will you ever find your way through this place? What direction should you go to reach your destination? And what if your Land Rover breaks down out here in the middle of nowhere?

Brian Tracy faced this bleak scene during his own struggle to cross the Sahara Desert. He and a fellow 21-year-old knew where they wanted to be in Africa. They had started out in Europe, trekking through France and Spain, and understood the Sahara stood between them and their ultimate destination.

Quitting wasn't an option. Give up in the Sahara and you die. He kept on going.

There was no road, exactly. Tracy explains that the French had embedded 55-gallon oil drums in the sand as markers spaced five kilometers apart, back when they controlled that part of the desert. He and his friend had to focus on those drums. Their ultimate goal was far away, but they carried on from one drum to the next.

The lesson took permanent root in Tracy's outlook on life and success: Set your direction and keep going. Once you know where you want to be, be persistent in achieving your goal.

Out there in the hot, desolate, windswept sandscape, Tracy learned the power of focusing on a destination and progressing toward it one step at a time. He also learned that the skill of focusing is complemented by the ability to be flexible and accept help—that being flexible when facing immediate challenges does not mean that you must weaken your ultimate mission.

Tracy recalls that at every step of their journey, people helped—with advice, with food, with assistance, with money, but especially with warmth, kindness, and generosity. There were the mechanics in Morocco and Algeria who helped with car repairs. There was the Frenchman who gave them a precious map that proved lifesaving when they were deep in the desert.

Tracy continued to be open to people he encountered on his travels, long after surviving his Sahara crossing. He met people from all walks of life as he made his way through some 90 countries. Although many people tend to overlook individuals they feel can't contribute to their success, Tracy learned from everyone he met—everyone from Dr. Albert Schweitzer to people who lived in grass huts.

"Synthesize good ideas from every source from all over the world," he advises. "Constantly look for insights."

The young Tracy could have allowed himself to become so discouraged out there in the Sahara that he might have pounded on those oil drums out of frustration instead of following them forward. He could have lost his focus and drifted with the shifting dunes, spurning the help and advice of others.

What he did, instead, led him to a life of astounding success as one of the top motivational speakers and authors in the world. He became the chief operating officer of a $265 million development company; started, built, managed, or turned around 22 different businesses; and has written 26 books and produced 300 audio and video programs. He even entered the race for governor of California during that state's 2003 special election.

Imagine focusing on your goals like Brian Tracy. Then imagine the success you can achieve, no matter how much sand the desert of life blows in your face. And don't give up.

Time after time we must decide between what we can do and what we must do. With luck and wisdom, we may choose a path that keeps our life in balance. Igor Khmelnitsky pursued his first passion for chess far enough to become an International Master and coach but gave up his full career potential in favor of a more normal life.

———•——

CHESS AND BALANCED LIFE CHOICES

IGOR KHMELNITSKY

When I was five years old, my father, Naum, taught me to play chess. During our first lesson, he told me I had to make conscious decisions—not just moves—and that these decisions would affect what happened next. After that first game, he asked me to explain every choice I made. He praised my good choices and showed me why the others were bad. That was my first lesson in making choices.

Little did my father know the impact chess would have on my life. Through the years of studying this great game, I have discovered that the process involved in formulating strategy and making moves in my chess battles also works in everyday problem solving and decision making.

The easiest decision I ever made was to come to the United States. Being Jewish in the Ukraine S.S.R., we were heavily discriminated against in all aspects of life. Being a Jew made it hard for me to get into college, find a job, even to join a junior chess team. So when we got a call from Uncle Sam (the real name of my uncle, who emigrated in 1978) offering to help us get to the United States, I didn't hesitate. My parents, Naum and Polina; my younger sister, Valerie; and I arrived in the United States as refugees in 1991, bringing nothing but our life experience, knowledge, and willingness to work hard to reach our American dream.

Facing a Tough Decision

At 23 years of age, I had to make a tough decision. What should I do with my life? By now I was an established chess player, having won a few international chess events in Europe. I also had two years of education at a small rural college in Ukraine.

I decided to put my chess training to work. I identified my ultimate goals (my "game strategy"), which were to have a family and children and to earn a comfortable living. I knew I would also want to travel, meet interesting people, teach chess to children, write, and, of course, continue competing in chess. But what if my goals were the impossible and unattainable dream?

I was able to identify two reasonable possibilities (or "moves-candidates"). I could pursue the chess career, which was my passion, something to which I had devoted 15 years of my life; or I could go to college and get a "real" profession, preferably in the financial world, which also had always interested me. I assessed the pros and cons; the professional career won. I knew that with hard work and a bit of luck, I could become one of the top five chess masters in the country in three to five years, but I didn't like the minimal financial security that chess offered. I also knew that I would have many competitive advantages in the business world due to my chess training—specifically, my ability to make concrete, sharp, quick decisions.

In the back of my mind, I realized that if I worked extra hard, I could manage to keep my chess skills from deteriorating while I focused on my professional career. While pursuing my B.A. at Temple University, I started teaching private classes in chess and lecturing about this wonderful passion of mine. This was very rewarding, both financially and emotionally. Not only was I able to support my family, but I could also share my chess knowledge with others. Through their successes in professional chess tournaments, I felt the experiences of competition and victory that I was afraid of losing.

I am often amazed at how one person's measure of success differs from that of the next person. Some of my students won tournaments and money prizes. Others gained rating points and improved their national and international rankings. But one of my happiest students turned out to be a fellow who began consistently beating his buddy at their lunch-break matches after suffering jokes and friendly insults during many years of losing.

Meanwhile, I worked hard to maintain my own chess skills. In college and during my first few years working for leading actuarial consulting firm Milliman and Robertson Inc., my challenge was to find time to study chess. My life became an example of having to balance important priorities: family, professional career, chess coaching, writing, and dealing with everyday challenges. Demanding job and family obligations were my top priority. Fortunately, I had mastered an efficient and effective training system, so I was able to keep up with the top U.S. players—full-time chess professionals. Twice, in 1995 and 1996, I was invited to play in the top chess event in the country, the U.S. Championship. These were exclusive events where only 14 players participated, and I was the only nonprofessional player among them. Others regularly study chess five to ten hours a day and play frequently. I spend barely five hours on chess per week, yet both times I scored a respectable five points and beat several strong grand masters.

Dealing with New Challenges

At the same time, I was advancing in my professional career. Thanks to chess, my analytical thinking skills helped me to do my job successfully. But the demands were increasing, and the time left for family and chess was constantly diminishing. My chess ranking continued deteriorating, from being counted in the top 20 in the U.S. to barely holding on to a spot on the top 50 list.

The birth of my son, Alec, placed even more strain on my already limited time. The situation threatened to get out of control; I had to make some new "moves" to help me better balance my life. After some strategic thinking, I made a "two-moves combination." On the professional front, I left the consulting firm, with its interesting but chaotic hours, and joined Aetna Inc., the leader in the health insurance industry. With a nine-to-five work schedule, balancing my daily routine became more manageable. I continued practicing and coaching chess, using my personally developed training techniques. I came home at regular times, spent time with family, and studied chess late at night in a quiet and peaceful house.

I regained my balance, but after a couple of years I began to miss chess battles. With so many things happening at work and at home, I was not sure how to break the routine again.

It took a major blow—the death of my 58-year-old father from cancer. He was my biggest fan and supporter in chess. Seeing him fight for his life against stomach cancer for a year, getting worse and worse every day, until he finally lost was terrifying. Right there I decided, in his memory, to work even harder on chess and to come back to play.

Making a Comeback

It took me almost two years of training and practice to feel ready to play at the tournament level again. Still, my life-balancing act was challenged—I had to help care for my mother and my ailing grandmother. My plate was full. Handling everything was not easy, but in 2001, after more than five years of chess retirement, I made my comeback.

What a joy it was to play again! The results were amazing. I shared first place at a major international chess event with more than ten grand masters and qualified to play in yet another U.S. Championship. My family, chess friends, co-workers, and managers fully supported me, and I had a great tournament. In my second game, I knocked out a grand master who was the former U.S. champion. I had draws with several strong grand masters and shared the lead for a while. In the end, I finished with a respectable tie for 16th place.

Looking at the decisions I've made over the years, I strongly believe that chess training is the best reason for my successes. Chess is the best simulator of life when you are considering life decisions. In my chess game of life, it is my move. Here is what I typically do:

- *Assess the situation.* Figure out the pluses, minuses, and major issues, review my memory to see if I've ever faced a similar situation, use my general knowledge and experience if this is a brand-new setting.
- *Develop a plan.* Consider the short term and decide whether I should attack or defend. Build in a long-term approach with the aim of building up my advantages. My extensive experience and

knowledge help me make correct assessments and choose the best plan.

- *Identify the dangers or threats that I am facing.*
- *Consider specific moves-candidates.* Based on earlier steps, I identify all possible options, then study them one by one and make a selection. I consider calculated risks and probabilities of various scenarios. Among my favorite methods is the process of elimination. This strategy works especially well when facing a threat or danger. I consider all the different ways I can deal with the risks and options: I can run away, defend, counterattack, or ignore.
- *Follow through on my plan.* As my father used to tell me, "Say B after you've said A." This is when I make my move with all the confidence of a correct selection process.
- *Repeat.* After I make my move and my opponent responds, it is back to step one again.

The process doesn't stop! It's the same in real life. Just replace *chess game* with *everyday life* in my earlier statement and see if you can use the same decision-making process. I use it all the time, and it works well in my other life experiences. The more important the decision, the more thoroughly I follow the process.

Analyzing My Choices

In chess, I've learned to analyze my games in great detail to find my mistakes and identify directions for improving subsequent games. In life, it is no different. I always look back at the critical choices I've made and try to analyze them in detail to make good lessons for myself. My dad used to say, "It is important to learn from your mistakes," and I always remember that. He added an interesting corollary: "It is even better to learn from the mistakes of others." That is why my slogan is "Never stop learning." I am constantly reading various books about chess, finance, health, marketing, and more to learn as much as I can. Learning helps me better understand the situations I am dealing with and improves my decision making.

Today, I have a great family that includes my beautiful wife, Svetlana, and my son, Alec. I have a satisfying job as an actuarial consultant for

127

Aetna Inc., a Fortune 500 company, and I maintain a strong presence in chess as a player, coach, and writer. I have traveled the world and met many interesting people. I have several celebrities among my current and former students, many of whom have become my friends.

I believe that the main reason for my successes has been my ability to make right decisions at the critical times and to strike a balance among the many challenging issues of my life. I believe that success must be obtained in every aspect of your life, not in just one specific area. I also believe that I must thank chess for becoming the best tool in my balanced and successful life. I know that every day will bring new challenges that require choices and brand-new decisions. But I have no fear. I am trained to look for the best move!

Adversity and
Risk Taking

The ultimate measure of a man is not where he stands in a
moment of comfort and convenience, but where he stands
at times of challenge and controversy.

—MARTIN LUTHER KING JR.

One law of human nature is to want more—more horse-power, more serenity, more intimacy, more money, more power, more life. But getting more is often an uncomfortable business. To reach the juiciest apples, we have to climb high, reach out, and risk falling off the ladder. Such risk taking tends to be uncomfortable—physically, financially, socially, especially emotionally. We spend a lot of time feeling awkward, inept, out of our element. Terror and exhilaration dance a reckless tango on our nerves.

Reaching for more takes learning, and learning makes us feel like children again, with all the excitement, wonder, and fear that spiced our earliest years. And it's not what we're learning, it's where we're starting from and how far we're trying to reach that make the difference. Learning is relative. The experience of a paraplegic rediscovering the complexities of walking is as intense as that of a teenager learning to drive, a downhill skier learning to snowboard the half-pipe, a manicurist learning to run her own shop. What is routine for one is unimaginable success for another.

In learning, we all start from adversity. We don't make enough money, can't stand our job, don't know enough, can't climb the mountain. Adversity may creep into our awareness as dissatisfaction, a natural manifestation of personal growth, or it may be forced on us by accident or catastrophic illness. Whatever the case, we desire intensely to move from adversity to triumph. And in moving, we encounter new ideas, learn new skills, acquire new beliefs, adopt new attitudes. We face down adversity and stretch ourselves toward success. We improve.

To improve, we must weigh the desired end against the pain of getting there. No risk, no gain. If we opt for comfort and ease, we forgo the rewards of accomplishment. But if we take to heart what professional athletes are taught and "do something every day that scares you a little," we stretch our boundaries and move into new territory. We gain in self-confidence, which makes it easier to push back the limits and tackle bigger challenges. We convert nervous energy—the jitters—into kinetic energy. We become unstoppable.

———•—•———

If the road to success were a straight line, almost everybody would get there as a matter of course and success would mean simply not making any mistakes. But small failures are an integral part of larger successes. In falling short, we learn what not to do, what obstacles to avoid, and how to do good things better. Derek Podorieszach, Canadian Olympic men's downhill ski coach, taught his racers, "When we start winning, our competitors aren't. But when they lose to us, they are forced to learn a better technique than ours."

PERFORMANCE CYCLES

DEREK PODORIESZACH

The world of sports and the world of business have one thing in common, and that's performance. Professionals, whether athletes or businesspeople, are constantly seeking to become better and move upward, fine-tuning and refining as they go to stay ahead. Nevertheless, performance is a very bumpy road of developing skills. Picturing long-term performance as a series of ups and downs as we progress up the hill of skill development helps us understand the continuous, ongoing process called "performance cycles."

A great misconception about long-term performance is the belief that a straight uphill climb can lead us to success and that any decline equals failure. Successful athletes and businesspeople have taught us otherwise. High performers picture the journey toward their objective as an uphill climb followed by a first peak and plateau. This eventually leads to a decline phase where new skills necessary for the next-higher performance phase are learned.

The best performers increase their strength through their defeats. Over time, the accumulated experience of overcoming numerous challenges makes them stronger. The professional understands and accepts these cyclical performance stages as valuable, healthy, and crucial to long-term progression. In the elite worlds of sports and business, every aspect of progression must be used to one's advantage.

Performance is mostly about aiming high and taking action. In the first stage of long-term performance, we are putting game plans into motion. We've studied, we've trained, and we're going for it! A little hard work and some sweat are created as we move along. By pushing the envelope of our performance, we progress and get closer to our objective. This first stage is exciting. We are enthusiastic about what we are doing and are experiencing concrete results. Our growth and gain confirm that our strategy will be successful.

As we keep at it, we eventually reach a first summit. This is stage two of performance. At this stage, motivation and energy levels are high; we feel on top of things; comfort slowly settles in. Ahead of the rest, we would find it easy to cruise along on a plateau and reap the benefits of our hard work and thoughtful planning. But great athletes and serious businesspeople all know that ongoing success is possible only when one is striving for progress by moving forward. If long-term success is what we're looking for, constantly improved performance is what we need. Our performance will improve for a certain time if we follow the training strategies we put in place earlier, using our newly acquired skills and mastering the use of proper equipment. But we truly progress and stretch our talents when we meet new challenges head-on.

The third phase can be pictured as a declining slope, a drop in performance. This phase almost always is awkward, uncomfortable, and sometimes scary. This is the time when we come face-to-face with our zone of discomfort. The challenges, feelings of awkwardness, and maybe even times of embarrassment we encounter must be embraced, as they are essential ingredients to our continued progress up the performance learning curve.

This phase is the most difficult, but also the most beneficial. In this segment of performance we innovate, create, and gain knowledge and experience. In no other part of the ongoing performance cycle can you learn as much. Forced to come out of our comfort zone, we discover that we'll need to confront these new challenges and change our ways. This is where we face the difficult task of mastering new skills and other elements that will allow us to reach the next plateau. As we develop new abilities and strengths, they become our new habits, allowing us to start the cycle all over again, secure in the knowledge that the next performance cycle will increase our strengths and our overall performance even more.

When Tiger Woods first arrived on the PGA Tour, he single-handedly forced the whole playing field into a decline cycle, causing them to reassess, rethink, and change their way of playing the game. His remarkable wins drove them to improve their own skills, which led to an overall improvement in the performance of pro golfers. Eventually, everyone is forced into this difficult stage, or else we must force ourselves into it. At the height of his game, Tiger Woods forced himself into this third decline or change phase of performance. After winning several prestigious tournaments and breaking many records, Tiger decided that it was time for him to change some techniques in his game. It wasn't easy, but he succeeded. He reassessed, rethought, and faced his new challenge of becoming better. He taught his competitors and still was ready to learn more.

Top-level teams, coaches, and athletes know not to fall into the trap of comfort. They look for tougher challenges, refine and redefine training, and constantly learn from defeat and adversity. These top performers come to love the zone of discomfort. At some point, all businesspeople and athletes need to go back to the drawing board.

Coming out of phase three and starting to move upward again is the most confidence-building experience of all. Phase three rewards us with experience and a much-needed boost in self-assurance needed to compete at higher levels. Becoming better and progressing is all about going full circle, constantly cycling through all three stages of performance. This ongoing road of ups and downs applies to each of us in varying degrees every year of our lives.

Using each stage of the performance cycle to our advantage is a skill we all can learn. The first step is to acknowledge that the road to success is always under construction. Go hard in the growth stage, congratulate yourself for reaching a certain summit, take care not to plateau for too long, and then get ready to learn, to change, and to reach higher goals!

———•—•———

The engine of achievement can be powered by internal or external combustion. There's the distant goal, beckoning and pulling; the innate ambition, stirring and pushing from within; and often, to goad and energize the striver, there's the challenge of a less-than-supportive audience to add fuel to the fire. Atlanta businesswoman Janice Malone discovered a world-class champion whose inspirational message tells us to go ahead and "just do it!"

———•—•———

JEAN DRISCOLL'S "PROVE YOU WRONG" ATTITUDE

JANICE MALONE

Lift the right foot slowly, move it an inch or two, then place it on the ground again. Oops! I will fall if I don't keep my balance. Steady now. Here goes! If I can just keep my mind on balancing my body so I don't fall down . . . . Now I'll lift my left foot and inch it along. Look at me, I'm on my way—one small step at a time!

It was this positive attitude, as well as penetrating focus from a very early age, that propelled Jean Driscoll to incredible accomplishments. *Sports Illustrated for Women* ranked her 25th among the top 100 women athletes of the 20th century—a two-time Olympic silver medalist, a 12-time medalist in the Paralympics, and the only person ever to win the Boston Marathon eight times.

Driscoll was born in the mid-1960s with both a cleft palate and spina bifida, an opening in the spine whose complications often prove fatal in childhood. She survived, but her doctors predicted that she would never walk or go to a regular school.

Then a remarkable thing happened: She set out to prove them wrong. At age two, she walked. Despite nerve damage that made it difficult for her to balance, she went to school with her brothers and sisters. "I could walk," she explains, "but my lower body muscles were weak, and I fell down a lot. But every time I fell down, I just got back up." Driscoll learned that if she got up more times than she fell down, she won.

"My big break was learning to ride a bike," she says. "That opened up a whole new world to me. I could go places on my own. I began to love the freedom."

Driscoll had discovered the secret of success at an early age. She realized that she alone was responsible for making her dreams come true—through a proper perspective, positive mental attitude, strong faith, and hard work.

She had to learn harder lessons, too, such as dealing with the inevitable setbacks. During her first year in high school, she "took a corner too sharp and crashed." Five hip surgeries later, she had to face reality. She could walk—with crutches—or she could get about in a wheelchair. The horizons closed in once more: she was now among life's "nonwalkers."

Watching TV with her father one day in 1984, she saw Sharon Hedrick, from the University of Illinois, win the first gold medal ever given to a wheelchair athlete at the Olympic Games. Her event was the 800-meter wheel race for women. "I want to do that someday," exclaimed Driscoll. Her father replied, "Don't get your hopes up too high."

It was time to prove her father wrong. Before long, a disabled friend introduced Driscoll to wheelchair sports. She was hooked. She lived for the days when she could play wheelchair soccer and wheelchair basketball. She regained her lost sense of freedom.

Seeing a limitless horizon once more, she applied to nursing school at the University of Wisconsin. After two years, though, she knew it wasn't the career for her. She flunked out and fell into a deep depression. Feeling that she was only an emotional and financial burden on her family, she considered suicide. In her despair, she began to think that those who had discouraged her were right after all.

Once again, however, her "prove you wrong" attitude prevailed, and with a renewed Christian faith, she put the pieces of her life together again. She began to play more and more wheelchair sports and was first noticed, then recruited, by coach Brad Hedrick to play at the University of Chicago. There was one condition: she had to bring her grades up. Here she learned another success lesson: Surrender yourself to your goal. Do everything necessary to achieve it, including the things you don't like to do.

Driscoll's racing coach, Marty Morse, who had also coached Sharon Hedrick, taught her that success requires goals, and that dreams are useful only if planning and effort follow. The inner creative consciousness he taught her, along with her relentless determination, began to breathe life into her dreams. He helped Driscoll regain the focus with which she had first learned to walk and direct it toward intense upper-body strength training. And she learned another life lesson: You can't do it alone.

Driscoll began to see herself as a great athlete, and the fire driving her toward that vision grew hotter. She felt she could be anything she wanted to be. That led her to a new realizaion: that visualizing success is crucial to achieving goals. The clearer the vision, the greater the chance of achieving the goal. With the help of Marty Morse, Driscoll not only acquired the skills, she learned to develop a plan that included all the steps needed to get to the next level, and the next, and the next. Part of the process was cultivating professional contacts and the sponsorships that are part of her support network. The woman who had once plotted her own suicide was now reaching for the stars.

Driscoll came to the world's attention suddenly, as a world-class athlete, Olympic medalist, and winner of the Boston Marathon wheelchair division seven years straight. What the world did not see was decades of overcoming pain and frustration, years of intense training, and years of climbing through higher and higher levels of competition to reach the top.

Driscoll now uses the sports arena to prove the world wrong about "disabled" people. She teaches the U.S. Army, Nike, Lucent Technologies, Easter Seals, and hundreds of other organizations the secrets of success that afforded her championship prestige. You may not be a corporate spokesperson for Ocean Spray, United Airlines, or Litehouse Foods like Jean Driscoll, but if you listen to her message, *success* might be a more familiar term in your life.

"The greatest limitations in life," she tells us, "are the ones we place on ourselves or the ones we allow others to place on us. All my life I constantly had people telling me that I couldn't do this and couldn't do that. This is what stoked the fires of proof deep within me, and helped to make my 'prove you wrong' attitude so strong."

———

"Life is like school. You have to pass one test to get

on to the next test."

—BETTY MORGAN

In times of emergency, leaders arise to take command. Sometimes these heroes are people wrenched from anonymity by crisis; sometimes they are known figures whose leadership is tested anew by unprecedented tragedy. In either case, the definition of success begins perilously close to survival. Lance Mead, a New Yorker, knows a lot about finding special people. His company, specializing in referral marketing, keeps a sharp lookout for talented people with extraordinary stories.

———

RUDY THE ROCK

J LANCE MEAD

We all hope to make a difference in the world. Some of us never get a chance; others come face-to-face with the opportunity through external forces—and in doing so, are forced to make a stand.

On September 11, 2001, the world changed for many of us. The very foundation that we had learned to take for granted was shaken. Nowhere in the world was the impact felt as much as by the people of New York City. The total destruction of the landmark World Trade Center towers destroyed lives, families, and companies, and continues to affect all our lives.

In the center of this devastation stood the mayor of New York City, Rudolph W. Giuliani. He had witnessed the courage, the heroism, and the loss of the brave people who served the public. He stayed on the scene throughout the aftermath. Giuliani, a cancer patient and not in the best of health, became the rock that New Yorkers depended on to persevere through the trying hours, days, weeks, and months following this event.

No one had ever faced such a single, overwhelming act of terrorism. Giuliani's task was to slow down the events that were a virtual whirlwind around him so that he could exert a calming influence on all who were helping to restore order in New York. Steps had to be taken immediately to coordinate the massive undertaking involving thousands of people in multiple departments, governmental agencies, and volunteer organizations. Communications and information flew nonstop, and the eyes and ears of the world were on New York every waking minute.

Giuliani attributes much of his ability to deal with September 11 to his early upbringing and training by his father. "All during that day," he says, "I could hear my father saying to me: 'In an emergency or a crisis, or if there's a fire, and everybody else around you gets very, very excited, you become the calmest person in the room, and you'll be able to figure your way out of it. Always become calmer. If you start to feel some form of panic, force yourself to put it aside for the time being; then say to yourself, I now have to be calm to figure my way out of this.'"

Although he became internationally known through the events of September 11, Giuliani had made a living by confronting the challenges others said couldn't be handled. As a prosecutor, he took on organized crime. He got elected mayor of New York as a Republican. He wrested the Fulton Fish Market from Mob control. He confronted the cabbies who threatened to bring traffic in Manhattan to a standstill. His life's commitment has been his sense of obligation to those who depend on him, his unwillingness to let them down.

In one of his last conversations with his father, who was dying of cancer, Giuliani asked him if he had ever been afraid. "I was always afraid," said his father. "It's not about being afraid. It's about doing what you have to do even though you are afraid. That's what courage really is." These words are a part of what makes him "Rudy the Rock."

Giuliani lived the lessons of his father, overcame the shock and horror of September 11, and transformed his own life success into New York City's defiant answer to terrorists: We are still here, and we are still strong.

He may have been afraid, but Giuliani had the courage to do what was required. "I've always understood that it's the management of fear, not the absence of fear, that helps us get through life," he says.

For a nation at war, success is victory; for the warrior, success is survival. Overcoming severe wounds adds another dimension to the definition; but the highest success is to come back not diminished but strengthened, capable of enjoying life, even inspiring others. Andrew Hall, a marketing expert in Great Britain, tells us of one man's decision to move forward in life against daunting odds.

139

THE MOST FAMOUS FACE IN BRITAIN

ANDREW HALL

The year was 1982, and Britain was embroiled in the Falklands War. Simon Weston was a private in the British army, a simple "squaddie," aboard the landing craft *Sir Galahad*. As Weston busied himself on deck, the alert sounded: "AIR RAID WARNING RED! GET DOWN! GET DOWN!" Weston glanced up, hoping to catch sight of an enemy plane. Over the hill raced a Skyhawk jet—just one at first, but then two, three, and four. Undefended, the *Sir Galahad* was the target. Weston could only watch as a bomb hurtled toward the vessel, ripped through the port side of the ship, and passed within ten feet of where he sat.

For a split second there was silence. Then the fireball erupted. In a moment, all of Weston's exposed nerve endings were torched. Comrades and friends he had spoken to moments before burst into flames before his eyes. A tough, hardened guardsman crumpled before him, melting hands outstretched, with his last words calling for his mum. Trying to help, Weston found his own hands useless, slipping as if covered in soap, his flesh liquefying from the heat.

Critically burned over half his body, Weston lingered close to death for weeks. His story attracted the attention of a documentary crew from the BBC, and as he underwent 75 major operations during the following years, a nation shared his pain and progress.

He was finally able to return home to the valleys of Wales, where it seemed that nothing much had changed. But for Weston, disfigured and with limited use of his hands, everything was different. Once a proud, tough, capable soldier, he now felt dependent, worthless, without purpose.

Like many servicemen in his situation, despite the love and support his family provided, he sank into depression. He became addicted to painkillers and edged into alcoholism. At the lowest ebb of his spirits, he attempted suicide.

And it was this bungled attempt on himself with a crossbow that jolted him in a new direction. As he struggled to arm the weapon, his weakened hands lost their grip and the string snapped back abruptly, almost removing his remaining fingers. It was a sharp reminder that he still had much to lose.

As so often happens in life, when the student is ready, the teacher will appear. Weston's greatest source of inspiration and motivation turned out to be someone not unlike himself, a man who had risen in total defiance against the realities of his injuries: his friend Jonathan. The IRA in Crossmaglen had shot Jonathan through the neck. Doctors told him that he would never walk again and could never father children, but Jonathan decided otherwise. Ignoring his doctor's assessment, he set off to the bar with Weston to get in his first round of drinks since his injury. Fueled by pride alone, Jonathan stumbled and lurched his way to his old group. Notes Weston, "By the time I finally got to the table, the drinks were half empty, but as sure as that, they were half full too." Today, Jonathan is the father of twins.

A new idea began to form in Weston's mind. He began to understand that "it is not what happens in life that matters, it is what you do about it that really counts in the end." Instead of seeing his disfigured face as a burden, he started to think of it as an asset: he now had the most recognizable face in Britain! With everyone from the Prince of Wales to the cabdrivers following his every step, he realized, opportunities to make a difference in the world were within his reach. All he had to do was act on them.

Like the first rugby player who picked up the ball and just kept on running, Simon Weston has been moving forward ever since. His disfigurment may have been an accident, but the way he has channeled tragedy into opportunity certainly has not been. Visit him today, and you find a man very much in control of his life and destiny. Weston has used to his advantage the political influence his unique position has given him. He is a successful public speaker and motivator, bestselling author of the autobiography, *Walking Tall*, and an inspiration to thousands of youngsters through his charity, Weston Spirit. Ask him today what made the difference, and he will repeat an observation made by one of his closest friends on the *Sir Galahad*: "The difference between you and me, Simon, is that you feel lucky to be alive. I feel lucky not to be dead."

Critical to his success is not just his positive outlook on life but also his refusal to become embroiled in the negative issues surrounding the Falklands War. The bombing of the *Sir Galahad* brought in its wake a mass of recriminations as a grieving nation sought to apportion blame. Weston leaves such issues alone and harbors no grudges, believing it has nothing to do with him. This attitude frees him to draw on the positive lessons he learned from that experience and use them as tools to "ensure that the past has a future."

Supported by a combination of steely resolve and a dark sense of humor, Simon Weston is driven by a unique set of motivators. One of his favorite stories is of a night out with two other desperately wounded men: "Noel," who lost both legs and an arm in an IRA bomb blast, and "Speedy," who broke his back in a hang-gliding accident. As this unlikely group made their way back to base, a voice came out of the shadows. It was a beggar, apparently able-bodied, who demanded: "Give us all yer money, lads. I need all of yer money." Incredulous at his nerve, the three injured men stared at him, then turned away, laughing. But the beggar was not finished; he called after them: "Just remember, fellers—there is always someone worse off than yerselves!"

Simon Weston never forgets.

———•◦•———

Finding success by doing what you're good at can be rewarding and fulfilling—but it is hardly surprising. The stiffest challenge is to become good at what you are not equipped to do, whether by nature or happenstance. As a business leader in California, Linda McCarthy seeks out success by looking in unlikely places.

———•◦•———

CAPABLE OF SUCCESS

LINDA MCCARTHY

This is a story about overcoming the odds, about doing exactly what others have said could not be done. It is a story about tragedy and prejudice turning to triumph and enlightenment.

Carol Leish has been overcoming the odds ever since she was ten months old, when a car accident left her with slurred speech, permanent hand tremors, and blindness in one eye. In 1963, the family Volkswagon Beetle was hit from behind by a drunk driver. This was before seat belt and infant car seat laws, and baby Carol was placed in the back storage well while her two older brothers rode in the backseat. Her mother and brothers suffered only minor injuries, but since Carol was in the far back she took the brunt of the collision. She suffered severe brain stem trauma and was unconscious for ten days. When she finally awoke, the doctors said she would never function as a "normal" person.

Just When You Think It's All Over, It's a Good Time to Start

As Leish grew up, family and friends treated her as just one of the kids. Her parents did not feel the need to place her in special education classes, thinking it would only slow her down. They wanted her to live up to the capabilities they knew she possessed, to develop the courage and confidence needed to lead a productive life.

As we are all aware, a child who is "different" will suffer socially. Leish grew up with the usual teasing and mimicking most kids suffer, but hers was magnified many times over. Friendships were few, hard-won, and far between, but because her upbringing molded her "capable" attitude, she kept her focus on the positive things in her life and valued the few friends she had.

As if her life challenges weren't difficult enough, her mom died suddenly from a serious illness just before Carol Leish's 14th birthday. This took its toll on her, and depression was added to her list of challenges. She began to see a counselor, who encouraged her to develop humor as a tonic against depression and negativity.

In high school, Leish challenged herself physically by taking piano lessons, working on hand control while learning to adapt chords to her playing capabilities. She made the junior varsity swim team and soon become the most improved team member. She began working with counselors from the state's department of rehabilitation, who put her through various hand-eye coordination tests, but she just couldn't pass them. When she started thinking about college, she was advised against it—even though she had never had any difficulty academically.

The Greatest Pleasure in Life Is Doing What Others Say You Cannot Do

Attitude is 100 percent of everything we do in life, and Leish's "capable" attitude kicked in once again. Ignoring the rehab agency's advice, she enrolled in college. Hand tremors made writing virtually impossible, so she took notes in class by recording lectures and using a portable typewriter. Proving the experts wrong once again, Leish graduated from college with a B average. She went on to earn her master's degree in education and counseling from California State University, San Bernardino, graduating with a GPA of 3.6.

Leish says many people mistake her condition for cerebral palsy, a condition characterized by impaired muscle control due to brain damage, usually at or prior to birth. They also assume she is deaf because she has slow, slurred speech (she gets signed to a lot) or that she isn't paying attention because her left eye wanders.

Assumptions like these prompted Leish to become a disability consultant, launching her business, Call Me Capable In-Services, in 1997. She realizes that people genuinely want to be helpful and courteous toward the disabled, so her program teaches them to be more sensitive and to broaden their perspectives. "My main goal," she says, "is to eradicate the prejudice that people have about people with physical disabilities. I hope that education in this area will help people to be more comfortable working with the disabled, and all of us will be more productive." Leish notes, however, that nondisabled people aren't the only ones who may need to change their attitudes. People with disabilities also need to focus on possibilities rather than limitations.

Focusing on those possibilities, Leish continues to gain recognition and has received several awards for her community achievements in promoting mutual understanding and respect of others. Among these awards are Top Outstanding Young American (California Finalist), 1998, from the U.S. Junior Chamber of Commerce; Outstanding Young Californian, 1998, from the California Junior Chamber of Commerce; and the Spirit of Networking Award, 1997–1998, from the Ventura County Professional Women's Network.

The future belongs to those who believe in the beauty of the dream.
—ELEANOR ROOSEVELT

Carol Leish has trained her slow, quivery voice to hold the attention of audiences at businesses, schools, hospitals, clubs, and nonprofit organizations. She invites audience members to join her on her personal journey of coping with visual and speech challenges. She uses her wry wit and genuineness to deal with this sensitive subject in a way that inspires and educates the listener. Ironically, one of her clients is the very same state rehabilitation agency that, back in high school, advised her to forget college.

An important part of Leish's presentation is Call Me Capable, a game she developed in college while earning her master's degree. The game is actually a noncompetitive discussion starter for both kids and adults. Players move around a board that prompts them to select cards with thought-provoking questions such as "How can you enjoy dancing if you cannot hear?" The game is both a fun experience and a way of fostering acceptance and empathy for people with disabilities.

It was Leish's dream to get this game published, and in November 2001, that dream came true. Through a networking connection, she was introduced to Franklin Learning Systems, which gave her the green light to get Call Me Capable on the national market.

God grant me the serenity to accept the things I cannot change, the courage to change the things I can, and the wisdom to know the difference.
—SERENITY PRAYER, REINHOLD NIEBUHR

Leish sees every challenge as an opportunity to find constructive solutions, ways to improvise, and the humor in each situation. There are many ironies in Leish's life: even with depression, she went out into the community and networked; with only one good eye and shaky hands, she went further in school than 90 percent of the population; and with her slurred, slow speech, she has become a motivational speaker.

She draws strength and inspiration from some of her favorite historic heroes. In the Bible, Exodus 4:10–16 tells that Moses had a speech impediment but delivered one of history's strongest messages about life. Helen Keller, who was blind and deaf, said, "I thank God for my handicaps, for through them I have found myself, my work, and my God." Thomas Edison had a learning disability; Abe Lincoln suffered from depression; and Beethoven was deaf when he composed his Ninth Symphony.

Leish accepts that God has an important mission for her, too. "Through the lessons of life, I have realized my goal to help others," she says. "Ralph Waldo Emerson said, 'Life is a succession of lessons that must be lived to be understood.' I have learned and continue to learn lessons that can educate others, making them more aware of everyone's capabilities. Thus, remember to *call me capable* and yourself *more* capable."

Success is most rewarding when the odds are stacked against you. That's why the greatest satisfaction comes from doing something well that you once did poorly. But to realize and appreciate fully the magnitude of your success, you will find nothing so sweet as using your hard-won mastery well in totally unexpected circumstances. Marty Laff, a financial advisor in Northridge, California, knows these rewards firsthand.

SOMETHING TO LAFF ABOUT

MARTHA "MARTY" LAFF, CLU

A few weeks ago, I watched as my friend Ruth, a well-known businessperson in my community, agonized over having to give her dear friend's eulogy. She missed him and wanted to express her love, understanding, and respect for him to those at his memorial service, but the thought of speaking in front of any group larger than three or four people terrified her. I could see how nervous she was and recognized the strength it took for her to pay tribute to her friend. Ruth's fear was a fear I knew all too well.

In 1978, I joined a women's networking group with about 50 women in attendance. After the opening remarks, we were told it was introduction time. I watched the 25 women before me give their introductions. They seemed comfortable, poised, and smart. Slowly, I began to panic. First my hands became moist. Then my mouth went dry. With each new introduction, I compared them to myself, counting off each of the reasons why I would fail: I was not prepared, I couldn't give the right information in the right amount of time, it just wasn't going to work. I watched and worried. Twenty minutes went by, and then it was my turn! Oh, my gosh, it was my turn!

I stood, knees shaking, still trying to gather just the right words. Taking a deep breath, I opened my mouth.

Nothing came out.

I struggled and choked, but not one intelligible word would come out of my mouth. I had lost my voice! I sat down, embarrassed and ashamed, wanting to fade away. I was near tears. After the meeting, some of the women were kind enough to come over and talk to me, and we exchanged business cards.

That night was a turning point for me. I decided right then and there that this speaking problem was something that had to be dealt with immediately if I was going to make it in business, much less succeed. My goal was to speak comfortably, naturally, and spontaneously in front of any group. But how on earth was I going to do this if I couldn't even form a sentence in front of people?

During the following weeks, many of the women in the networking group came to my rescue. They comforted me and identified with me, saying they had faced similar upsets. When I asked them for suggestions, they recommended that I try some breathing and relaxation exercises as well as writing out my introduction, visualizing success, and practicing every day in front of a mirror. I was encouraged to use a tape recorder and critique myself for self-improvement.

They were so caring. Their coaching made me feel a part of their group. The next month, after working hard at their suggestions, I returned to the meeting. When it came my turn to introduce myself, I got up and succeeded at least in telling the group my name and what business I was in. For some people, this would barely register on the success meter, but to me it was monumental. It wasn't easy, and it certainly wasn't perfect, but the small step I had taken in breaking through the barrier of my fear put me on a path toward further successes in public speaking.

That's not the end of this story, though.

In the following years, I attended other networking meetings and watched other speakers perform in front of their audiences. I then asked them questions, copied or mirrored their styles, and looked for small speaking opportunities where I could continue practicing my new craft. I learned to volunteer at organizations, help with meetings, get on committees, create marketing talks, and generally add value to the group where possible.

About four years later, I volunteered to help organize the first chapter of the Los Angeles Women Life Underwriters' Confederation. Within a year, I was the Los Angeles chapter president.

The following year, as the past president, I organized a very special membership meeting, designed to attract more support from the Los Angeles area insurance agencies. About 70 people attended, including some of the most important agency managers and sales associates in Los Angeles.

The guest speaker was a member of the Million Dollar Round Table. We had corporate sponsors and vendor booths. The morning had success in the air. We had created a positive energy, and it felt good just to be there. My own manager was seated across from me. As the chairperson, my job was to provide the welcome and opening remarks.

At the moment I stood to give my presentation, the waistband broke on my very expensive and beautiful suede skirt, and the skirt fell to my ankles. My manager and the entire audience held their breath. How could this happen?! What could I do? Time stood still.

I gathered my focus and directed it entirely at what would be best for my group. We needed respect; we needed to be seen as peers. We wanted to be accepted and recognized as talented representatives of our industry. In the flash of a moment, I assessed my options. To panic. To leave the stage. To cry. No, none of those options would help move us toward our goal.

Instead, I bent over and picked up my skirt; holding it in place, I stepped up to the podium, put on a small smile, looked around the group, and spoke into the microphone. My comment at that moment came easily and with only a slight blush to my cheeks: "Now that I've got your attention, don't you think it would be worth the cost of the membership dues today, to be able to come to our meeting next month to see how we'll follow this act?"

It took only an instant, but the laughter began and then grew louder. Some even applauded. It was actually quite funny. The tension left the room, and I gave my ten-minute introduction speech. I think they listened just a little more carefully and a little more attentively than usual, and at the end I received a standing ovation. Our chapter accepted several new member applications from agents, and we were recognized in the industry from that day on.

I was very honored that my agency manager had personally attended that morning event. Always the gentleman, he never commented to me about what had happened, even after his retirement several years ago. Recently, one of the staff members from our agency told me how he had shared the story of what happened. He said that I was quite a lady and he knew I would be successful. That was the best award I've received so far. I survived the one experience that is probably most people's worst nightmare about speaking in public.

Looking back, it's hard to believe that the same person who had lost her voice just trying to mention her name in front of a group had handled such an embarrassing experience so gracefully. Some days are easier than others, of course, but the lessons I've learned along the way have made me a successful public speaker. Oh, and I've learned always to carry an extra safety pin.

—◆—

Sometimes success comes from just doing one thing after another and ignoring everyone's hollering, like a draft horse wearing blinkers. Success stories, such as the following that inspire small-business owners to higher achievement are the stock-in-trade of journalist Jim Blasingame, described by Fortune Small Business *magazine as one of the top small-business resources in America. Blasingame is the author of* Small Business Is Like a Bunch of Bananas *and host of* The Small-Business Advocate Show *on radio and the Internet.*

—◆—

DAVE WAS A HORSE

JIM BLASINGAME

Dave was born the fifth of 12 children during the Great Depression. His father worked at a sawmill and was a part-time basket weaver.

Dave had some personal problems: He was a stutterer, he had epilepsy, plus he had a learning disorder, all of which prevented him from graduating high school until he was 21.

How do you like Dave's chances in life so far?

Dave Takes a Chance

Dave was a good employee—a Fuller Brush salesman and the route man for two bakeries. And then, with all of his personal challenges, he purchased and successfully ran two businesses, a restaurant and a grocery store.

Remember his father's part-time basket weaving? Well, Dave started selling baskets. First those made by his father's hands, and later from Dave's factory—the basket factory that he sold his two very successful businesses to buy. Turns out Dave had serious entrepreneurial sap rising in his bark.

His friends, family, and bankers were incredulous. Why leave a successful and sure thing to make baskets? By the way, they knew Dave didn't know anything about how to make baskets himself.

Would you have invested in Dave?

Dave Had Vision

Turns out Dave also had vision. He envisioned a world that would need baskets—lots of baskets. And Dave Longaberger wanted to fill that need.

Over the next 25 years, Longaberger Baskets grew from selling a handful of Dave's father's baskets to more than $1 billion worth of the woven wonders annually. Not too shabby for the stuttering, epileptic, learning-disabled son of a sawmill worker who took 15 years to get out of school.

What Dave Longaberger lacked in education he made up for with uncanny instincts. Any lack of sophistication he had was more than compensated for with an innate leadership ability that made employees love him and customers want to do business with him.

His daughter, Tami, who now runs the company, told me her father liked to say, "Your success will ultimately depend on the relationships you build with people." I know some highly educated folks who still need to learn that lesson.

Education is important. But an educated entrepreneur without instincts and leadership ability is like a jeweled Spanish saddle with no horse to put it on. As we say of someone who possesses awesome ability, Dave was an entrepreneurial horse.

Next time you feel deficient because you don't have an MBA, ask yourself what Dave would have done. When you are tempted to have a pity party because you've had it tough, imagine what Dave would have said if you tried to lay a whiny attitude on him.

The Longaberger Company is privately held. If they ever go public, I want in, don't you?

Write This on a Rock . . .

Dave Longaberger has won praise from the state of Ohio: "Perhaps as much as any other company, any other entrepreneur, Dave Longaberger is Ohio's ambassador for how business is done in Ohio."

But we'll let Dave have the last word: "Your success will ultimately depend on the relationships you build with people."

———•◦•———

Dealing with personal tragedy is, for most of us, the bitterest of life's challenges. Success in these terms can come down to simply facing overwhelming grief and going ahead with the business of living. But the noblest success is to transcend loss by rescuing the spirit of the life that was as a lamp for the future. Visionary entrepreneur Niraj Shah, who speaks and writes about the unconscious mind, success psychology, and peak performance, faced calamity and found another way of looking at life.

———•◦•———

"WE CANNOT CHANGE THE DIRECTION OF THE WIND, BUT WE CAN ADJUST THE SAILS!"

NIRAJ SHAH

Some moments we will remember forever. The most powerful and enduring of these moments are the ones where we faced great adversity and against all odds reached within us to turn it around. These character-defining moments are the ones we remember most clearly. Each of us will have an obituary, with two dates—the day we were born and the day we died. There is a simple dash that separates these two dates. This dash represents how we conducted ourselves between our birth and death. Much of this dash will be a reflection of how we conducted ourselves in the face of overwhelming adversity and who we became as a result.

My defining moment came on May 15, 2001, a day on which I had to face the unthinkable. It marked the end of a fairy tale and the beginning of a nightmare. It began just after my wife, Sheetal, and I left our office in Nairobi around 6 P.M. It was always a tense moment leaving at this time. There were not many people around, as most businesses closed between 5 and 5:30 P.M. Security was a concern, given the road layout. We were more vigilant at this time for anything suspicious.

We had driven barely 100 meters. The potholes were particularly bad and were covered in muddy water. About 15 meters ahead, there was a small kiosk on my right. I decided to cut to the left of a huge pothole and headed slowly for the footpath on the left.

Suddenly, I saw a man pointing something at us. It seemed as if he were directing us. It struck me as odd. Then I realized that he was pointing a gun right at us! I immediately shifted my attention to the right, and saw another gunman about ten meters away. I saw more men running out of the kiosk and shouting. There were about eight or nine men, all of them armed. We were being ambushed! I had already stopped the car and tried to put it into reverse. They opened fire. I heard a bang from the guy on my left. Simultaneously, the man on my right fired and I saw the bullet come through the bottom of the windscreen.

The rest of what followed seemed to happen in slow motion. I saw a bullet go straight toward my wife. It struck her just below her throat, and the impact flung her forward. The seat belt activated and jerked her backward. I watched in utter horror. Blood started gushing from a hole the size of a quarter. Her head drooped forward and she went into shock. She never said a single word. She never even had time to scream.

In that moment, I came face-to-face with my greatest fear. Sheetal, my lover, my best friend, my soul mate, died in my arms. I felt an anguish that penetrated the very depths of my soul. I cried until I could simply cry no more. Suddenly I felt so lonely. We would never be able to share all those little things that gave us so much joy, to do all those things that we had dreamt of doing together.

You must be aware of the meaning that you attach to such horrific events, as they will continue to shape your life for the future. When such shocking events occur, your mind is riveted to what is happening. At this point, the entire mind is instantly activated and photographs or records everything in terms of the senses. Our minds become fixated and continually replay these movies because of the emotional weight we attach to these events. Most of my attention was captured by this movie, and subsequently, very little of my potential was available to do anything else. Our reality becomes the same as our constant thoughts.

One morning some time after this event, I awoke with a strong impression of one single word in my mind: *Anekantvad* (ane-kant-vad). It temporarily distracted me from loading my habitual-thought film. I had no idea what the word meant as it wasn't in English.

That evening a relative happened to visit me. I related the unusual events of the morning and was delighted to find out that he knew what this word meant! I learned that it was an important Sanskrit word within the Jain Indian philosophy. He explained what Anekantvad meant using a wonderful parable:

> There was an elephant that came to a village. No one had ever
> seen an elephant before, and all the villagers were very excited.
> There were five blind men who also lived in the village, and they

were also excited to hear about this elephant, so they converged at the place where the crowd had gathered to see it. The crowd made way so that they could get close to the elephant and touch it. They were all thrilled with the experience, and on their way back home they started discussing it.

The first man said, "An elephant seems very much like a snake—long, thick, and moving about!"

The second man said, "My friend, maybe you are mistaken. An elephant is very much like a short, thin rope!"

The third man disagreed, "You are both wrong. My elephant was flat and thin and it moved slowly, producing a gentle wind. An elephant is very much like a large flat fan!"

The fourth man said, "Absolutely not, an elephant is like a solid wall!"

The fifth man said, "My friends, your sense of touch is not what it used to be. An elephant is round and solid like a thick pillar!"

Of course, all of them were right—each had felt a different part of the elephant. I immediately understood what Anekantvad meant. It meant: open up your perspective!

I realized that a sense of loss has a valid purpose in relation to death. Loss itself is not the only meaning. Sometimes we hold on to the trunk and think that's the whole elephant. Sometimes we are too close to understand the full meaning of what has happened.

During my quest, I found a very practical way to open my perspective that dissolved my fixed-thought film and led to profound insights that subsequently have shaped my life. I started using my five senses to become fully present and ever aware of everything that was going on around me. I found that entrance into reality was through the present moment. I started to practice living in the Now.

A simple way for me to live in the Now was to do the things that I really enjoyed. I found myself reentering the flow of life. My mind was more relaxed, and as a result, my awareness naturally expanded. I rediscovered more of my potential so that I was more able to do things important to living rather than being trapped in the false reality created by my thought film. Living in the Now switches you out of your thoughts and into reality. It allows you to experience what is actually there, rather than what you think is there.

It is easy to say, "Live in the Now," but I know it is hard to accomplish when one's mind is so involved with a past-thought film. The way I created change in my life and reduced the dominance of my thought film was serendipitous.

One day I was clearing our flat, and I came across Sheetal's diary. I was astounded by the contents. In one part she had written the following:

> *Emotional Fitness.* My life is filled with fun, laughter, profound happiness, deep love and respect and compassion for everyone. I am an ever-smiling person who cheers up everyone and this gives me a lot of joy.
>
> *Forever Friendships.* To be a lover of people, a supporter, a fun companion, an angel in need, a loyal friend. Reach out and touch someone.
>
> *Spiritual Life.* To honor the privilege of the life I have been allowed to have by devoting my time and life to my God, spending some time in prayer daily to thank him for each day.

Her words moved me profoundly. I was so proud of her for being a person who really "walked her talk"! I pondered her words deeply and realized that these same qualities were ones that I aspired to myself. Suddenly I felt a deep sense of peace washing over me. I couldn't quite understand what had just happened. I did know that I now understood something deeply, but I wasn't yet conscious of its full meaning.

As my quest for answers continued, this understanding finally came to the light of my consciousness. I now understand that part of our identity is invested in the ones we love. The more we love someone, the more our identity is invested in them.

As I later toyed with this concept, I began to understand a far greater truth, and the pieces of the puzzle fell into place. When we grieve, we suffer two losses. One is the physical loss of that person. This loss is most immediate to our conscious thought. The second loss has a far more powerful impact but is one that we are not immediately aware of.

This second loss is actually the loss of our own identity. This second loss is the area we understand the least. This is why grief affects us so profoundly, especially when we experience the loss of someone very close.

It is like looking in the mirror and not being able to see our own reflection. It feels like we have lost ourselves. But of course we can never lose ourselves. This feeling is just a case of temporary amnesia resulting from the shock of a loved one's death. We are fixated on the single thought film. We don't realize that we also are experiencing a loss of our own identity. Our personal identity gives us an understanding of who we are, and it is one of the most powerful factors in our life.

I finally discovered a way to transform grief in such a way that we restore our true identity and at the same time honor the person who has passed away.

The Key to Transforming and Integrating Your Grief

The first key is to recognize that the qualities you love about that person are also the same ones you aspire to. When I read Sheetal's diary, I began to understand this phenomenon.

The second key is to make the qualities you admired about the person you loved a part of you. By doing so, you will manifest the very best of that person in your everyday life.

What an incredible way to honor the ones that we love. Now the very best of Sheetal becomes a part of me and continues to live through me every day! I started cultivating her fun, happy, joyous, loving, and compassionate attitude every day. I started injecting these qualities into the way I live and interact with people. I now live in a way that honors Sheetal and respects how she lived. In doing so, I am now a better person. Once you understand this way of grieving, there will be no other way. When you find something of greater value than your pain, you drop the pain. This is the way of the phoenix. Just as an alchemist transforms base metal into gold, the phoenix transforms suffering into empowerment and enlightenment.

It takes only three simple steps to become a phoenix:

1. Open up your perspective.
2. Transform the negative meaning (fixed thoughts) into an empowering one.
3. Integrate the new meaning within you in a way that allows you to live life fully.

I want to leave you with this amazing metaphor that helped me in my quest:

> I am reading an epic novel in which the heroine has just died and the hero is left alive. We know that he is coping well and has learned many spiritual lessons since his beloved passed away. I turn over the page, and it's blank. In fact, all the pages are blank thereafter, except for a small yellow sticky note on the first blank page upon which is written:
> It is up to you to finish the rest!

———•·•———

Seeing the goal is a prerequisite for success; believing in the goal, knowing absolutely that you're going to get there, is how you achieve success beyond the long-odds challenges. Few know this more surely than Lou Holtz, a coach known for winning an amazing number of football games against stacked decks in his 30-year career.

———•·•———

SEE THE SHOT BEFORE YOU MAKE THE SHOT

LOU HOLTZ

All the great golfers I have known visualize their success before it happens. They never entertain doubts. If they miss a putt, they will always tap down a spike mark, giving you the impression that it is never their fault. You must have the same self-confidence to compete on their level. I don't care what you do, never question your ability. Do everything you can to improve your performance, but when game time comes, take the field thinking you are the best.

This Turtle Could Play

When people choose happiness and success, nothing can stop them. Great things are bound to happen. For example, during my early years at Notre Dame, we had a player from Baltimore named Mike Brennan. He came to us as a tight end. Mike was six feet, four inches and 210 pounds—an average weight for his height—yet he may have been the slowest athlete I have ever coached. Naturally, the players nicknamed him Turtle. This was very disparaging . . . to turtles. I mean, those reptiles were relatively quick compared to Mike. Heck, I've seen corpses that could have spotted him five yards and still beat him in a sprint.

After his first season, I doubted he would ever play for us, but I liked having him on the team. He had a wonderful spirit and worked harder than anyone. Mike could have focused on his shortcomings and quit. Who would have blamed him? Instead, he chose to believe in himself. He was always the first one on the practice field and the last to leave. Mike rehearsed all his assignments until he had them down perfectly. His self-confidence, backed by his all-out effort, made all the difference. Mike not only eventually won a starting position with us, he went on to play four seasons as an offensive lineman in the NFL. He provided us with some of our best evidence of the power of positive thinking.

Don't Flinch

In 1987, I drove to Chicago to have lunch with Carl Pohlad. During our meal, Carl said, "Successful people don't flinch."

In the Eye of a Hurricane

Winners exude self-confidence. Watching a football game, you can usually predict early in the contest who is going to win just by observing how each team carries itself. Certain teams set up as if they know they have you beaten before the game even starts. A club like that can destroy an opponent's morale.

When Notre Dame played coach Jimmy Johnson and his University of Miami Hurricanes in 1987, they had an outstanding receiver named Michael Irvin. Every time he had a good play—something he did often—Michael incited the crowd with antics that most of us would call hotdogging. You see players do this all the time. They run into the end zone for a touchdown, then spike the ball while breaking into a flash-dance. Some players indulge in this choreography just to call attention to themselves, but for Michael, hotdogging was a weapon. He used it to challenge and intimidate, to let his opponents know he was going to beat them all afternoon.

Michael and his Miami teammates did top us that day. However, by the following year, our team had developed the attitude that we could vanquish anybody. I'm sure Jimmy and the Hurricanes felt the same way. They came into our 1988 rematch ready to defend the longest regular-season winning streak of any college football team in the country.

We held the home-field advantage for that game. The night before the contest, I got up to speak at a pep rally in front of 25,000 students. I kept my remarks brief. I asked the fans to do three things for our team. First, I wanted them to cheer louder for Notre Dame at this game than they had ever cheered before. Second, I wanted them to comport themselves with class, as they always did. Third, I wanted them to let Jimmy Johnson and his team know that we were going to beat them like an old yard dog.

By the time I had addressed that throng, it had been so late in the evening that I didn't expect my comments to hit the morning papers. Was

I wrong! I woke up the next day to headlines blaring, "Lou Holtz Predicts Victory over Hurricanes." My first reaction was that I had pulled one of the all-time rock-headed blunders. Miami was awfully good; they didn't need any help from me to get psyched for this game. I could just picture my words being posted throughout their locker room.

Then I thought, "Heck, what difference does it make? The Hurricanes are going to be up to play us no matter what I said." Jimmy Johnson could have given motivation lessons to Dale Carnegie. He was, and still is, an outstanding coach who would have his team completely prepared for any game of this magnitude. The more I thought about those headlines, the less they concerned me.

Besides, I had accomplished exactly what I wanted. My outlandish comments at the pep rally—outlandish because they were so out of character for me—weren't aimed at the fans or even the Miami football team. The Fighting Irish of Notre Dame were my targets. I wanted all of our players to realize how much confidence I had in them. This was not smoke I was blowing. I believed with every fiber of my being that we were going to be victorious.

At first, my players had no idea what I was doing. To be honest, I wasn't completely sure myself. But when we gathered for our team meeting, I explained why I thought we would win the game. I pointed out how our team had vastly improved since last season. No one could dispute that. Then I asked how many members of our offense were going to fumble the ball or throw an interception. No one raised a hand. I asked which member of our defense was going to make an interception or recover a fumble. Quite a few hands went up. We went through a litany of assignments. Every time a player's hand rose, I wrote his name on the blackboard alongside the task he had promised to carry out. An exercise such as this encourages your people to make a visual commitment to winning. By the time this meeting was over, our squad believed it was unbeatable.

Two obdurate football teams took the field the next day. Not a player on either side could spell the word *yield*. With the score tied at the end of the first quarter, the two teams exchanged ends of the field. As they passed each other, one of Miami's tackles said to our linebacker, Frank Stamms,

"This game is going to the wire, isn't it?" He knew. Miami went into every game certain it would prevail, but now they were facing a team just as confident. We staged our version of Armageddon throughout the afternoon. It was a brute of a football game and, yes, it did go down to the final second. We beat them by a single point. That was a victory that could have gone either way, because neither team knew how to flinch.

In life, be a participant, not a spectator.

—LOU HOLTZ

From *Winning Every Day* by Lou Holtz, copyright ©1998, published by HarperCollins Publishers Inc. Used by permission of Lou Holtz.

Social Capital

Everyone thinks of changing the world, but no one thinks of changing himself.

—LEO TOLSTOY

A business grows through the relationships it establishes and maintains with its employees, customers, suppliers, advisors, and others. For lasting success, it must keep customers coming back to buy its products or services. People will bring you repeat business if they believe you consistently give them excellent value in return.

It's the same with individual relationships. Each party must provide value to the other, or else the glue of exchanged value no longer binds them together. Whether within a family, a company, a community organization, or a coaching relationship, if the bond is not mutually beneficial, the relationship will end.

The days of the lone entrepreneur risking all to gain the objective, bravely bucking the odds against survival, are gone. Life and commerce in a modern society are too complex. The solo pioneer cannot keep up with the information available on the booming Internet and in the thousand books published daily, cannot understand all the factors and perform all the tasks needed to succeed. Success comes through teamwork. No one gets to the top alone—not a headlined CEO, not a sports star, not an international leader. Corporate acquisitions and mergers are less about power than survival; even large companies are less able to go it alone in the increasingly interconnected age of information.

Starting a new relationship or assembling a success team means giving others good reasons to join up. Money can jump-start the process, but it takes more than that to keep a relationship alive. What brings us together is the perception that we could share in and benefit from each other's strengths and resources. What holds us together over the long term is that we create and maintain this relationship of mutual benefit. As we climb toward success, gaining skills and knowledge and insight, it's wise to follow the rule of sharing: On your way up the ladder of success, don't step on the person below you or pull down the person above you.

There are many examples of mutually beneficial relationships involving more than two individuals. In a business networking group, members gain access to one another's information, knowledge, contacts, and other resources. People join Toastmasters in order to learn from one another the skills of public speaking. Such groups offer support, access to information, and collective strength through teamwork.

Being active in a relationship-based network is like depositing money in a bank account: the more you put in, the more there is to draw upon when needed. The concept becomes clearer if you substitute *social capital* for *money*. By making deposits to your account—referrals, expertise, public service—you build your social capital. It's a way of marketing yourself: you are the product, and you can help others by supplying this product.

In the end, what benefit do you derive from the social capital you amass? First, you'll find that helping others achieve their goals becomes a benefit in itself. Second, when you base relationships on mutual value, your growing social capital will attract others who can help you achieve your own goals.

———•◦•———

When living is not about money or fame but simply about making it from one day into the next, social capital can spell the difference between life and death. Americans had banked considerable social capital in the Philippines that, after the Japanese overran the Allied forces in 1942, paid interest that helped many prisoners of war survive the ordeal in surprising ways. Brian Alcorn, a network specialist in West Virginia, recounts his father's extraordinary survival story.

———•◦•———

NETWORKING FOR SURVIVAL

BRIAN ALCORN

It's 5:00 A.M., and you're roused from sleep, covered with another night's rash of mosquito bites. The heat hangs in the predawn air just waiting to spring to full life with the rising sun. You grab your morning shower, along with about 75 other guys, and line up for breakfast. The smell of ham and eggs fills your mind, but fades when you stare into the cup of watery rice in your hands. Hell, you never liked ham and eggs back home, anyway.

Now you're lining up and counting off. Everyone's here. No escapes last night. You don't feel fully awake yet, but your feet are marching you forward, step and step and step, along a dirt road.

The guards are probably no more awake than you, but they have guns. You keep marching. Some distance along you pass a roadside fruit market. The Spanish lady who runs the market glances at the procession and smiles. Your guards take no notice. There's a little sign in front of her market today. The sign says, "WE."

You trudge on. Lots of local folks line the road. Your guards pay them no heed. About 50 feet ahead you spot a different lady holding an inconspicuous little sign. It says, "WON."

More steps. Another lady. Another sign: "AT."

If today were your first day in this steaming place, you might think you'd already begun to lose your mind. Or you might wonder what language these people speak, since you could swear these are English words you're seeing along the side of this mud-lined road. Or you could just ignore the signals and keep marching straight ahead.

But this isn't your first day. Your name is Ed Alcorn, and you're not losing your mind. You got here to the Philippines on February 14, 1940—Valentine's Day!—courtesy of the U.S. government. Uncle Sam made you Sergeant Ed Alcorn and designated you a platoon leader in the 60th Coast Artillery, Battery M, of the U.S. Army. In 1941, the invading Japanese military took offense at your presence in this area. It's a complicated story, but the bottom line is that you and hundreds of your colleagues got herded into an involuntary labor pool for a certain distant emperor.

How you got here barely matters anymore. You just know you're marching down a road for another day's backbreaking work, building an airport with a pick and shovel.

As you march, you spot yet another local woman holding a little sign: "MIDWAY."

Shouting "Hooray!" is an unwise gesture during your daily hour-long march to work and back. So you suppress the temptation to celebrate any good news, silently letting this day's roadside serial news-flash—"We won at Midway"—fill your spirit like a bowlful of your favorite strawberry ice cream.

You make this trip six days a week for nearly three years (before getting shipped to a work camp in Japan for the war's final year), watching some of your fellow prisoners drop to the sun-baked ground from lack of food, disease, or total exhaustion. You have no electricity, precious little clean water, and a trench in the ground that would make an outhouse seem luxurious by comparison.

You and the guys are so damn hungry that every conversation is about food. Talk might start out at Betty Grable's legs, but it's sure to end up at Betty Crocker's cookies.

There never are any cookies. And some days there are no signs. Yet you keep marching. Even on the day you see the ladies holding up a series of words flashing General Douglas MacArthur's promise—"I SHALL RETURN"—you never really know what to expect. The war could all end in a moment, or go on for years.

One thing is clear. You know that information from the outside world is helping you and the men plan for survival and think about rescue. You discover that these women by the road—your links to reality—are part of a network. The Spanish lady at the fruit market married your POW work leader—a U.S. Navy chief petty officer—back before the Japanese invasion. The women down the road from the market are her cousins.

As the chief's second in command, you develop a way to send intelligence out of the prison camp through this network of brave people. You split a small block of wood down the middle and hollow out an area large enough to store a note. Every day, you and your men write a note giving information about your captors and other details, placing the paper in the wood block and sealing the package with mud. At the end of the day, you drop the wood block in a dump that is accessible at night to the locals.

The chief had hired a local 16-year-old boy before the war to help his wife with housework. Though young, this boy is part of the network helping POWs. He has the task of picking up the wood block each evening, taking out the note, replacing it with a message written by the chief's wife, then leaving it for you to pick up the next day. Through the chief's wife, you and the men learn about successful naval battles, guerrilla activity in the area, and international talk about retaking the Philippines.

Sometimes the wood block contains money. You and the men use the gift to barter with the Japanese soldiers for supplies, such as pony sugar (so-called because it is usually fed to the ponies that pull taxicab buggies and not especially meant for human consumption). The boy often leaves food along with the block, too.

Months pass. You keep marching. You keep reading. You keep writing. In spite of the dismal odds, you never feel that your number is up. You believe you will survive.

Then one day you open the block and find it empty. No message. You wonder what happened.

This motivated network is a key to your and your fellow POWs' survival. These local friends are intertwined with your fate, and you with theirs. The possibilities of success and the consequences of failure are mutually shared—and profoundly personal.

After all, you could have ignored their signs. Worse, you could have not believed them. You chose, instead, not only to value their messages, but also to respond in kind, sealing the bond.

You won't know, until after the war, that the enemy captured that boy, tortured him, interrogated him, and executed him for helping you and your friends. And you won't know, until after the war, that he never talked, saving you and the other POWs from probable execution.

The cloak of night closes in and sends you and your fellow prisoners to the straw mats that serve as beds, your gut as hungry as the mosquitoes. And all you can know now is that your network—your friends and their unseen sacrifices—is helping you and hundreds more stay alive and dare to hope.

Substance abuse is mostly a solitary affliction, crippling and isolating the individual from society. Recovery is partly a function of social support and encouragement. The result is often a person who is more in touch with friends, associates, and community than ever before, and more capable of contributing social capital for those who follow. Tom Fleming is a business coach and marketing advisor in Florida.

IT'S ABOUT COLLABORATION, NOT COMPETITION

TOM FLEMING

No man is an island.

—JOHN DONNE

Bill Frederick was lucky. He came from a good home where his family supported his physical, mental, and spiritual development. He was somewhat shy and unassuming, but he was also intelligent and a good athlete. Anyone who met Frederick would say that he was a great kid with a great life. But his luck was about to change.

In high school, Frederick was introduced to alcohol. He drank socially, like all the other kids, but with him it was somehow different. It was as if a switch got flipped, and he found himself unable to control the amounts of alcohol he drank. Once he started, he was unable to stop.

As alcohol became more prominent in Frederick's life, he became more headstrong and stubborn. He pictured himself as a John Wayne character from the movies: fierce and independent. His mind clouded by the effects of alcohol, Frederick never thought he needed anyone's help. He had never been more wrong. As often happens with alcohol abuse, things in Frederick's life began to slip away. He lost his job, his girlfriend, and his home. His life was rapidly spiraling out of control.

The more the pieces of Frederick's normal life slipped away, the more he replaced them with alcohol, up to a liter of vodka a day. His health began to fail; he found himself on the verge of alcohol-induced hepatitis. He was forced to share a room in a two-bedroom apartment in South Boston, and since all of his money was going toward alcohol, he couldn't afford a bed. During the heat of summer he slept on two plastic trash bags filled with his winter clothes, and in the cold of winter, two trash bags filled with his summer clothes. Reduced to fleeting moments of sobriety, Frederick hit rock bottom. He finally realized that he had only two choices: recover or die.

Fortunately for Frederick, the only thing that could ultimately save him was the one thing he had left. He still dreamed of a normal life filled with love, companionship, and a family. He was desperate to get his girl-friend, Ann, to come back to him, and it was this goal that gave him the light to find the way through his own darkness.

The road was never easy. Each day was a struggle to avoid the sharp claws of alcohol, but he was determined to take it one day at a time. Tired of his John Wayne act, Frederick began to ask for help and discovered that the community called humanity was more than willing to support and accept him. He found a fellowship program that understood his problems and people who were willing to guide him on the long road to sobriety. He started taking care of himself physically and financially, and slowly he began to regain the life of which he dreamed.

Through his new support team, Frederick was offered a job in the medical supply field making deliveries. He maintained his sobriety and moved into an inside sales position. Frederick was very good at his job, at one point producing an idea that earned the company $250,000. But when he asked for a raise, his boss told him that he "could not psychologically bring himself" to give him the $1 more per hour. This triggered something in Frederick. He determined that no longer would he allow others to put a value on his worth. He decided to start his own company.

With his increasing confidence and determination to bring his life back into focus, Frederick was able to launch Allcare Medical Supply, a company offering hope to thousands of sick and elderly individuals by providing the equipment for a higher quality of life. With no experience owning a business, he found the first months more than just a challenge. One of the guiding principles Frederick began to embrace was that "in business and in life, there is no such thing as competition, only opportunities for collaboration." He started to rely on family, new business associates, and friends in his 12-step alcoholism program for both mentoring and support. Not surprisingly, his newfound faith and trust in people began yielding success.

One day, Frederick received a call from a potential client looking for a particular product. The prospect explained that a national distributor had discontinued it and he was looking for an alternate supplier. Frederick had access to the product and was happy to support his new client. But he recognized an opportunity and decided to take it one step further. He called the branch manager of the national distributor, his "competitor," and suggested that he help the customers who were no longer able to purchase the discontinued product line. The branch manager saw this as a great chance to establish goodwill among his customer base and gave Frederick the discontinued line's client list.

This one collaborative deal increased Allcare's sales 76 percent on a monthly basis over the course of four months. This same large distributor also referred Frederick to one of its shipping companies, cutting Frederick's shipping costs by 35 percent while saving him and his assistant countless hours of driving and delivery time. By having faith in people and living his life in community and collaboration rather than in isolation and competition, Frederick increased his sales 1,000 percent in two years. According to Frederick, "Success is all about losing the John Wayne attitude."

He has embraced collaboration not just as a business charter but also as a life philosophy. He has been married to Ann for ten years now, and they have two young boys. He has achieved his dream. Frederick cherishes his family, feels blessed by what has become a tremendously successful company, and is humbled by all those he calls friends.

Frederick's collaborative philosophy continues to reap benefits. A short time ago, that same national distributor called to tell him the company was getting out of four more lines of business and asked him to pick up its customers for those lines. His company and life continue to sky-rocket. Bill Frederick is lucky once again.

———•·•———

It's surprising how quickly a small investment of energy and effort can increase your social capital, even when the original modest goal is not achieved. As any investor will tell you, you have to stick to your investment plan for a while before you begin to see results—and then the payoff may grow beyond your most ambitious expectations. Linda Macedonio stuck with her new business until her reputation and business savvy led to the purchase of a large marketing franchise in the Northeast. Rachelle Dionne-Coury, a free-lance writer with a personal interest in heart health, helped enthusiastically with this project.

———•·•———

GREAT THINGS HAVE HUMBLE BEGINNINGS

LINDA MACEDONIO AND RACHELLE DIONNE-COURY

Sometimes great things start from humble beginnings. Jason Feid is a physical education teacher at North Attleboro Middle School in North Attleboro, Massachusetts. In 1999, an opportunity to acquire funding for gym equipment for the new middle school crossed his desk. Hoops for Heart was a basketball fundraising program sponsored by the American Heart Association. For each dollar raised, the program gave participating schools the chance to earn gift certificates for physical education equipment. To Feid, this was a win-win situation. The kids would benefit from new equipment and from participating in a community event that promoted exercise and heart health. At the same time, the money raised for the AHA through the Hoops for Heart program would be used to fund research and educational programs on heart disease and stroke, which are leading causes of mortality and morbidity.

Feid enlisted fellow teacher John Dempsey to help him organize the event. In their first year, with 30 kids participating, they raised $630. Unfortunately, this was not enough to qualify for gym equipment. Discouraged by his results, Feid felt he had let down both his students and the American Heart Association.

The following year, Feid was invited to sponsor and organize the event once more. He couldn't imagine why they would want him to do it again, but deep down he knew he could do a better job, so with the encouragement of the AHA he agreed. He created a new plan and managed to recruit 160 kids to participate. This time they were able to raise $2,732—a vast improvement! By the third year, Feid's and Dempsey's dedication really began to pay off. They attracted 353 student volunteers, generating a $16,811 donation to the American Heart Association.

The year 2002 became the proving ground. With the knowledge and experience they had gained during three years with Hoops for Heart, the two teachers and the enthusiastic staff of North Attleboro Middle School rallied and pulled out all the stops. With the help of 522 students, their parents, and the community, they made their event the number-one Hoops for Heart fundraiser in the country by raising an amazing $30,722.

By now, the group was generating some real momentum. They established a 2003 goal of $40,000. Perhaps they should have set their goal higher. On April 16, 2003, a record 793 students, more than three-quarters of the student body, worked with Feid and the faculty to raise a total of $58,709.24.

With such dramatic results, there had to be some secret to their success. So what were the key ingredients to this community's successful program? According to Feid, it's all about the relationships. "As the event has grown each year, so have the relationships between staff members, between staff and students, and between students themselves," he says.

"The kids have so much fun that they tell others, and then those kids sign up. Faculty and students get to see each other in an atmosphere that is fun, and they see each other in a different light. Getting to know each other better builds relationships. Good relationships build loyalty." And loyalty raises money. When asked about his plans for 2004, Feid replied, "The plan is to have a physical activity fair and involve area businesses. Our fundraising goal is $100,000."

It would be easy to assume that Feid measures the success of his program by the amount of money raised for the American Heart Association, but that couldn't be farther from the truth. He feels that the money is more like the icing on the cake. The real success comes in the time he spends with the students, the bonds that are forged between the school and the community, and the level of awareness that is raised about two very significant and deadly diseases: heart disease and stroke.

Over the course of his fundraising efforts and with each year's gain, Feid became an example and a resource for others. He was called upon by other school districts to share his knowledge of the Hoops for Heart program so they might follow in his footsteps and achieve similar success. Feid receives calls from all over the country seeking his assistance or asking him to speak to various groups and organizations. Recently, the American Heart Association asked him to be the coordinator for the New England region Hoops for Heart program. "I never thought it would get to this point," he says. He also never expected that he and co-coordinator John Dempsey would be invited to the White House for the National Health Fair. Feid and Dempsey brought T-shirts signed by the kids at North Attleboro Middle School to present to President and Mrs. Bush. Mrs. Bush accepted them personally.

In 2003, several regional directors of the AHA from New England made the trip to North Attleboro Middle School to observe the event firsthand. Obviously, the system for success Feid has created has generated a lot of interest. He says his level of success could be duplicated in any school setting using the system he's developed.

National prominence has changed Feid's perception of what is attainable, but it hasn't changed his perception of himself. As far as he's concerned, he's just doing his job as an educator: teaching and providing students with a positive role model. Working with children is Feid's passion, and teaching is something he had planned to do ever since his own high school experience. His goal in life was simply to do what he loved, have fun doing it, and never settle for less.

This creed is also his message to his students. Aching from a humble desire to improve the quality of his students' education, Jason Feid has succeeded in doing so much more. His job as an educator has now expanded beyond the confines of his classroom. He educates people across the country for the American Heart Association and helps them to help others. He's taught his students that they have the ability to contribute to their community and can affect the lives of others in a positive way regardless of their age. He's motivated a school and brought a community together with his enthusiasm and determination.

Feid is a leader and an achiever. When asked what being a "master of success" means to him, he responds, "It's mastering the success of whatever you are involved in. That could include parenting, volunteering, or your career. I feel that if I want to do something, if I put my mind to it, I will accomplish it!" A valuable lesson from a remarkable teacher.

Loyalty is a two-way street, with trust flowing in both directions—something many companies forget at their own risk. This form of social capital can be your most durable and important asset. When others undermine you by making sudden withdrawals from their accounts, you can turn for help to those whose trust you have earned by your steady investment of loyalty. Terry Misfeldt's company, Simply Success Ltd. in Wisconsin, specializes in public relations and marketing for other business entrepreneurs.

———•·•———

FIRED UP

TERRY MISFELDT

Shake-up-minded companies, beware: How you treat your people will come back to you in spades.

When Lincoln National Insurance Company fired Ron Weyers and Wally Hilliard, it did the deed in a way that soon drove its best talent into the waiting arms of its competition.

Who did the competition turn out to be? A new company formed by the jilted Weyers and Hilliard.

The pair started their corporate adventure in the basement of Weyer's home. Their original firm, Employers Health Insurance of Green Bay, proved so successful that they sold it in 1982 to Fireman's Fund. The sale price: a cool $10 million. Plus Weyers and Hilliard stayed on to run the new company.

Not bad for two guys who started in a basement. Or so they thought, until Fireman's Fund Employers Health Insurance Company was sold five years later for $215 million. "We didn't know much about selling a company," Weyers jokes.

The buyer: Lincoln National Insurance Company. Again, the duo remained in their management posts. There were nine months left on their noncompete agreement when Lincoln National took over, and the new parent waived the noncompete clause.

A meeting was scheduled at Lincoln National's Fort Wayne, Indiana, headquarters so Weyers and Hilliard could update the new parent on its acquisition. The two were flown to Fort Wayne—at which time things got interesting.

According to Weyers, he and Hilliard were fired, then left stranded while Lincoln National's president flew back to Green Bay to tell the employees he'd "accepted resignations" from Weyers and Hilliard—while the two shocked execs were forced to drive back to Wisconsin.

176

Wham bam. They were out.

"Getting fired was the best thing that ever happened to us," says Weyers, a farm boy who joined the army at 18, then chose sales as his post-service career, moving from vacuum cleaners to life insurance and then to health insurance. "I thought about retirement, but Wally wanted to try again, and I didn't want to go out as having been fired into retirement."

They were like kids again. They certainly weren't ready to retire—at age 48 for Weyers and 46 for Hilliard—and they now had something to prove.

The partners picked themselves up, dusted themselves off, and launched their new venture: a health insurance firm named American Medical Security.

The way they were fired did not sit well with their loyal former employees—much less with their former customers. Within months, roughly 170 of their original 200 employees migrated to American Medical Security, including 10 of 13 regional sales managers.

"We picked out the field representatives we really wanted," Weyers says. "We gave the employees the same benefits they had before and let them keep seniority, and we even set up a good profit-sharing program for them. The employees who came with us were a godsend."

American Medical Security hit the ground running. The sales force was in place. The systems were identical but improved.

Their firing had one important benefit, Weyers believes. It helped American Medical Security get in touch with its agents and clients to determine what they really wanted. "It got us back in touch with the grass roots," Weyers says.

"You have to know what your customer wants," he insists, "whether that customer is the independent insurance agent who wants to talk to *you*, even if you're the president of the company, or the customer who has a question about his claim." The Weyers approach had always been to manage by walking around, long before MBWA became popular. He had processed claims, sold policies, and done all the jobs he was asking others to do, so he learned just to listen to what the customers said and what the employees needed.

"It was also important to have a partner like Wally," Weyers adds. "Executives need someone they can go nose-to-nose with, even senior management, because you can become so engrossed in your idea that you don't look at the backside of it, and it's very important to have people around you to do that.

"And you have to be good to your people, because it costs a lot to find new customers if you lose them."

The same holds true for employees, which is why American Medical Security offers its employees a day-care facility, an in-office health spa, and a training staff that offers workshops on listening skills, time management, and other beneficial skills in addition to those on understanding health insurance products.

All of Weyers and Hilliard's people-valuing steps helped the firm grow to more than 2,000 employees by 1994, when *Inc.* magazine dubbed it the 21st-fastest-growing company in the United States.

Weyers believes that a true entrepreneur is one who sees a need as an opportunity and then meets that need. From processing their own claims in Weyers's basement to landing on their feet and building a new insurance industry powerhouse, he and Hilliard achieved success by listening to people—and treating them as they wished to be treated themselves. It's a lesson any company, especially one that's tempted to buy one-way plane tickets for a couple of execs, would be wise to heed.

————•◦•————

In chaos theory, a small input can produce an enormous and unforeseeable output: the downdraft off a butterfly's wing steers a typhoon to Taiwan. But can you be ready to harvest good results from chance winds if you are willing to step outside your comfort zone, try something new, and watch for the unexpected opportunity? Mary Jo Sherwood, a successful marketing consultant of 25 years, believes in in maximizing small chance encounters. Not content with opportunities arising from 24 years of marriage and raising three children, she also serves on several boards of directors throughout the midwestern United States—ready to turn small contacts into great advantages.

———•·•———

SUCCESS HAPPENS BECAUSE...

MARY JO SHERWOOD

One of my children's favorite bedtime storybooks is *Because a Little Bug Went Ka-choo!* by Rosetta Stone. The refrain is classic, the rhythm is infectious, the pictures are funny, and the message is one that bears repeating. Doors open, opportunities develop, and the world changes *because* of something as seemingly insignificant as the little bug's sneeze in the story. The book sums up the result of the bug going "ka-choo" with these thoughts: "And that started something they'll never forget. And as far as I know it is going on yet."

Today, as a successful business owner with four years of organized networking experience, I know this to be true. Doors have opened, opportunities have arisen, and my world has changed, just *because.*

Early in my career, when I worked for a Fortune 500 corporation, an event occurred that changed my life. My boss wanted me to network with some very important clients on the golf course. I was not a golfer. Not only that, I wasn't the least bit interested in golf. But my boss was persuasive, especially when he mentioned that the opportunity would benefit my career. He further encouraged me by saying, "We can't have Friday staff meetings on the golf course because you don't play golf."

He suggested that I contact a newly formed golf organization dedicated to serving professional women. He said they were hosting a clinic in a couple of weeks, and he was sure they could help me. I said I would give it a try, which made my boss very happy. This guy, I decided, was committed to having Friday meetings on the golf course.

The clinic was run by the Executive Women's Golf Association (EWG), which was planning to start a new chapter in our area. Along with 22 other professional women, I attended the first planning meeting—and soon found myself on the group's new board of directors. I didn't know anything about golf, but I volunteered to run events because I was interested in what the organization had to offer.

Two months later, the board president resigned, and before I knew what was happening, I was made president of the Executive Women's Golf Association of Minnesota. I had yet to play my first round of golf—but through my contacts in my company, we were able to get media coverage for our new golf organization, not only locally, but nationally on ESPN. As a result, we grew from 22 members to more than 300 in our first year!

Over the next several years, I did learn to play golf. I also determined that I wanted to start my own business. Part of my business plan was to use business networking as a central component of my marketing efforts. One afternoon, as I played golf with a woman from EWG, I mentioned that I needed a way to increase my business contacts. This woman, who was a member of a business networking organization, invited me to their weekly meeting as her guest. Not only did I join the group, Business Network International—where my business began to flourish—I also became president of our BNI chapter and went on to become a director for BNI Minnesota.

All of this happened *because* someone "strongly suggested" that I move out of my comfort zone and learn to play golf! The success lesson I learned is that a past action or decision will often open future doors at the most unexpected times—but you must be prepared to enter unknown territory.

You, too, can find success—if you are willing to do things *just because!*

———•—•———

We are prone to believe that success comes to ordinary people who just happened to be in the right place at the right time. As the great French writer, artist, and filmmaker Jean Cocteau said, "We must believe in luck. For how else can we explain the success of those we don't like?" But let us heed Ralph Waldo Emerson: "Good luck is another name for tenacity of purpose." Susan DeLoren is the BNI franchise owner for Oklahoma and for San Antonio, Texas, the launching pad of one of the world's most successful business operators.

COLLEEN BARRETT: SERVICE TO OTHERS

SUSAN DELOREN

Colleen Barrett's office is full of playthings. Stuffed animals are piled on the wall of shelves behind her massive desk. Toys and games are strewn on the big table in the corner and the coffee table in front of the sofa. And, of course, there are the airplanes: models of the Southwest Airlines jets, painted in riotous colors, hanging by thin wires from the ceiling, swaying slowly as the air conditioning silently cycles on and off. Hearts of every description, from paper to cut-glass to hand-painted porcelain ones brought from Germany, are everywhere. After all, this is the office of Colleen Barrett, the president and chief operating officer of Southwest Airlines—the LUV airline.

The woman behind the desk has a permanent smile on her face. Her round, wire-rimmed glasses and waist-length gray hair, pulled back in a ponytail, give Barrett—or Colleen, as everyone at the airline calls her—an air of informality and welcoming eagerness to pull you into the corporate culture at Southwest: work hard, have fun, and join in the journey to self-discovery. She's the den mother and head cheerleader of the company.

Colleen Barrett's own journey to self-discovery has been a 35-year trek from the small Vermont town of Bellows Falls to the executive offices of the most consistently profitable and successful airline in the United States. Told by her mother while still a child that it was inappropriate and unbecoming to judge another person without having lived in his or her circumstances, Barrett is understanding and accepting and believes people deserve the opportunity to grow beyond their circumstances and realize their own potential for success. She has shaped the culture at Southwest to provide this opportunity to its employees, and the result has been a fiercely loyal work force steeped in the philosophy that one gains what one wants only by giving to others.

Barrett has always known that in order to be successful, a person must prepare to take advantage of opportunities when they arise. She has lived her life believing that if anyone works to better himself, favorable circumstances for success will present themselves. During the summer between her junior and senior years in high school, she realized that there would be no money for her to attend college. So she spent that last year taking a double load of business courses—typing, shorthand, accounting, and related classes—to prepare herself to make her own living.

Once prepared, she was able to walk through the door of opportunity when it opened in 1965. Married shortly after her high school graduation, Barrett moved with her new husband to San Antonio, Texas, where he began basic training at Lackland Air Force Base while she hit the streets looking for a job. She was down to her last dime and desperate when she walked into a downtown law firm, determined to get a secretarial job even if she had to get down on her knees and beg for it. They didn't need a secretary, but she wouldn't leave the office, persisting until she was finally given a job working for one of the firm's attorneys, Herb Kelleher.

Kelleher didn't have a secretary and didn't think he needed one. But when Barrett saw the mounds of paperwork stacked on every flat surface in his office—on the floor, falling off shelves, hanging out of cabinets—she knew better. She read every piece of paper, organized it all into a coherent system, and filed it away. It took weeks, during which Kelleher was out of the office on vacation. When he returned, he realized Colleen Barrett possessed qualities that perfectly complemented his freewheeling, driven style: a sense of structure, attention to minute detail, and an enormous need for order.

The two also realized they shared a basic philosophy about work, believing that success came from a sense of idealism and service to others, and the best way of getting what you wanted in life was to help other people get what they wanted. Recognizing the dignity of individuals and treating people with fairness and respect would guarantee success for all, they reasoned. And when Kelleher and one of his law partners, in 1966, sketched out the idea for a Texas airline to serve the state's three major cities, yet another door of opportunity opened for her.

During the next few years, as Kelleher appeared in court to face the challenges brought by other air carriers to kill the upstart airline, Barrett was there with boxes of perfectly organized files, briefs, and planning documentation. Kelleher trusted her unconditionally, and because they shared the same philosophy—including a demanding work ethic that included having enormous fun—she became an invaluable asset to the organization that was taking shape. She became a charter member of the Southwest family.

The word *family* at Southwest is taken quite seriously and embraced as a way of doing business. From the beginning, Barrett has ardently promoted the concept of the Southwest family. No one at the airline has done more to celebrate the achievements of everyone who works there. She believes her highest calling is to demonstrate the company's commitment to its employees—its family members.

Colleen Barrett likes to say that the business of Southwest Airlines is built on the following priorities, in order of importance: the company's employees, its customers, then its shareholders. The priorities are working. The airline was started in 1971, and after the first two tumultuous years of buying planes and hiring employees, Southwest has been profitable for 30 consecutive years and has the lowest employee turnover rate in the industry. The awards, accolades, and recognition ceremonies for employees come streaming out of Barrett's office at an astonishing rate, always carried out in a pervasive atmosphere of festivity. "I can't count the number of ceremonies and celebrations we've held over the years," she says. "Families celebrate the accomplishments of their members—they have parties and recognize the successes of their members. We encourage our Southwest family members to set goals, and when those goals are realized, we party!"

Barrett believes that listening to the needs and wants of employees and giving them the knowledge of how company departments work, how the company makes its money, and how it meets its obligations is absolutely necessary for those employees to have a stake in the company's success. The freedom to develop solutions to problems in the workplace is the most important motivational tool at her disposal. "Motivation comes from showing people you believe in them," she often remarks.

Often going against accepted business hierarchy to empower the airline's workers, Barrett has seen her trust rewarded over and over as workers devise more productive and successful ways of getting the job done than any executive committee could. "Collaboration is essential," she says. "The people on the front lines are the ones who face the challenges every day. They are in the best position to work together to come up with solutions."

By developing employee committees charged with solving company problems (employees, often to their disappointment, are limited to a two-year appointment to a committee); by building teams to plan festivities ranging from departmental awards ceremonies to company-wide extravaganzas; and by creating a mentoring plan to help employees attain both personal and professional goals, Colleen Barrett has become the beloved matriarch of an enormously successful organization.

"It all stems from a desire to help others," she insists. "Respecting people, believing in their abilities, and giving them the freedom to reach beyond themselves is the key. Rarely, very rarely, does an employee let us down. When they realize that the success of the company is tied to their own personal success, that we're all in this together, everybody wins.

"The Southwest story," she concludes, "is the story of our employees—their commitment to delivering the most thoughtful customer service, to helping each other, and to making the company the best at what we do."

Most of all, Colleen Barrett believes in the power of love—or LUV, as it's spelled at Southwest. Southwest Airlines is the house that love built, and all those hearts in the president's office are just another manifestation of this woman's idealism.

———•·•———

In The Driving Force, *from which the following is excerpted, Peter Schutz tells us a leadership secret he learned early in his career: the success of a company rides not so much on its products, services, factories, and offices as on its human resources. Social capital is not a stack of bills in a bank; it is the knowledge, wisdom, and goodwill in people's minds. Peter Schutz is a former CEO of Porsche and now heads his own company, Harris & Schutz Inc. He speaks on management and marketing to business audiences worldwide.*

———•·•———

THE CULTURE OF EXCELLENCE

PETER W. SCHUTZ

A business culture built on excellence will most frequently outperform a culture in which success is the singular objective. It is easy to conclude that excellence and success are the same, but they are not.

Success in business is often measured by material accomplishments, money, and assets. The criteria change constantly and are often compared to the perceived success of others. People focused on success can be burdened by an obsession with it, frequently leading to a focus on short-term

185

results. For such people, the daily stock price and the performance of the business in the most recent quarter become overriding objectives.

Managers focused on success, particularly short-term success, will frequently fail to mobilize the real driving force, the committed passion of people that can result in extraordinary performance. For such impatient and compulsive managers, the future is short term.

Success must come quickly and may be fleeting and fickle.

Managers focused on success want to be known as winners above all. At times, they look for a single transaction to catapult them into fame. The pressure for short-term results, particularly in the eyes of others, is exhausting and can cost such a person his health, to say nothing of happiness or fulfillment.

Excellence is lasting and dependable.

Excellence is largely under the control of the manager. Managers striving for excellence and high quality tend to be patient because their focus is on the longer term. They lead with a quiet confidence because they know they will win in the longer term. This is due in part to the fact that their opinion of themselves matters more than the opinion others have of them. This can, at times, be perceived as an inner arrogance that may be difficult for others to understand.

Success does not obsess such managers in the short term. The daily bottom-line results do not cause them to rejoice, panic, or scream. They will frequently shrug off a short-term setback and focus on the lessons to be learned instead. They know that a focus on excellence and quality will more likely activate the driving force of the business and bring positive results in the longer term.

Managers focused on success are frequently so competitive that they feel threatened by the success of others, even members of their own business teams. They may actually resent real excellence.

In contrast, a manager committed to excellence and quality is invigorated by these qualities in others. Being surpassed is not feared but nurtured in the effort to excel.

An obsession for success can burn up the manager who seeks it.
Excellence will build the manager who strives for it.

Catastrophe in the business news is often the result of a business success story gone wrong. The difference between excellence and success is not always easy to grasp. A business that has focused on success to the exclusion of excellence and ethics can fall prey to disaster.

At Porsche, we were striving for a culture of excellence above all. When I admonished the racing group that we would never enter a race we didn't intend to win, I was calling on them to embrace a quest for excellence. If I had said, "We will never *lose* a race," it would have been a call to success rather than excellence. We might have won the first race, but it could have been a shortsighted pursuit of success. Excellence is the appropriate focus of leaders who wish to create and sustain driving force.

A Champion Never Quits

At the 1984 Le Mans race, Jacky Ickx spun the number-one Porsche 956 at the end of the Mulsanne-straight on the very first lap. Al Holbert, driving the number-three Porsche 956, passed Ickx to take the race lead. Holbert and Hurley Haywood led the race from that point on, but not without major challenges. In the middle of the night, Holbert was at full speed on the Mulsanne-straight when the right door of his 956 came open. Beyond creating incredible noise, the partly open door deflected cooling air away from the right-side radiator. The engine overheated; the door had to be closed.

The car came into the pits, and the badly damaged door was bolted shut and taped over. Holbert returned to the track and was immediately ordered back into the pit area by the race marshals. Doors on cars had to be mounted so they could be opened in case of an emergency; it was not acceptable to bolt the door shut.

The door was remounted with an emergency hinge. Shortly thereafter, the door simply disappeared at full speed on the Mulsanne-straight. It flew off at more than 200 miles per hour into the bordering woods. To the best of my knowledge, that door was never found.

A new door was installed. It simply would not stay shut. It rode slightly open, about an inch or so. This was enough to interfere with the engine cooling on the right side of the engine. (Each side of the flat-six engine had its own radiator.)

Holbert managed to hold Ickx off and maintain the lead in the race. Inevitably, he lost ground to Ickx. Holbert's 956 was clearly losing power. Lap after lap, Ickx closed in on Holbert. With two laps to go, Ickx had Holbert in sight and was gaining steadily. Holbert battled back with his badly overheating and clearly failing engine.

Coming through two chicanes before the straight stretch to the finish line, Holbert's tired engine gave up and seized.

Holbert disengaged the clutch quickly to conserve as much speed as possible, put the transmission in low gear, and re-engaged the clutch. This broke the engine loose and gave him at least a little power to work with. With thick black smoke pouring out the right exhaust stack, he crossed the finish line just before Ickx caught up and flashed by.

Holbert had won the race by a few yards as a result of his last-minute efforts to keep the car moving.

This never-give-up performance typified the Porsche culture.

Keeping the Faith through Highs and Lows

Racing is dangerous, and we had our incredibly bitter moments.

One of the brightest young stars among race drivers in the 1980s was Stefan Bellof. There was little question that he was headed for stardom in Formula I racing, the top of the race driving profession. Bellof was fast, as fast as any of our drivers.

Bellof often drove for the Porsche factory team. In Spa, Belgium, he drove a privately owned Porsche 956. Ickx drove one of the factory team Porsche 956s. Ickx, the veteran champion, and Bellof, the up-and-coming young tiger, were incredibly competitive. The Spa racetrack is one of our favorites. It is set in the beautiful hilly forests of northern Belgium, and since Ickx is Belgian, it was his track. This raised competitive fever to a high pitch.

At the end of a downhill straight run past the pits is a rather difficult curve followed by a climb up a steep hill. The curve is the famous Aux Rouge curve. The Aux Rouge *cannot* be driven side by side. Ickx and Bellof roared past the pits toward Aux Rouge alongside each other. Someone would have to yield. Bellof attempted to intimidate Ickx, but Ickx would not be intimidated. They entered Aux Rouge side by side.

Both lost control of their cars. Ickx spun up the hill past the curve. Bellof hit a concrete barrier at full speed. There was little left of his Porsche 956. Our Stefan had no chance of surviving and was killed in that incredible impact.

To the best of my knowledge, Ickx never raced again after that accident; we lost both Bellof and Ickx that day in Belgium.

Two race driver fatalities had a major impact on the Porsche racing program. Rolf Stommelin lost his life in a horrendous crash in Minnesota in 1983. The Porsche 953 he was driving was hit by another car and lost the rear wing (spoiler). Losing control of the car at more than 200 miles per hour, Stommelin struck a concrete barrier with incredible force.

The "cage" surrounding him was not penetrated. There was not a single scratch on him, and all of the restraining belts were in place and intact. Every safety device had functioned perfectly, but Stommelin was dead!

The deceleration of the crash was so great that his heart was thrown against the inside of his rib cage, severing the aorta and killing him instantly.

The following spring, Stefan Bellof died in Belgium. Once again, a driver struck a concrete barrier at more than 200 miles per hour and died instantly.

Helmut Bott, Porsche director of technology, decided: "That's enough!" He initiated a study of race-car deceleration upon impact with an unyielding barrier.

About seven Porsche race cars were driven into a concrete barrier with the following energy-absorbing materials placed in front of the concrete:
- tire stacks consisting of five tires banded into a stack
- tire stacks consisting of five tires filled with bags of sand
- tire stacks consisting of five tires filled with plastic foam

The amount of energy that could be absorbed was significant. The foam-filled tires worked so well that we at Porsche decided *we would no longer expose our drivers to the hazards of a track in which concrete retaining barriers were not protected by energy-absorbing devices.*

The NASCAR incident that cost Dale Earnhardt his life also involved an unprotected concrete barrier.

Restraining the driver, providing energy-absorbing crash zones in the body of the car, and other means of keeping the driver in the car during a crash are important; but when the deceleration exceeds a certain value, the human body comes apart internally. Extensive (and more sophisticated) tests at the University of Nebraska have confirmed much of what was learned at Porsche almost 20 years before. Modern electronic instrumentation resulted in credible data about performance of available energy-absorbing materials and their effective reduction of deceleration forces.

At the running of the 2002 Indianapolis 500, energy-absorbing material was installed at critical points of the track retaining walls. An increasing number of tracks are equipped with sand traps and other measures to increase the survivability of racing accidents.

I am confident that in the face of increased speeds, automobile racing is safer today due in part to the safety measures Porsche initiated in the mid-1980s. The loss of two of our drivers was the low-water mark, at least for me. There were plenty of highs, too. A high-water mark of Porsche sports-car racing in the 1980s was the Le Mans 1983 finish. In 1983, our advertising poster said it best:

LE MANS 1983: NOBODY'S PERFECT
1st	Porsche
2nd	Porsche
3rd	Porsche
4th	Porsche
5th	Porsche
6th	Porsche
7th	Porsche
8th	Porsche
9th	BMW–Sauber
10th	Porsche

From *The Driving Force: Extraordinary Results with Ordinary People* by Peter W. Schutz, copyright ©2003 Peter Schutz, published by Entrepreneur Press. Used by permission of Peter Schutz.

It's a good idea to listen to high achievers who have been recognized and rewarded for their contributions. These big names are just like the rest of us, except that many more people recognize their deeds. A few use past accomplishments to tackle the new challenge of helping others succeed. Bill Byrd teaches networking to business owners and is especially interested in finding outstanding examples of networking mastery.

FROM SUCCESS TO SIGNIFICANCE

BILL BYRD

Nido Qubein came to America at the age of 17. He had $50 in his pocket, had no connections, and knew no English.

Today he is a multimillionaire, CEO of an international consulting firm, chairman of Great Harvest Bread Company (175 stores in 34 states), a director of 15 organizations including a Fortune 500 financial institution with $75 billion in assets, and recipient of many prestigious awards, including the Ellis Island Medal of Honor.

The author of numerous books, Qubein—winner of the Toastmasters International Golden Gavel Award and an inductee into the Speakers Hall of Fame—is in high demand for his speaking and consulting services. His resume and accomplishments extend beyond the space available in this chapter. Nonetheless, you get the point. Sounds like a pretty successful guy.

Ask Qubein directly about his success, however, and the picture is not so clear-cut. "I believe you're a successful person when you have something worthwhile to do, when you have someone to love, and when you have somewhere important to be," he says.

He doesn't believe so much in success as he does in significance. When a person becomes significant in another person's life, he suggests, then success follows. He believes that although there are many successful people in the world—and that success is certainly admirable—being significant in other people's lives is even more important.

Qubein offers these simple rules for achieving success through significance. If they don't sound like the kind of rules you'd readily think of, remember: Qubein is anything but typical.

Rule #1: Make a Transformational Impact on Others

"Facts tell; emotions sell," he explains. "You can't simply be a dispenser of information in today's world, you have to be transactional. To truly make a connection with people, you must create an environment in which they can relate to you on a deeper level."

Rule #2: Position Your Value

"In the marketplace of life," says Qubein, "the seller can set the price, but the buyer always determines the value." Successful people interpret their value for others through positioning. You position yourself in numerous ways, but the most important method is by building trust. When your customers trust you, they tell others how important you are in their lives.

Rule #3: Understand Behavioral Economics

"If we don't tie what we do to economics, we have no way to quantify it," Qubein observes. He notes that 60 percent of American households are one paycheck away from bankruptcy, and 80 percent have a net worth of under $75,000. Immigrants are four times more likely than born Americans to be millionaires. Why? Because immigrants don't come to America thinking that this *might* be the place to make it—they already believe it is. Beliefs lead to behavior, and behavior leads to results.

Rule #4: Achieve Balanced Living

People can be so focused on "success" that they miss the whole point of life. Qubein cautions against charging headlong toward success. Having a balanced life that includes work, family, and friends will help you reach your goals much more quickly. He says there are lots of successful people in the world—but many of them are the least happy people he knows. Creating balance between work and life comes about through knowing when to work on each area.

Balanced living also means giving back. "We shouldn't think of it as 'giving back,'" he elaborates. "We should just give. Give unconditionally." He quotes William Barclay, Scottish theologian, to make his point: "Always give without remembering; always receive without forgetting."

Qubein is a director of Business Network International (BNI) and feels the motto of "givers gain" sums up his philosophy succinctly. He feels that the help of countless individuals over the years has enabled him to achieve his own success. He has, in turn, helped many others—especially young people—start solidly down successful, significant paths. His Qubein Foundation provides scholarships to 45 deserving young people each year and has, to date, granted more than 500 scholarships totaling more than $2 million.

Qubein understands that pursuing a life of success, a life of significance, requires change—and that change does not come easily to most people. He says the only person in the world who readily accepts change is a baby in wet diapers. The rest of us resist until the pain of remaining the same exceeds the pain of changing.

To counter this resistance, Qubein urges students of success to invest in themselves and work hard at being valuable to those around them. People wouldn't think anything about spending money on a night on the town with friends, notes Qubein, but the same people look down on spending that money for personal development.

Such misplaced priorities can be banished by making a commitment to excellence. Quoting Aristotle, Qubein observes, "Excellence is not an act; it's a habit."

From his humble beginnings as a teenager new to America's shores, Nido Qubein learned—and lived—his rules for success. He proves in his own life that through striving every day for excellence and significance, great things happen.

—•—

An aura of accomplishment and recognition can serve you well in networking your success to others. Recognition itself is a transferable asset; those who look to accomplished people for leadership gain motivation from personal attention. Thus are the effects of success multiplied. Karla Kay Lenkiewicz started her successful career as an excited and enthusiastic student and is now teaching others.

MARY KAY: EMPOWERING OTHERS

KARLA KAY LENKIEWICZ

For what seemed like the hundredth time that week, I laced up my sneakers and headed out the door toward the mailbox. I felt like a small child waiting impatiently for Santa to bring gifts worth a year of good behavior. I took my time opening the box for fear of finding nothing once again, thinking: Please be there, please be there, please be there! To my astonishment and boundless relief, there it was: one small white package. Struggling with the wrapping, I tried to suppress my anticipation. Why do they make these things so hard to open? I managed to tear the last of the wrapping off the package and took a deep breath. This was what I'd been waiting for. I opened the card and started to read:

Congratulations on your accomplishment as a Star Consultant! By achieving your dreams, you've earned this 40th anniversary pin—a beautiful symbol of women helping women. Wear it close to your heart as a reminder that you're passing on the Mary Kay spirit by inspiring beauty and enriching lives!

How long I sat holding that little message in my hand without even looking at the gift itself, I'll never know. My mind sped back to one of my favorite memories, and I relived every single moment of it.

• • •

The year was 1981, and I had set my sights on becoming a sales director for Mary Kay Cosmetics. In those days, before someone could even begin the qualification process for that position, she had to attend a week-long training session in Dallas. It was something I'd looked forward to for a long time. I knew that Mary Kay would be teaching in person and I'd get a once-in-a-lifetime chance to learn from this master of cosmetic success. I was excited beyond words. The butterflies didn't show up, however, until my friend and mentor, Norma McKinney, told me that not only would I be trained by Mary Kay, I would be invited to her home and have the opportunity to speak with her personally. You mean, like one-to-one quality time?" I asked.

"Sure," she answered, "and you'll eat cookies she baked and have your picture taken with her as well."

I about died right then and there. What in the world would I say to this legend, this icon of womanhood? I couldn't eat. I couldn't sleep. I couldn't think of anything else. Finally, I made one of the best decisions of my life. I decided that I would pretend to be a reporter during our time together and go to that interview prepared. I knew I would be awestruck, so I left nothing to chance. Instead of just thinking of questions to ask and memorizing them, I wrote them down. The butterflies didn't disappear, but preparing myself did get them all "flying in formation," as Mary Kay used to say.

Just as I'd planned, I sat in the front row during the class that Mary Kay taught. I didn't just sit in the front row; I sat on the edge of my seat. Consulting my notes for my first question, I remembered that someone had once told me that our successes (or lack of them) are always in direct proportion to the people skills we possess. Knowing that Mary Kay seemed to be a people magnet, I wanted to know if she had one tip to give me to hone my people skills.

"Absolutely," she replied, cupping both of her hands over mine and piercing my right eye with both of hers (she used to tell us that it's a form of mild hypnotism). "Just pretend that every person you meet has a sign hanging around their neck that says, 'Make Me Feel Important.' More often than not, people just need someone who'll listen. To give someone your undivided attention without letting your mind wander or looking over his or her shoulder to see who else is there is definitely an art worth practicing. It's not a secret, really, but I'm just amazed at how few people understand how important this is."

I asked her whether she thought that was the reason she was so highly respected, not just within our company but throughout the business world. She smiled, then answered in a tone that was completely humble, "Well, I think it may be because I've never asked someone to do something I haven't already done myself, or wouldn't be willing to do. I've heard it said that there are only three ways to lead: by example, by example, and by example. That's a great philosophy."

I nodded in agreement. Not because I was living that way, but because she was nodding. I couldn't help myself. I was captivated by her sincerity and her charm.

Thoughtfully, she went on, "People follow best, Karla, when they are shown the way. Can I count on you to lead your own people like that?"

"Yes, Mary Kay, of course you can!" I promised without giving it a second thought. Then I added, softly and again without thinking, "But . . ." To this day, I'm surprised she even heard it.

"But what?" she asked, and I kid you not, her eyebrows shot up about an inch. I was beginning to understand why people referred to her as a grand combination of velvet and steel.

The truth was, I was scared. Before I could even censor myself, I told her how terrified I was, and asked if she had any advice for someone like me. Where in the world had that come from? Suddenly my prepared questions were left behind. Words were jumping out of my mouth as if they had a life of their own, perspiration was popping out on my forehead, and my heart was beating double-time.

I felt her hands tighten around mine as she explained that "fear can only settle in when our focus is inward." She told me to take my mind off myself and strive to help others: "Make that your purpose, and when you've helped enough other people reach their goals, you'll find that you've reached your own. I know you can do it."

I thought she'd teach me about cosmetics that day. Instead she reached out, touched my life, and changed it forever. She taught me the difference between people and things. She taught me how to be a better wife, mother, friend, and citizen. She taught me values that continue to mold and direct me. Although she never asked for it, she gets the credit for who I am today. It's because of her that I only think, "I can," and it's because of her that I'll never quit. The impact she made on my life keeps me continually growing into someone more.

In a nutshell, she challenged me to live outside my "I" zone just as she had always done. No matter what question I asked her, "others" was always at the center of the answer. Cosmetics may have been the vehicle she used, but Mary Kay was all about reaching out to others, touching and changing lives. Although she passed away on Thanksgiving Day in 2002, the legacy she left behind is timeless and very much alive today. That's the way of a master. And that's the beauty of Mary Kay.

• • •

I put the note down and pulled the 40th anniversary pin out of the package. It was a lovely silver rose with a golden heart in the center. Just like Mary Kay, a rose in full bloom. I pinned it close to my heart as a reminder.

———•·•———

Human beings like to change things, to make them better. They are endowed with curiosity and reason and use these tools to learn about the world and think up ways to modify it. Anything that interests you can become your full-time field of expertise, and the degree of your interest—your passion— brings you ever nearer your goal of making a difference. Tony Alessandra is a high-touch, high-tech advisor in the areas of sales, marketing, and relation-ship building.

WHAT DO YOU REALLY CARE ABOUT?

TONY ALESSANDRA, PH.D.

What do you feel passionate about? What do you care really deeply about? Whatever your objective—whether it's ending world hunger or ensuring better care for stray animals—you'll never influence anyone to change their ideas or take action if you don't feel strongly about it yourself.

How do you get such passionate vision? Well, the process probably varies somewhat from person to person. But for starters, a common denominator is recognizing what I call the need gap.

That's the gap between *what is* and *what could be.* This disparity is the breeding ground for vision. This ability to see deficiencies in existing situations and act on them is one of the skills that separates the charismatic leader from, say, just a manager or an administrator. The manager can, so to speak, make the buses run on time. But the charismatic leader sees the need for whole new routes—or maybe even whole new modes of transportation.

Consider Bill W. and Dr. Bob. They started out in the 1950s in a small Midwest steel town with nothing but their own shattered lives—and an idea. They founded Alcoholics Anonymous. The simplicity of its 12-step program, with its credo of "love and service," was a vision that has changed millions of lives.

Or take Carl Stotz, an almost penniless Williamsport, Pennsylvania, baseball fan who during the Depression liked to play ball with his two young nephews. As historian Garry Wills recounts in his book *Certain Trumpets*, Stotz wondered why the boys had to use clumsy grown-up gloves, swing a bat that was far too big for them, and do an imaginary play-by-play "broadcast."

So he acted on his vision. He found an unused lot and devised the dimensions of a kid-size field. He asked around for other boys to play and other men to coach or maybe to umpire. He went to 56 companies before he found one willing to cough up the $30 it took to field a youth team in 1938.

He then persuaded local sportswriters to cover the early games and recruited friends, relatives, and fellow volunteers to build bleachers, embroider team names on uniforms, and perform dozens of other tasks. He drew up rules that would let all boys play, even if it meant having four outfielders rather than an extra kid sitting on the bench.

His modest concept grew into—you've probably guessed it by now—Little League, a sports program that has affected more lives than any other. Baseball had risen from an old child's game in the 19th century to become the modern sport for the American masses. Stotz's vision returned it to the children.

A purist, Stotz eventually became estranged from the Little League organization as it grew into a big business and the sport became more of a high-pressure pastime. But until his death in 1992, he could take pride that it was his vision—and energy and hard work—that had created recreation and character-building opportunities for millions of young people.

The Steps to Creating Vision

I think there are three stages to arriving at a vision that'll help make you a charismatic leader. The first is your *defining moment*. That's when, as the saying goes, "the lightbulb goes on." Something clicks in your skull. You realize you're on to something really exciting.

This can occur in the throes of a busy day at work, but often it's a solitary experience. "If we are to survive, we must have ideas, vision, and courage," historian Arthur M. Schlesinger Jr. wrote in *The Decline of Heroes.* "These things are rarely produced by committees. Everything that matters in our intellectual and moral life begins with an individual confronting his own mind and conscience in a room by himself."

About 15 years ago, for example, it occurred to Robert L. Johnson, a black businessman who worked for the National Cable Television Association, that someone was going to target black media consumers. "I figured," he later said, "why not me?"

An associate describes Johnson this way: "He is the kind of person who is able to create a vision or an idea of what he wants to accomplish, and once he has, he's fantastic at persuading other businesspeople to support him." Johnson's BET Holdings Inc. (for Black Entertainment Television) aims to be to African American consumers what the Walt Disney Company is to families in general, and already BET reaches 40 million households. Meanwhile, Johnson is transferring the BET brand to magazines, radio, film production, electronic retailing, and other interests. Aiming at becoming a one-stop shopping spot for advertisers to reach black consumers, BET employs 450 people and brings in $115 million in annual sales—all from Robert Johnson's idea that there was a need for black programming and his "Why not me?" approach.

Filling an Existing Need

Not every idea you have will be a breakthrough, a defining moment, though. Your idea might be initially exciting to you. But to qualify as visionary, it must appeal to the values and needs of the people you're seeking to lead.

Remember, a big part of charisma is chemistry between the leader and the led. So you'll have little luck in the long term if you merely have a solution in search of a problem. The Edsel automobile. The "new" Coca-Cola. The rush to get the United States to adopt the metric system for all its measurements. These were all ideas somebody had, but they were ideas that didn't fill a widespread need.

So if you exaggerate the need gap, or try to create a phony one, you'll lose credibility. What's required is some serious study to make sure you're filling an existing need, not a manufactured one or one that appeals to you alone.

Molly Wetzel's defining moment, for example, came after much work and worry. A business consultant and single mother in Berkeley, California, she watched helplessly as her once middle-class neighborhood fell into decay. A house nearby, owned by an absentee landlord, had become a haven for prostitutes, drug dealers, and other criminals. Her teenage daughter couldn't walk down the street without getting solicited for sex, and her young son was robbed of 75 cents at gunpoint. "It was a nightmare," Wetzel says.

For 18 months, she and her neighbors appealed to police and local politicians, but to no avail. Then one day she read an article about a California appellate court decision that declared small-claims court to be a proper place for settling disputes involving complex social issues. That was her defining moment. She knew the need, knew it very well. And now she knew the answer.

Though she had no legal background, she soon corralled 18 neighbors—ranging in age from 3 to 65—and together they sued the absentee property owner for destroying the neighborhood. They won. Wetzel and the neighbors were awarded $2,000 each, and within two weeks the property owner had evicted the drug dealers. Today the neighborhood is thriving—and so is Safe Streets Now!, a nonprofit organization Wetzel formed to help other neighborhoods fight crime by using small-claims courts or the threat of lawsuits.

"After we won the case, my phone never stopped ringing," Wetzel says. At last count, Safe Streets Now! had 23 chapters from California to Massachusetts, and their actions had resulted in the shutting down of 485 trouble spots, such as drug houses, liquor stores, and motels that were hangouts for criminals.

Wetzel's efforts have been lauded by Harvard University's Kennedy School of Government and others. But apart from the statistics and the kudos, the real triumph, Wetzel says, is what neighbors learned about themselves and each other: "New leaders emerge. When they fight crime successfully, they realize that they can improve the parks and the schools—they can do anything." And the greatest lesson of all, she says, is that children watch their parents solve problems without violence.

Though she lacked an impressive title or the backing of a large organization, Molly Wetzel believed strongly in what she was offering, could explain how it filled a need, and was willing to work hard to develop the idea.

From *Charisma* by Tony Alessandra, copyright ©1998, published by Warner Books. Used by permission of Tony Alessandra.

Leverage Your Achievements to Heighten Your Success

Failure is the opportunity to begin
again more intelligently.

—HENRY FORD

Success may be a lasting accomplishment, but the thrill of success is transitory; much of the joy is in the journey. Once it's over, we begin to wonder, "What's next?" This feeling of emptiness cues us to step up and get ready for the next level, for success goes on as long as we keep building new steps. We graduate from one level and, equipped with what we've learned, go on to new accomplishments in the next. Each accomplishment becomes something we can stand on to reach higher. We can leverage our success.

Small successes can add up to major leverage. Each experience, each skill learned or honed, each new technology adopted multiplies the results of our efforts. The achievements leveraged can be our own, or those of other contributors in a team effort. Those who work alone against tall odds to accomplish what others might consider mundane achievements often end up amassing powerful capabilities. However they are combined, the whole can be greater than the sum of the parts if used to full effect.

The resources we find most useful as levers depend on both our immediate and our long-term goals. Many are specialized, closely identified with a particular field or profession or industry. Trial lawyers, politicians, and motivational speakers cultivate forensic skills, the ability to sway audiences. This is a vital resource that can be transferred from one project to another, even in different fields. The same goes for marketing skills, management expertise, and most leadership skills. The more success we have achieved, the more easily we can apply these resources toward achieving new ends.

As a lever, success is also portable to others. We can use it not only to help ourselves reach our own goals but to also help our associates, friends, colleagues, family members, even worthy strangers reach their goals. Success contains many valuable and transferable components: experience, skills, wisdom, insight, confidence, enthusiasm, energy, money, reputation, sometimes just the outsize influence of fame. These assets can be mobilized in pursuit of different ends, including the needs of others. All that is necessary is to choose a worthy goal and turn the momentum of success in a new direction.

Networking is a structured system for leveraging success and thereby sharing its benefits. Helping others achieve their goals not only leverages a person's success for the benefit of others, but also brings the leverage full circle: what goes around comes around. Although it springs from an initial good given without expectation of recompense, an altruistic act for a network contact accrues social capital. The benefits provided eventually come back to the giver.

The ultimate leveraging of success is the philanthropy of those whose accomplishments have made them rich and who look for ways to give back to individuals who helped them and to the community that nurtured their success. Their rewards come not in the form of superfluous money or fame but in the prosperity of those they help and in the goodwill and approval of the community. This is success of a whole new order—social immortality.

Success is an elusive concept. It comes in many forms and disguises. Many things we commonly think of as essential to success turn out to be unimportant. Success, it seems, has more to do with putting together and using to full advantage whatever assets come to hand, a combination unique to the individual. Ron and Joanna Stark, writers and professional entrepreneurs in Arizona, recognize the strengths of one uniquely accomplished woman.

A WOMAN OF VISION

RON AND JOANNA STARK

You don't notice it at first because when Betty Clark Mong walks into a room, heads still turn. She is petite and elegant with a mischievously enchanting smile and twinkling eyes. Her blond hair is coifed, makeup expertly applied to her alabaster skin. The designer suit looks as if it were made just for her svelte figure. She is a picture of grace, beauty, and success.

She appears confident but approachable, intelligent yet fun-loving. And those eyes. There is something about those sparkling aqua eyes. Then you see it. In her right hand is a slender white cane with a red tip, and you realize: Betty is blind.

When she was a toddler of 15 months, Betty's parents discovered that she suffered from juvenile arthritis. She wasn't able to walk until she was four years old. By then, the arthritis had spread to her eyes and she was left with only 2 percent vision. "Despite the vision loss," she explains, "I still had some light perception, could follow someone around who was wearing bright-colored clothing, and could usually walk into a room and find a chair."

Betty's parents were loving and supportive during her childhood, encouraging her to be independent and adventurous. She was given the same responsibilities as her sighted younger brother, and that included helping in the family's large confectionery business, working in the factory as well as in retail sales.

During World War II, Betty volunteered at the Hollywood Canteen entertaining military men on leave. She and her girlfriends spent free evenings at the Hollywood Palladium, where she met Stuart Mong, a young soldier who was waiting for his orders. The two dated until he shipped out. Eventually they lost touch and went on with their separate lives.

Betty married another man in 1945 and continued working with her family in the confectionery factory. In 1971, after volunteering for a couple of years, she became a full-time employee in public relations at the Braille Institute of America in Los Angeles. Public speaking became a passion of hers, and she was able to leverage her position at the Braille Institute so that thousands of people, of all ages and backgrounds, were able to hear her motivational and educational presentations. She provided medical, business, civic, and social groups with insight on living with blindness, and she served as a consultant to writers, producers, and actors in the television and film industry. Betty was an inspiration to all who heard her speak, winning a host of awards—everything from a Paul Harris Fellowship from Rotary International to a Letter of Recognition from the White House.

Betty's marriage ended after 17 years, and she began dating again. She soon realized that there was still a little piece of her heart that belonged to

Stuart Mong, the wonderful soldier she had met at the Palladium so many years ago. On a whim, she obtained his sister's phone number through the college she had attended years before. His sister told Betty that Stuart was now the director of an art museum in Green Bay, Wisconsin. This was followed by a phone call from Stuart himself, and a long-distance romance began. He moved to Los Angeles, and the two were married some months later in a joyous ceremony at the Ritz-Carlton in Rancho Mirage, California.

It was a time of great happiness for Betty. She had carved out a successful career as a respected and sought-after inspirational speaker. She was married to the love of her life. And finally, there was hope that she would see again: the doctors at the Doheny Eye Institute agreed that she was an excellent candidate for corneal transplant surgery.

Betty underwent two successful surgeries, and her vision was nearly completely restored. Stuart and Betty were overjoyed. As Stuart drove her home from the hospital, Betty was astounded by all the different colors. So many bright and shiny cars!

The couple decided to see all they could and began by touring Europe. They visited museums, art galleries, and historical sites. What intrigued Betty most were the beautiful portraits painted by different artists. "It made me cry to see so much beauty," she recalls. "It was overwhelming at times, but it brought me such joy."

Upon returning home, Stuart and Betty enjoyed an evening out to celebrate nine months of sighted life together. As they left the restaurant, Betty tumbled down a flight of stairs and hit her head. Days later, she began having trouble seeing. Doctors confirmed what she had feared. Her retinas were becoming detached, and despite all surgical efforts, blindness was enveloping her once again. Nothing could be done to stop the loss of vision a second time.

When Betty tells this part of her story, her audiences visibly despair. Heads bow, shoulders fall, and cheeks grow moist. How could this happen to such a lovely woman? How does one survive losing her sight not once, but twice?

"My mother was desperately ill at the time," Betty explains. "I was so concerned for her that I could not become self-pitying or depressed. In fact,

I really did not suffer depression at all, though I did have times of frustration. When tragedy happens, you really find out what you are made of.

"I wish I were not blind, but I have met and made some great friends because of my blindness. I have nothing to complain about. I have an absolutely wonderful life." She speaks with such easy sincerity that one has no choice but to believe her statement. Her self-assurance and sense of humor do not inspire pity.

Betty's self-assurance comes from the fact that she has never let her blindness limit her. She feels that when you lose one of your senses, you can strengthen another. Betty discovered she had a talent for hand-weaving beautiful fabrics for everything from formal table linens to evening gowns; a handwoven stole she made for Nancy Reagan and a flag for Betty Ford hang in the archives of gifts to the White House. Betty is also an accomplished gourmet chef, a talented singer, and an avid dancer—all talents she might never have developed had she been able to see.

Betty and Stuart, a gem of a man in his own right, still live a devoted and loving life together creating their own adventures. She continues to work at the Braille Institute, now at the Desert Center in Rancho Mirage, as coordinator of community activities.

"My life has been a success," she states. "But what success means to me might not be the same as success would be for you. My success is found in developing relationships with all kinds of people. And, though it may sound strange, I sense energy in a room and relate to people based on that. Nothing in life is more important than your relationships with others. On a personal level, being visually limited is a lifelong challenge. I know I can do nothing about the past, but for today alone I have the privilege of doing something to help another and enjoy life to the fullest. Then, possibly, I may be able to help again tomorrow. Now, that is success."

Betty's ready smile, ageless beauty, boundless energy, kind nature, and endless optimism prove that she is truly a woman of great success and unlimited vision.

Success always requires an investment of time, energy, or money. But equal investments don't necessarily mean equal returns. How successful you are in the long run depends in large part on how intelligently and efficiently you invest your resources—and those of your teammates—for greatest effect. Bestselling authors Mark Victor Hansen and Robert G. Allen elaborate.

LEVERAGING SUCCESS

MARK VICTOR HANSEN AND ROBERT G. ALLEN

Leverage equals speed. If you want to create wealth, you need leverage. Lots of it. There are three parts to leverage. The first part is the objective (the Dream) that you intend to bring into reality. The Enlightened Millionaire focuses on a dream that advances humanity; it adds value. In this way, every dollar earned is an "enlightened" one. In addition, the precessional events are always positive, and, as the dollars mount to millions, a sense of gratitude permeates the Enlightened Millionaire's being.

The second part is the fulcrum. That is you. You are the object upon which the level pivots. Without you, there is no height to the lever, and the objective will never move, no matter how long the lever or how much force is applied to the lever.

The third part is the lever itself. When the objective and the fulcrum are in place, success depends on the length and strength of the lever. Assuming the lever is strong, it is all about the length of the lever. The longer the lever, the *less* force that is needed to move the object. A long lever works easier and faster than a short one.

Enlightened Millionaires know that speed is the new currency of business. Hence, Enlightened Millionaires create very long and strong levers.

> *Give me a lever long enough and a place to stand and*
> *I will move the entire earth.*
>
> —ARCHIMEDES

A movie star makes a movie once. The leverage comes when thousands of prints are made and the movie is shown all over the world. The money comes when millions of people pay to view it.

A baseball player plays baseball. The leverage comes when he is watched by tens of thousands of fans at the stadium and viewed nationally on television. The large salary a ballplayer makes comes from the revenues of this leverage.

Teachers, on the other hand, usually have 25 to 40 students per class. They have very little leverage, and thus their salary is relatively low. Both the baseball player and the teacher add value (with the teacher generally seen as adding more value), yet the baseball player has the greater leverage and thus is able to demand and receive more money for his services than the teacher.

All large sums of money embrace the generalized principle of leverage. For example, the first volume of *Chicken Soup for the Soul* added lots of value. It was a book that was written once, yet it was purchased by millions. Once the book became a hit, the authors were able to leverage the Chicken Soup brand into many other books (e.g., *Chicken Soup for the Teenage Soul*) as well as other products, such as the Chicken Soup calendars. Tens of millions of these products have been and continue to be sold. This leverage creates continuous income streams not only to the authors but also to the publishers, distributors, bookstores, and many others.

The book *Nothing Down* explains the power of leverage in real estate. For example, if you put 10 percent down on a $200,000 home that goes up in value by 5 percent in one year, then the property is worth $210,000. You get the leverage not only on your $20,000 but also on the remaining $180,000 that you have borrowed. Your $20,000 investment has earned you $10,000 and a 50 percent return on your money.

When you are able to buy real estate for no money down and it goes up in value, you have created a return on someone else's money. Of course, some time and effort are involved. However, computing a financial return on no money invested shows an infinite return. That is infinite leverage.

The Awesome Power of Leverage

Leverage is the power to control a lot with just a little. Big doors swing on little hinges. In the business world, there are five kinds of leverage.

OPM—OTHER PEOPLE'S MONEY

In real estate investing, we buy residential real estate with 10 percent down, and yet we control 100 percent of the property. The classic investment book *Nothing Down* teaches how to achieve ultimate leverage: how to buy property with little or no money down. Thousands of people have become millionaires using this system.

OPE—OTHER PEOPLE'S EXPERIENCE

It takes too long to learn it yourself, so borrow or learn from others. The easiest way to become rich is to apprentice personally with someone who is rich. Learn all they know, meet all their contacts, and do what they do—do it even better. If this isn't possible, read their books, listen to their tapes, watch their videos, interview them if possible, and attend their seminars. One idea you learn can save you ten years of work effort. Leverage is about maximizing your results in a minimum amount of time. Therefore, absorb lifetime bodies of information and insight—compressed into instant usability just for you—in the forms of books, tapes, CDs, films, videos, and seminars. This is the cheapest and quickest way to gain OPE.

OPI—OTHER PEOPLE'S IDEAS

When Mark wanted to become a professional speaker, he attended the National Speakers Association meeting in 1974. Cavett Robert, the "dean of speakers" and co-founder of this association, talked about how to create multi-authored books. Within a month, Mark had adopted the idea and created a book with Keith DeGreen called *Stand Up, Speak Out, and*

Win. They enrolled 14 co-contributors who each invested $2,000 to obtain 1,000 books each. It was Mark's first zero-cash investment. He capitalized on someone else's idea to personally earn $200,000 in that year (selling 20,000 copies at $10 each). Your objective is to associate with people who can share with you their powerful moneymaking ideas.

OPT—OTHER PEOPLE'S TIME

Individuals will sometimes volunteer their time in certain circumstances, but most will sell you their time, talent, connections, resources, and know-how relatively inexpensively. Leverage yourself with professionals who are excellent and unique at employing their abilities.

OPW—OTHER PEOPLE'S WORK

Most people want a job. They want security, rather than opportunity. Hire and delegate to them everything that you don't want to or can't do as well. Leverage yourself through other people and grow.

Millionaires are masters at using all five kinds of leverage.

From *The One Minute Millionaire* by Mark Victor Hansen and Robert G. Allen, copyright ©2002. Used by permission of Harmony Books, a division of Random House Inc.

———•·•———

The qualities of a leader come from within—either qualities that are inborn or capabilities learned and made part of a way of dealing with life. The same principle applies to all achievements: to reach goals that are outside yourself, you have to start by leveraging the capabilities inside you. Niri Patel, a networking coach in Great Britain, tells how leadership brings improvement.

———•·•———

LEADERSHIP

NIRI PATEL

Success is about making things better. Whether you want to be a success in your career, business, finances, health and fitness, or relationships, your circumstances have to improve. These improvements come through making changes.

In 1992, I was dissatisfied with my lot in life. Because of the health problems that had plagued me for almost two years, I was forced to quit my well-paid job. My health was suffering, my finances were dire, and I found myself without a career. Wallowing in my misery, I couldn't understand why all of this had happened to me. How had it all gone so wrong?

Later that year at a personal development seminar, I heard the following words: " For things to change, you've got to change. For things to get better, you've got to get better."

It made sense. As unhappy as I was with my life, I couldn't expect things to get better by complaining about my circumstances. Nor could I expect things to get better by blaming others around me. I decided that day that some things needed to change in my life and *I* was going to change them.

But how would I change them? An understanding of what creates change is crucial. I realized that what creates change is not action. Nor is it persistence, making a decision, commitment, or faith. All these things expedite change. They are necessary for change to occur, but they do not create change itself. What actually creates change is a *change in thinking*. When our life conditions change, we need to change our thinking in order to accommodate or overcome the change.

Today my life is totally transformed. I am happily married, and we are expecting our first child. We have two very successful businesses that make a positive impact on people's business and personal lives and are surrounded by some amazing friends. What a difference a decade makes!

What turned my life around was the understanding that creating change is about stepping up and becoming a leader. Leaders show up in government, business, religious groups, sports teams, and even at home. At a recent speaking engagement, I addressed an audience that included a preschool teacher and a housewife who was on long-term maternity leave to look after her eight-month-old daughter. I started off by informing these two women that they were the most important leaders in the room because they needed to be leaders for the children around them. After all, if they were not going to influence these children positively, then who was? I went on to share some of my personal insights about leadership with the audience, mainly by posing a number of questions. I would like to share these with you in the hope that you will find them as beneficial as I have.

What Is Leadership?

Leadership is the constant study of how to create a new future. Leaders are persons of significant influence. Their thoughts, feelings, and emotions influence the people around them and can lead to change. Leaders engage people and get them to believe that they are no longer creatures of circumstance. General Norman Schwarzkopf defines a leader as "someone who gets people to willingly do more than they would ordinarily do themselves."

What Qualities Does a Leader Need to Possess?

The four qualities a person must have in order to be a leader are:

1. *Vision.* A leader is a person who looks forward and is a student of the road ahead.

2. *Presence.* A leader is a person who projects certainty that the goal will be attained. The best leaders also genuinely care about those around them.

3. *Standards.* A leader is a person with higher standards. Leaders will not settle for what others around them are willing to accept as the norm.

4. *Strategies.* A leader is a person with some skills and strategies that other people require but do not possess.

How Do I Start if I Want to Be a Leader?

Start by leading yourself. Make the necessary changes in your own life to become a better version of yourself. Beyond this, there are three levels of leadership:

Leadership Level 1. A leader with followers. Once you come to grips with leading yourself, it's time to lead others. At this level, the leader has followers. Followers differ from crowds. The crowd serves no useful purpose other than to fuel the so-called leader's ego. Followers, by contrast, carry on the leader's message.

Leadership Level 2. A leader of leaders with followers. At this level you are able to identify leaders within your group of followers or bring them in from outside the existing group. This increases your influence because you can reach more people with the help of your leaders.

Leadership Level 3. A leader of leaders who lead leaders to lead people! It may sound like a tongue twister, but it's really quite simple. The greatest leaders will have their work continue even after they change jobs or even pass away. They believe in succession planning.

How does a leader create a new reality in people who hold on to an old reality?

There are three things a leader can do:

1. *Get people to participate at a greater level.* Leaders get people to look beyond their life circumstances and create a new vision. They help them create a compelling future that inspires them to greater levels of success by becoming more resourceful. What people generally lack are not resources but resourcefulness! This is how a teacher can take an unconfident child and help him flourish in school and ultimately in his life. It is also how Mahatma Gandhi helped India gain independence from Britain and how Martin Luther King Jr. motivated so many with his dream.

2. *Demonstrate a desire and motive to serve.* A person's intent affects her ability to influence people positively. If significance and self-importance dominate over service and contribution, weak people will be attracted. This invariably results in failure. If, on the other hand, people feel that you are really there for them, they will not only listen to you but also will act in response to your leadership. This is why Mother Teresa had so many people travel from all over the world to help her care for the homeless and needy in Calcutta.

3. *Help others to understand the laws of life.* There is only one certainty in life, and that is change itself. If things did not change, leaders would not be required. Only managers would be needed! Leaders anticipate change and understand that the best time to handle a problem is before it becomes one. Winston Churchill warned of the dangers looming across Europe long before the rest of the world came to know them as reality.

Becoming a good leader, whether of others or simply of yourself, is the best way to improve your life. I've often heard it said, "If we always do what we've always done, we'll always get what we've always got." It's only through change that we can truly find success.

———•·•———

Success itself is a leverage tool. By achieving ambitious goals, you can attract the attention of others who wish to emulate your success and magnify the effect of your leadership. Most striking are the achievements of those who leverage their success to reshape their professions in profoundly beneficial ways. Connie Hinton, a marketing expert from Seattle and a NASCAR racing aficionado, writes about a champion's legacy to his sport.

———•·•———

SUCCESS DRIVES A FAST BLACK CAR, OR, SOMETIMES GOOD GUYS DON'T WEAR WHITE

CONNIE HINTON

It's the last lap of NASCAR's Daytona 500, February 2001. Michael Waltrip and Dale Earnhardt Jr. are running first and second, respectively. Dale

Earnhardt Sr. (known as the Intimidator for his aggressive driving style) is immediately behind them with a pack of race cars fast approaching his back bumper. At speeds approaching 170 mph, the senior Earnhardt dodges and weaves in front of the trailing cars, shielding the two young drivers as they are about to cross the finish line.

As the cars race into the final turn, one of the approaching race cars bumps Dale Senior, sending him out of control just as Waltrip and Dale Junior cross the finish line to a roar from the crowd. Their celebration is short-lived. Everyone quickly realizes that the black number-three car, Dale Senior's car, is in the wall and there is no movement from the driver. Drivers and fans alike hold their breath to see if the Intimidator will walk away from yet another racing accident. But this time there is no happy ending at Daytona for the man in black. The racetrack that had given him the highest highs and some of the lowest lows in his racing career would be his last.

This icon of motor sports met with an end all race-car drivers face whenever they strap into their cars. As tragic as his death was, what he brought to the sport of stock-car racing will be long remembered. Dale Earnhardt Sr. was an inspiration to both his fellow race-car drivers and his millions of fans, teaching them the true meaning of success. Throughout his victorious career, he believed in following five basic principles.

First, Earnhardt wasn't afraid to speak out for improvements in the sport he loved. His biggest concern was driver safety, especially as the races got faster and more competitive. He saw too many friends and fellow drivers lose their lives or be critically injured in races where heavy restrictions resulted in cars (running at almost 200 miles per hour) being bunched together so tightly that the slightest driver error would create a multiple-car pileup. He was a fan favorite; reporters flocked around him for post-race interviews at Daytona or the Talladega Superspeedway. He always used these opportunities to express his concerns. By making people aware of the issue, Earnhardt helped bring driver safety in stock-car racing to a new level.

Second, Earnhardt knew it was the small accomplishments in each race that would lead toward his goal of winning the championship. Drivers are awarded points for reaching goals at weekly races, and these points are added to a driver's record throughout the season. For Earnhardt, the most obvious points in each race came with just showing up. He couldn't earn points toward the championship if he didn't start the first lap, so on many occasions he would crawl into his car with a wince due to injuries received in a previous crash. Additionally, points are awarded for being the fastest car to qualify (referred to as the pole position), leading a lap, being the leader at the halfway point, and the finishing position. Every point counts in a sport where, in many years, the difference between being NASCAR champion and coming in second is less than ten points. Seven-time NASCAR champion Dale Earnhardt knew it was the small things that happen each day that add up to the final result.

Earnhardt's third principle was to focus entirely on the task at hand. He recognized that without complete concentration on succeeding at the immediate objective, the long-range goal of the championship would remain out of reach. In August 1996, he took the pole position at Watkins Glen, New York, barely a week after a crash broke his sternum and collarbone. Explaining his ability to work through the pain, he said, "When you're going after something big like qualifying, you're focused on that. You don't feel the pain as much." Tunnel vision toward a short-term goal was what got Earnhardt into the winner's circle time after time.

Earnhardt's fourth principle was to market his business both on and off the racetrack. Racing is an expensive sport, and it takes major sponsorship to maintain a competitive car. Despite Earnhardt's reputation as the Intimidator on the racetrack, off-track he was really a very shy person. Still, he understood the importance of making personal appearances on behalf of his sponsors and interacting with the fans. He chose to work outside his comfort zone to ensure his success. While many NASCAR drivers struggle to find sponsors, Earnhardt's dedication to marketing, coupled with his impressive driving record and strong ties to his fans, led to a long-term relationship with GM Goodwrench—a name now synonymous with the black number-three car.

His final principle was to prepare for the future of his business. Through Dale Earnhardt Inc., he trained and mentored young drivers to become the next champions. Even in the last moments of his life, he sheltered his legacy by protecting Michael Waltrip and Dale Junior from being passed. In a recent interview, Steve Parks, another Earnhardt team driver, said, "He's taught us all to be winners, and that's something you just can't replace." Through his confidence in and support of these young men, Earnhardt assured a winning succession in his beloved sport of stock-car racing.

Looking back on his approach to his career, it's easy to see how Dale Earnhardt achieved such great success and brought ever-increasing popularity to NASCAR. His concepts are universal, and regardless of your profession, Earnhardt's five principles for success still apply:

1. Work for improvement in your profession.
2. Do the small things each day that add to your success.
3. Focus on the task at hand.
4. Market yourself or your business even if it's out of your comfort zone.
5. Prepare for succession in your business or life.

Dale Earnhardt left his permanent stamp on the world of racing, affecting his fellow racers and fans for generations to come. His dedication and example prove that sometimes good guys don't wear white—they drive a fast, black car.

———•◦•———

Only a few decades into the information revolution, we are daily finding new ways to leverage the powers of our newborn computer and communication technology. A case in point is the convergence of mass media, emergency communication, public transportation, and Internet technologies with an enlightened concern for the community. Brian Roach, a partner in Evolve Partners, is an expert in the application of technology to problem solving.

———•◦•———

SUCCESS INSIGHTS FROM TECH-SAVVY COMMUNITIES

BRIAN ROACH

Success lessons sometimes come from unexpected sources. As we pursue success in our personal, family, and business lives, we can benefit by looking at a venue that's easy to take for granted: our community.

The community provides support systems—law enforcement, for example—on which we depend for our basic safety and survival. The consequences of an individual's success or failure are often limited to that one individual, perhaps rippling out to family members or a small circle of stakeholders. The consequences of a community's success or failure, however, affect hundreds, thousands, or millions of people.

Communities are increasingly using technology to perform at higher levels of effectiveness—that is, leveraging advances in technology to become more successful. While we each share in the consequences of our own community's successes and failures, let's single out one group to illustrate the point: parents of young children. A community's successful use of technology can make a life-or-death difference when disaster strikes.

Picture a father, successful by all accounts, who happens to live near a big town in the year 1870. He arrives home one day to discover his wife distraught, tearfully explaining that their daughter is nowhere to be found. In fact, she fears that two men on horseback whom she had seen riding nearby kidnapped the little girl. Alarmed, the husband runs out to find the sheriff. The sympathetic sheriff can form a posse, but it will take many hours for a search to begin.

Fast-forward to 1925. A father answers his office telephone. The operator on the line puts through a call from his panicked wife. She says a man has just kidnapped their daughter right off their front porch and sped away in a black sedan. She's called the police. The responding officer says he will phone a description to nearby precincts. He hopes an officer on the beat will get lucky and spot the girl—but he knows the odds are low. After all, most sedans are painted black in the 1920s. And crucial hours will pass before the word can circulate to every precinct.

Jump to the year 1996. A bright little nine-year-old girl named Amber Hagerman is kidnapped while riding her bicycle in Arlington, Texas. She is later found, brutally murdered. Outraged residents contact radio stations in the area and suggest that, in the event of future child abductions, the stations broadcast special alerts over the airwaves. The Dallas–Fort Worth Association of Radio Managers teams up with local law enforcement agencies to develop a first-of-its-kind early warning system to help find abducted children.

Named after the slain little girl, the AMBER Alert system—which also stands for "America's Missing: Broadcast Emergency Response"—offers a gift unavailable to prior generations of desperate parents and concerned communities: speed. The U.S. Department of Justice estimates that 74 percent of the children who are kidnapped and later found murdered were killed within the first three hours after their abduction. The AMBER Alert system can inform a community within minutes that a child has been kidnapped. Now the community has something better than a posse, better than a telephone, and—as technology improves—even better than radio alone.

In July 2002, a man approached five-year-old Samantha Runnion as she sat with a friend near her house in Orange County, California. "Did you see a little Chihuahua?" the man asked. He didn't wait for an answer before grabbing Samantha, carrying her as she kicked and screamed to his car, then escaping into an ocean of traffic.

An AMBER Alert quickly went to radio and TV news media. This would be one of three occasions on which the state of California would use its version of the system in a pilot phase before implementing it statewide. In addition to news alerts, California used the electronic signs along its interstate highways, which ordinarily display traffic updates, to flash descriptions of the getaway vehicle and suspect.

The manhunt that resulted from this abduction represented a paradigm shift in the way Californians would come together as a community and use technology to help find the criminal responsible for this unthinkable act. Because most motorists listen to their radio while driving and the electronic message signs are ubiquitous on southern California freeways, hopes ran high that someone would see the child, the kidnapper, the vehicle, or something that would help police find Samantha.

The ordeal turned into heartache about 24 hours later when investigators reported the discovery in a nearby county of a little body that closely resembled Samantha. Confirmation came the next day.

The AMBER Alert was not yet done with its work, however, as it produced thousands of calls with hundreds of leads for the police. Within days, authorities had a suspect in custody, and officers were crediting the system for quickly leading to his apprehension.

The AMBER Alert helped prevent the worst from occurring in two other child abductions during its pilot phase in California. In one case, a child was safely recovered in Mexico. Another situation arose with the kidnapping of two teenage girls in southern California by a parolee who had an outstanding warrant for rape; the vehicle the parolee was driving was spotted within hours, and law officers were able to rescue the girls.

The State of California expanded the AMBER Alert program from its pilot phase to cover the entire state. In October 2002, Attorney General Bill Lockyer, California Highway Patrol Commissioner D.O. "Spike" Helmick, and California Broadcasters Association president Stan Statham announced distribution of the AMBER Alert manual and other resources to assist communities in developing and implementing local AMBER Alert plans. The manual was developed by the California Department of Justice, the California Highway Patrol, and the California Governor's Office of Emergency Services.

AMBER Alerts are being adopted by a rapidly growing number of jurisdictions throughout the United States and Canada. The system has even moved onto the Internet, with the August 23, 2002, launch of CodeAmber.org. More than 83,000 Web sites had joined Code Amber, and more than 26.5 million AMBER Alert tickers had been displayed as of October 2003.

Technology has long been a way to innovate, achieve the unimaginable, provide quicker delivery time, communicate more effectively, and make shifts and changes in the way society solves problems. The simple yet ingenious use of technology in the AMBER Alert system enables communities to knit the caring, watchful eyes of ordinary individuals into a safety net that can, with the occasional miracle, save children from the fate of Amber Hagerman and Samantha Runnion. And when the worst happens, this net of justice can at least help ensnare the criminal so that others might be spared.

For students of success, our communities' use of technology, illustrated by the AMBER Alert system, offers a valuable lesson. As we review the building blocks of a successful endeavor—"*Enthusiasm*? Check. *Vision*? Check. *System*? Check. *Clear goals*? Check"—we have to remember to apply the best technology available, then leverage that technology for all it's worth.

———————

Despite much talk to the contrary, the space age has not come and gone. The extraterrestrial achievements and sacrifices of scientists, technicians, and astronauts over the last half-century will soon lead to new adventures on the last physical frontier. Success will be measured by how commonplace space travel becomes. Buzz Aldrin, one of the first two men to walk on the Moon, talks about the wide-open future of space travel with Elisabeth Misner, a business writer in Los Angeles.

———————

SEE YOU IN SPACE

BUZZ ALDRIN WITH ELISABETH MISNER

The images of that day are burned in my memory—the magnificent desolation of the lunar surface, the soft glow of planet Earth, floating like

223

a space flower over the horizon of a dead Moon—images with depth and clarity, a frameless immensity that cannot be adequately captured on film.

People always ask me what it's like to have been "out of this world," to have walked on the Moon. The answer for me, and for everyone else who's been up there, is simply that it's the greatest experience of my life.

In fact, it's such an extraordinary experience to circle the globe in 90 minutes that I'm amazed so few people have enjoyed it. I believe that this is wrong! Why shouldn't everyone have the chance? I don't want the achievement of space travel to define my success. I would like to use the greatest experience of my life to serve as a jumping-off point for even more success for others in the space industry.

I first began to think about this ten years ago, and an idea formed that I have been developing ever since. It would take innovative marketing, but I know that there are thousands of people who would be willing to spend a significant proportion of their assets on a once-in-a-lifetime spaceflight. I want to be a part of the team to make that happen.

First, we need to make people more motivated. Not too long ago, I started a nonprofit organization called ShareSpace as a way of getting ordinary people more interested and involved in space and space travel.

ShareSpace would conduct a sort of lottery, giving people the chance to win opportunities to attend space camp, witness a shuttle launch, experience a high-altitude zero-gravity flight—and very soon, I hope, win a ride into Earth orbit.

I want people to become inspired and realize that space travel is not just a dream for some, but an opportunity for all of us—an experience available not only to the wealthy, but also to some with just good fortune! With creativity and imagination, we could see this dream come to life.

Space exploration is a costly undertaking, so we do need new ideas to make it easier and put it within our reach. Imagine if every time you took a flight across the country or across the ocean, they threw away the airplane. That's what we did to get to the Moon. We flew up on a 360-foot-tall rocket and splashed down in a space capsule not much bigger than a Volkswagen.

That's why I'm working today with others to design and implement what I call Starbooster rockets. These are reusable rocket boosters that

of their good fortune. Gillian Lawson and her husband developed and own one of the fastest-growing referral marketing firms in the United Kingdom, and she is very involved in charitable fundraising in London.

THE GIFTS OF JOSÉ CARRERAS

GILLIAN LAWSON

José Carreras, the charismatic, world-renowned tenor, had been enjoying a sparkling musical career for nearly two decades when he was diagnosed with leukemia in July 1987. Natural talent combined with determination and hard work had taken him from his opera debut at the age of 11 to principal roles in opera houses all over the world. But over the following 11 months, Carreras reached the depths of pain, exhaustion, and despair with two series of chemotherapy sessions, the extraction of his bone marrow for cleansing and reinjection, then more chemotherapy and radiation therapy with their painful and distressing side effects.

Then came the transplant operation itself—by which time his immune system had completely shut down—and an anxious wait to find out if it had been successful. Only a couple of weeks after the transplant, the new bone marrow stopped working, stopped regenerating blood cells, and he was left, as he says in his autobiography, "poised on the edge of an abyss." But he was one of the first patients to receive a new drug that kick-started his bone marrow into action and initiated the slow process of recovery.

Interviewed for this book in June 2003 in London, Carreras talked frankly about how he found the motivation and strength to get through such an appalling and challenging time.

He was secure in the knowledge that he was in the hands of an experienced medical team, experts in their field, and would have to let them get on with what they needed to do, he says. It was on the emotional front that he needed some backup. He was fortunate to be able to rely on the support of his family. And as a world-famous singer, he also had an army of fans concerned for his health, who provided a "constant proof of solidarity and affection and generosity from all over the world" that gave him great reassurance.

But most of us, if we become ill or face other challenges in life, cannot rely on the support of devoted admirers among the general public. Was there something he did, something that helped, that could serve as an inspiration for those of us without an international fan base?

Carreras admitted that the real motivation and commitment he needed came from within, allied with the support of his loved ones. "From the very first moment," he says, "the doctors were talking about percentages, possibilities of success, of overcoming the disease. It was this treatment or that treatment, chemotherapy or radiotherapy, bone marrow transplants that can be done in this way or that way. But with all this talk about percentages of success, I thought that if there is only one chance in a million, that is my chance, and I am going to fight for that and believe that I can make it. However, this determination also came from the help I received from others. If I had to do it on my own, I don't know if I would have made it."

But there are times when things are bad, whether it is illness or some other serious crisis being faced, when the dark thoughts close in and there seems to be no hope left. At these moments, even the support of loved ones might not be enough. "The help of others is absolutely fundamental, but only up to a certain point," says Carreras. "Then, as we say in Spain, you have to take the bull by the horns."

Carreras's version of taking the bull by the horns involved an intensely personal internal challenge. He walked slowly to the hospital bathroom, trailing all the wires that attached him to various machines, and looked in the mirror. Perhaps this doesn't sound like much—most people face the mirror every morning. But Carreras looked into his own reflected eyes and understood that this was it. The doctors were doing all they could, but he had to take responsibility for the part of the process that he still had control over—the part that each of us, whatever the challenges, has control over, even though we sometimes don't want to acknowledge it. That part was his mind. Many of us would prefer to face any number of external challenges than to look deep into ourselves, to face up to whatever is going on and take responsibility for our thoughts.

He recalls, "I looked in that mirror and said, 'Now, José, don't be stupid. Fight. Go on until the very last possibility, and if it doesn't work, then—so what? What would be so terrible?'" He had experienced a wonderful 40 years so far, had a loving family, and would be devastated not to see his children grow up. What he understood that day was that there was no reason not to keep fighting in his mind.

For a man to whom music was such an essential part of life, it was not enough just to get better. Carreras had to sing again. His first concert after recovery, singing to a crowd of 150,000 in his hometown of Barcelona, was almost exactly a year after he was first diagnosed. It took, he says, a lot of courage. "I knew that I had my voice, but I didn't know if I would have the physical and mental strength to go in front of an audience and sing again. Eleven months in hospital affects you mentally as well as physically. But I had such an incredible desire to go back to what I loved so much and what had always been such an important part of my life.

"It was an emotional moment. I remember climbing up onto the stage that had been built for the occasion, and I stopped and thought, 'I can't do this, I'm going to be overemotional.' So I had to play cynical with myself. I told myself, 'Oh, all these people are here, I suppose I can give them a little bit of my time.' It would have been impossible for me to articulate any more. That concert was one of the most special evenings, not only of my career, but of my life. That day I knew I had made it, much more than walking out of the hospital."

Asked if his experiences of making it as an opera singer helped him find the strength to face his illness, Carreras plays them down. "Maybe unconsciously, the fact that I knew what it was to go onstage and face an audience helped," he says. "But all through those 11 months in hospital, the artist part of me was parked somewhere else. When you are facing such a situation, it's you as a pure person, the personality completely naked, just what you are as a human being."

Walking onto a stage and facing rows of expectant faces, however, are only the very public aspects of his career and his success. His illness was a private challenge, which is why these public elements played little part. What he is perhaps modestly leaving out are the commitment, determination, and taking of personal responsibility required to do the countless hours of practice, year after year, that are necessary to turn a natural talent into one that is world-class. And it seems these qualities got him through the psychological impact of his fight with leukemia while the doctors were doing their essential work on the physical battleground of his body.

Even as he resumed his life and his career, simply getting back to singing did not satisfy him. "When I was in hospital in Barcelona and talking to the nurses, I told them that the day I got out I was going to sing a concert for all of them. But then when the moment came, I thought that was not enough," he says.

With support from the scientific community and business contacts, he set up the José Carreras International Leukaemia Foundation in Barcelona, which now has partner organizations in the United States, Switzerland, and Germany. The foundation supports clinical research by providing scholarships to promising researchers from anywhere in the world; runs a bone marrow donation network, searching for matches for those needing transplants; supports the research and clinical facilities of leading international institutions and hospitals in Eastern Europe; and helps leukemia patients and their families, mainly by providing accommodation for families near transplant centers so they can be nearby during the long process of treatment. The main source of money for these activities continues to be Carreras's charity recitals and concerts, which attract generous corporate sponsorship.

A voice like Carreras's is given to only a few souls on the planet at any one time. But everyone can choose to exercise the commitment and determination that supported his career and kept him emotionally strong when he most needed to be. And everyone can learn from his example to share the good fortune of his successful recovery with the community that made possible his career and restored his health.

For more information about the José Carreras International Leukaemia Foundation, visit www.carrerasfoundation.org.

CHAPTER

EIGHT

Prescriptions
for Success

I can't imagine a person becoming a success who doesn't
give this game of life everything he's got.

—WALTER CRONKITE

I f you don't believe success is all luck, just ask any failure. But if
you believe in taking your cues from successful people, like
those you've read about so far in this book, you'll understand
that success comes in a variety of forms, is measured in diverse ways,
and is arrived at by many different routes. You'll see that successful
people have many traits in common, often including an inner drive,

passion, perseverance, goal-setting skills, a capacity for overcoming and profiting from adversity, a talent for establishing and maintaining good relationships, and a knack for leveraging their success. Sure, luck is sometimes involved—finding the nugget in the dust, not being where the meteor falls—but for the most part, successful people are those who keep on moving toward the goal, stay alert for unexpected opportunities, and make the best of whatever happens along the way.

The leveraging of success—using the achievement of one goal as a lever for achieving other goals—has interesting implications. If success can become merely another tool, is there any such thing as a final goal? Many of the most successful among us think not. They live for the joy of achieving one goal after another. Their success is measured not by the satisfaction of the goals achieved—although that is not an inconsiderable reward—but by the thrill of achieving them, a pleasure that fades when there is no next goal in sight.

There is no magic recipe for success because success is a different dish for each person on the planet, and our individual cooking styles are culturally influenced. The basic ingredients can be combined in different ways, however, to produce a tasty, nutritious, and satisfying creation for each person who cares to spend some time in the kitchen.

In any case, it is helpful to pay attention to those who have achieved some measure of success, especially when they summarize and set priorities for what they consider the essentials. Mahatma Gandhi, Winston Churchill, Martin Luther King Jr., and many, many others stand as beacons for our aspirations. The tools and strategies they have used are available to everyone; they are in common use by individuals, groups, organizations, and healthy, vibrant societies.

Success, you may remember, has been described as the result of the uncommon application of common knowledge. We may not be able to replicate the accomplishments of the greats who went before, but we can learn plenty from the choices they made—and in most cases, build on what they accomplished.

 You've got the tools. Success is in your hands.

Sometimes it helps to condense a formula for success into a set of simple, positive statements that have proven more conducive to success than negative thinking. At any given time, any one of these may have greater resonance than the others.

Together, they can constitute a free-form primer for achievement, an antidote to the poison of futility. Author Larry Elder, a popular black radio personality, knows the value of keeping a positive mind-set.

AFFIRMATIVE ATTITUDE

LARRY ELDER

A poll in the *Los Angeles Times* asked whether, in America, "everyone has the power to succeed." Low-income whites were more likely to say yes to that statement than blacks earning $50,000 or more!

At American dinner tables all across the country, parents urge their children to work hard, study hard, and prepare. But in black households, how much dinner table talk revolves around "the white man done me wrong" rather than focusing on grit, hard work, and preparation?

The formula for success is simple. Implementation is hard. As a high school friend put it, "Anybody can talk the talk. But it takes a whole other set of nuts to walk the walk." So regardless of your race, gender, or circumstance, get ahead and stay ahead by following these 32 things—my Personal Pledge 32.

Personal Pledge 32

1. There is no excuse for lack of effort.
2. Although I may be unhappy with my circumstances, and although racism and sexism and other "isms" exist, I know that things are better now than ever, and the future is even brighter.
3. While I may be unhappy with my circumstances, I have the power to change and improve my life. I refuse to be a victim.

4. Others may have been blessed with more money, better connections, a better home environment, and even better looks, but I can succeed through hard work, perseverance, and education.

5. I may be a product of a single- or no-parent household, but I will not hold anyone responsible for my present or allow anyone to interfere with my future. Others succeed under conditions far worse than mine.

6. Some schools and teachers are better than others, but my level of effort, dedication, curiosity, and willingness to grow determine what I learn.

7. Ambition is the key to growth.

8. I will set apart some time each day to think about where I want to go and how I intend to get there. A goal without a plan is just a wish.

9. "Luck" is what happens when preparation meets opportunity.

10. If suitable role models are not nearby, I will seek them out.

11. A role model is someone who, through hard work and a positive outlook, has achieved.

12. A role model may be a parent, relative, friend, church member, judge, doctor, attorney, businessperson, or someone I've read about in the newspaper or seen on the local news.

13. I will contact role models and seek their advice, guidance, and counsel. People remember when they were my age and are eager to help.

14. I will seek out recommended magazines, articles, books, biographies, videos, and motivational and how-to books, and use them for education and motivation.

15. The light is always green. You cannot go full speed with one foot on the brake.

16. I am always "in school," and I will not waste my summer by failing to read about and speak to people who can inspire me.

17. I will avoid friendship with people who do not share my goals and commitments. Nonsupportive relationships waste time and energy.

18. I will not seek immediate results, as I understand life is a journey and not a destination.
19. I will read a newspaper each day.
20. I will entertain myself in ways that challenge and expand my mind. As someone said, a mind once expanded never returns to its original size.
21. I will pay attention to my diet and overall fitness, as they are the keys to a healthy and productive body and an enthusiastic mind.
22. Drugs are stupid. People who believe in drugs don't believe in themselves.
23. I understand the jobs of the future require more preparation and training than ever, and I am determined to obtain the necessary background.
24. A well-rounded, competent student studies math and science.
25. People are not born "deficient in mathematical ability." Through hard work and dedication, the subject can be mastered.
26. It is essential that I learn to speak and write standard English. This is not "acting white," but acting smart.
27. A strong vocabulary is the key to communication, and I will read books on vocabulary enrichment.
28. I expect sometimes to be teased, even ridiculed. This will not stop me; it will only make me stronger and more determined.
29. I control my body and will not create a child until I am spiritually, psychologically, educationally, and financially capable of assuming this awesome responsibility.
30. Life is difficult. I expect setbacks and will learn from them. Struggle creates strength.
31. Every day is precious, and one without growth is squandered.
32. There is only one me, and I'm it!

From *The Ten Things You Can't Say in America* by Larry Elder, copyright ©2000 by Larry Elder. Used by permission of St. Martin's Press.

The road to success is a road of learning, but learning comes not so much from success as from stumbles and mistakes. A good road map, drawn from the mistakes and successes of others, can make the journey easier. Nancy Holland Morgan, a two-time Olympic competitor once ranked among the world's top ten skiers, takes her message of striving for excellence to marketing clients worldwide.

SEVEN COMMONALITIES OF CHAMPIONS

NANCY HOLLAND MORGAN

What is a champion? By definition, it's someone who excels above all others. Generally, the term refers to a world-class athlete, but it could just as easily apply to a top businessperson, significant religious leader, or public celebrity. The study of great champions shows seven commonalities that combine attitudes with other attributes to achieve success. These seven characteristics help us understand how we too can get to the top of our game and become champions.

ENTHUSIASM ABOUT YOUR EVENT

You have to *really* like what you are doing. If you can't acquire a love of the activity, an enthusiasm that turns into a burning, white-hot desire, then it may be time to sit down and reassess your life's interest. You will not have the passion necessary to maintain the drive. Fortunately, doing what you are passionate about doesn't seem like work; it's what you love doing for 12 to 15 hours a day! Without passion, none of the other characteristics will even matter.

COMMITMENT TO LEARNING THE FUNDAMENTALS

Achieving success invariably means having to learn new techniques, master skills, develop new strengths, or obtain new knowledge. But more often than not, when we learn new techniques and skills, we don't get it right the first time. Have you ever watched professional athletes practice for their event? They'll do the same thing over and over again until they perfect that one move. Then they move on to the next movement. Repetition, practice, review, effort, critical feedback, and analysis all go into learning the fundamentals. Commitment to training is an absolute necessity for improvement in *any* activity, whether it is an athletic event or a business function.

PURSUIT OF GOALS, OBJECTIVES, AND PLANS

Combine your desire with commitment to training, and you begin to formulate a thoughtful plan to improve your performance. But all the desire and commitment in the world won't do you any good unless you have a goal. Champions set goals based on their strengths and weaknesses. Their plans revolve around reaching new thresholds based on increasing their strengths and ameliorating their weaknesses. True champions analyze their full event in its parts and then set improvement objectives relative to each of the components. Champions know that paying attention to all the small details of improving one area will help build momentum in other areas. Whether the aim is weight training, dieting, or even psychological training, champions know that to compete seriously for their personal best, they must surrender themselves to the goal.

TENACITY

The first three characteristics prepare us for the fourth characteristic: tenacity. Life is a series of tests: we have to pass each one to go on to the next. As we move higher on the mastery scale, we take the chance of falling harder and longer. The falls are always painful. Fortunately, we accumulate a set of small positive experiences and successes to build our self-confidence enough to drive us through the larger challenges. If we learn to get up after each fall, we can move ever closer to the destination of perfection.

A PERSONAL NETWORK

No one today makes it to the top alone. All champions surround themselves with a support team. The strength of others is crucial to achieving the goal of championship status. Your support team may be only your closest family members, it may be a friendship circle, or it may consist of a paid staff of advisors. The members of your support team will fill in the gaps of your performance. You still have to do the work, put in the effort, and be a driving force, but members of your support team will allow you to focus in the right areas, your strong areas. The team must be carefully chosen; the right team will propel you forward, but the wrong team will drag you down. As you achieve one objective after another, your team may have to change with your own changing goal directions. Your team's job is to keep you in the right attitude as you gain in altitude.

ZONE OF DISCOMFORT

Do something every day that scares you just a little—not something that is life-threatening, but something that causes enough discomfort that you will become accustomed to pushing the envelope of your performance. Get to love your zone of discomfort. Being in the discomfort zone means that we are in an awkward phase of learning a new skill or strategy to help us achieve a higher level of performance. Human nature wants to stay within the comfort zone, but doing so will only keep us in the status quo. To move forward, we must enter our zone of discomfort at least a little and in progressive steps. With each awkward step, we get just a little better. The next time you feel awkward, understand that you have been given the opportunity of learning to increase a strength. Feeling a little awkward is a natural outcome of gaining new strengths. Some people seem to move in and out of the discomfort zone more easily. This is generally either because they have more experience living in the zone of discomfort or they have learned to fake it better than others!

PERSONAL MARKETING AND SELF-PROMOTION

People like to be around those who have an aura of self-confidence and positive self-esteem. Self-confidence means you believe in the potential of achieving your goals. High self-esteem means you are satisfied with your talents and are able to recognize and appreciate the talents of others. This is not about being arrogant, but rather a more humble expression that you are comfortable with yourself, your accomplishments, and your talents.

Good personal marketers communicate that they enjoy their events and are capable of high levels of performance. <u>These people remain positive and attract others to join their support</u> teams. Regardless of how disappointed or discouraged they may feel, they cannot allow themselves the luxury of wallowing in their own misery. Team members will not stay for long around those who are masters at complaint.

Becoming a champion starts from and ends within. To achieve success, you must start with a strong desire and end with the courage to maintain positive self-esteem and confidence in your ability. But in between is where the real work takes place. Champion status takes every bit of inner strength and external leveraging you can muster. With hard work, the rewards will be those of a champion.

Step-by-step is fine in the abstract, but sometimes, and for some people, it's most helpful to hear a straightforward tale of success told by the person who achieved it. You can decide for yourself what the lessons are but pay attention to the simple, positive, "let's try something new" attitude of the following writer—Ina von Koenig, who built a successful business in a nontraditional field for women simply by going where her interests led her.

I GOT THE IDEA WHILE SKIING

INA VON KOENIG

All of us have certain aptitudes, inclinations, and qualities that carry us forward, provided we develop them properly. My interest in unconventional ideas and my sense of adventure are like an inner fire. Again and again throughout my life, they have driven me to follow my own path and sometimes even to do extraordinary things. Anyone who goes through life with eyes open finds special corners where business ideas can evolve. Ideas can come to you at any point, even during a skiing holiday.

In 1965, some friends invited me to go helicopter skiing in France. I had just turned 21, and this was the beginning of my lifelong fascination with helicopters. This miracle of technology interested me, even then, more than skiing in the wonderful scenery. The timing was perfect. I had just finished my commercial training, had completed my studies in foreign languages, and was looking for something meaningful to do. Suddenly, there was this helicopter. I had a thousand ideas about how it might be used profitably. I couldn't stop thinking about it. Less than a year later, I founded my first company, LTD Helicopters, in Stuttgart, Germany.

It was hard at first. My career as an independent businesswoman began at an old desk in a ten-square-meter office, where I sold all sorts of transport flights. Among other things, I organized scenic helicopter trips at public festivals. I carried the heavy iron rods from my basement to the helicopter landing area myself, so that a sign saying "Helicopter Rides" could be fastened to them. I sold the tickets, explained the safety regulations to the passengers, and helped them get in and out. The entire ground crew consisted of one person: me.

The external conditions in the highly competitive business of selling flying hours were far from ideal for a newcomer with not much capital and mostly male rivals at her back. But the competition drove me further, forcing me to provide more than my competitors. I offered extra services unique in Germany, such as camera attachments that made it possible for me to guarantee photographers, advertising agents, cartographers and survey offices steady, unblurred aerial photographs. My approach worked. With greater turnover, I was able to add new branches to my business and work toward realizing my vision: entering the international oil business.

It was certainly a bold ambition for a small helicopter company to get involved in a business that had always been the domain of big international companies. The fact that I was a woman didn't help either. On one occasion, an executive was so disappointed to discover that I was in charge that he told me to bring a pilot with me to the meeting. Of course, he meant a male pilot. Despite these potential roadblocks, or maybe because of them, I chose to rely on my strengths. My focus on marketing consistently led to improvements, and I used this as an argument in many sales discussions.

Because there was no one to show me the ropes, I had to make my own path. I taught myself to work hard, take punishment, yet always present my services in a friendly way. I often set out at three o'clock in the morning in my VW car (in which I traveled all over Germany, driving 60,000 kilometers a year) so I could get to my first meeting punctually at eight. I drove back home the same day because I couldn't afford to stay the night anywhere. Marathon working days like that—sometimes with ten meetings in one day—brought me close to the limits of my physical endurance. It was a total investment. It demanded endless amounts of industriousness, conviction, and determination, not to mention the luck involved in presenting the right idea to the right decision-maker at the right time. But, with hindsight, the really important qualities were my tireless enthusiasm and the unshakable conviction that my services would mean added value for the customer.

The huge effort that was necessary to give the customer more value than my competitors at the same price ultimately led to my breakthrough. After about two years of acquisition discussions, I received an order from Deminex, the parent organization for all German oil prospecting companies, to take over the offshore supply flights to the oil rigs in the Gulf of Suez. I was to work with Heli Air Egypt, a company formed especially for that purpose. To finally achieve my vision, getting into the international oil business as the only German helicopter enterprise, was my greatest reward as a businesswoman.

Meanwhile, my firm was growing rapidly. I now employed about 100 workers, used 12 of my own helicopters, and visited my customers in my own private helicopter. A key task for any helicopter enterprise is to optimize the use of capacity with booked flying hours. My method for generating additional bookings was simple: I looked for new ways to use my helicopters. For some time, I had been watching the successful model of the Swiss flying ambulance service and wondering if the same concept could be institutionalized in Germany. Like the Swiss, I wanted to develop an organization that coordinated the actions for ambulances at road accidents and returned injured and sick people from other countries. Whether it was chance or fate, I spoke about this Swiss institution with a good friend at just the right moment. "Simply do that here in Germany," he advised me. That was just the encouragement I needed, and from someone who really knew, a remarkably successful businessman from a well-known industrial family. At that very moment I decided to put my idea into practice. And so I founded the Deutsche Rettungsflugwacht.

At first I acted without the support of the government ministries and humanitarian organizations, who reacted to my initiative with skepticism. But nothing is as powerful as an idea whose time has come. After a mere two years, we were supported by 50,000 members paying a sponsorship contribution. Today there are more than 300,000. For me it was obvious from the beginning that this system, which worked so well in Switzerland, would also justify itself in Germany.

I managed to win over the president of the Swiss flying ambulance service for this huge project. By cooperating with us, the Swiss ambulance jets were able to make better use of their capacity, which, of course, was very welcome. We, in turn, were able to profit from the 25 years of experience of the Swiss. It was a win-win situation. As early as 1972, I developed one of the first alarm centers in Germany, which could be reached 24 hours a day. Today that is taken for granted; but then, more than 30 years ago, it was a great achievement in the ambulance service.

I have to admit that I am a bit proud of creating something permanent, a wonderfully helpful institution for people in difficulties. I devoted myself totally to this humanitarian project for many years, putting my commercial interests in the background. But even as the proprietor of a profit-making helicopter company, I sometimes gave myself the pleasure of providing free trips around the Alps for paraplegic patients. This social effect enriched my life enormously and brought me valuable experiences.

Later, I founded the company flyingdoctors Global Network with head offices in Hong Kong and Liechtenstein, giving it all my knowledge gained from experience in the field of flying ambulances. The brand name flyingdoctors Global Network is now protected in 40 European countries and in Japan, Russia, and Cuba, both as a text and as a logo. Exploiting these trademark rights in partnership with interested parties—an ideal one would be a major insurance company—and making use of today's opportunities for telemedicine (cardiology) are topics I want to busy myself with in the future.

I believe the key to my long-term success is that I always saw what I had achieved as nothing more than a confirmation of the path I was following. I have always been and still am a pioneer, and the same fire is still burning inside me to enter new domains and to cross boundaries. I will always have an unbroken enthusiasm for original ideas and the same willingness to take risks and enjoy adventures. The sky's the limit!

If the road to success is truly a road, then the turnoff to your particular destination may one day present itself without warning. That's when you take what you've learned so far and turn the corner in a new direction—if you're primed for the opportunity like Debbie Allen, who turned a vague desire to not continue down the same path into a flaming career. Now known as the Who's Who of Marketing Experts, she is featured in Entrepreneur, Selling Power, Sales and Marketing Excellence, *and* Franchise *magazines. Allen wrote the award winning* Confessions of Shameless Self Promotions *and other books targeted toward inspiring her audiences around the world with acute business perspectives that lead toward success.*

THEY TOLD ME I WAS CRAZY

DEBBIE ALLEN

The alarm buzzed that annoying 6 A.M. sound, just as it had every work-day for the past 14 years. As I tried to wake up, my body and mind kept telling me not to go in to work that day. That was exactly what it was, I thought. It was just work, not my true life's ambition. I had learned a lot from my family's car rental and mini-storage business, but I had the feeling it was time for me to move on. But what else could I do?

I was fortunate to have the experience of a strong family-business background. My father, a true entrepreneur, loved starting new businesses, and did just that about every six months. This taught me how to deal with growth and a lot about crisis management because, unfortunately, those new businesses eventually got dumped into my lap to run.

Because I always dealt with the last business venture's problems while Dad went on to the next, his latest brainstorm became the catalyst for my exit from the family business. This morning, Dad said, "We're going to start a port-a-potty rental business. Oh, look, they're arriving right now." I looked out the office window to see a semi full of brand-new portable toilets. At that moment, a picture flashed before my eyes. I could see myself cleaning out these houses of convenience on the weekends when my employees did not show up for work. Now I knew for sure it was time to make a career change—I did not want to become an "entre-manure."

After 14 years in the family business, I had no idea what I was going to do, but I resolved to take the next opportunity that came knocking on my door. That opportunity turned out to be a women's apparel store. But there were obstacles: the store had never turned a profit in its six years of existence, and I had never worked a day in retail. What was I going to do with a retail store? I did not know the answer to that yet. I just knew I needed a change and believed that, for some reason, this opportunity was it.

Just about everyone I knew told me I was crazy. "I don't know how you think you're going to make this work!" "You have no experience. Why would you leave a career that pays you well to do something you know nothing about?" "How do you think you're going to get a bank loan and make any money out of a losing business?" With comments like these, it's a wonder I took the risk at all.

When I thought about it, some of these comments actually made sense. Maybe I was crazy. I almost held back, but the feelings inside me were burning to get out. I was passionate about starting my own business and making a difference in people's lives. Dad had taught me well. I wanted to own *my* business. I wanted to make 100 percent of the decisions.

Unfortunately, I had to make 100 percent of the mistakes along with it. On my route to success, I had many more lessons to learn. Here are five of those strong lessons.

Lesson #1
Have an unstoppable belief system and the commitment to make it work.

I took my fears and frustration and turned them into motivation. I wanted that dream of owning my own business, and no one was going to stop me, even if it did sound crazy. It was the early '80s, and retail made sense to me. The economy was good, and small retail boutiques were all the rage. There would be no more early morning hours and no boring office work. I began to look forward to going to work every day, something I had not done for years. I vowed never to have to work another day in my life—because I believe that when you find something you truly love to do, it's no longer work. It drives you and feeds your spirit to succeed.

OK, so now I was motivated and feeding my spirit. But I also had to feed my stomach. My excitement began to dull somewhat when I realized that no money was coming into the business. I started to question myself. How was I going to turn this store around? Fortunately, my father's gift of a true entrepreneurial spirit and a strong belief system kept me headstrong and motivated to go on. I made a commitment to myself to make it work no matter what it took.

Lesson #2
Many heads are better than one. Network and build a strategic alliance of mentors, coaches, teachers, and motivating friends.

I soon discovered that a strong belief system and motivation were good, but not enough to get me past the next obstacle—to learn the business, and learn it fast.

Knock, knock! Another opportunity came my way, to join a group of networking retailers. Every retailer in this group had more than ten years of experience. I had only six months' experience at the time. They were sharing so much with me that I became a sponge for knowledge. They became my mentors, teachers, coaches, and friends. But networking is about sharing. What did I have to share with them? I did not have the knowledge, but I did have something else, something that many of them had lost over their many years in the business: enthusiasm! My enthusiasm was contagious and they wanted to catch it.

Combining the invaluable knowledge and resources I gained from networking with my enthusiasm caused my business to grow quickly. Within three short years, I had expanded my new venture from $87,000 to nearly $2 million annually. Years later, after building and successfully selling my retail stores, I was honored with the prestigious Blue Chip Enterprise Award sponsored by the National Chamber of Commerce. I was one of just a handful of business owners across the nation who had received such an award for overcoming adversity in their businesses. Those "crazy" comments quickly changed to "Debbie, you are so lucky, everything you touch turns to gold!"

Lesson #3
Luck is a residue of design. You find your own luck through the opportunities you seek and act upon.

I have learned that you can create your own luck through opportunities that come your way. If you have a true passion and commitment to making something work and continually seek more opportunities to make that happen, anything is possible! When that next big opportunity comes knocking, clanging, and banging at your door, are you going to jump up and open the door or just ignore it? You will never know if it is the right opportunity unless you take a chance.

Lesson #4

Set big, crazy, or even unrealistic goals to stretch yourself.

Back then, I did not know about goal-setting, but I did have expectations, and I exceeded my expectations many times over. Actually, if I had set goals back then, I probably would have set them too low. Because I didn't know much about the business I was in, I didn't know what I could really do. Give yourself permission to have some crazy, maybe even unrealistic, goals at times. If your goals are not a little far-fetched and even darn scary, they probably are not stretching you to your highest level of success!

Lesson #5

When you do what you love and make a difference in people's lives, you will never have to go to work *ever again.*

Today, a genie jumped out of a bottle to grant me a wish, a wish to have any career that I could dream of creating. I had to tell her to get back in that bottle because I'm already doing it. After successfully building and selling a number of retail stores, I now have the privilege of a platform. Today, I get to share my knowledge and passion for business with others as a professional speaker, consultant, coach, and author. It is another dream come true for me. And they told me I was crazy!

* • *

The lessons of success are sometimes most eloquently spoken by those who have made the long journey and had time to think about it. Be ready to listen—these heroes may be known only to ourselves and a few others, and their wisdom may be passed only to those who are paying close attention. Kirstie Bjorn, a sports psychologist and tennis professional, learned at her grandfather's knee success secrets she will pass along to her own children.

———•·•———

A LIFE OF SUCCESS YOUR OWN WAY

KIRSTIE BJORN

The most successful person I have ever known was my grandfather, Dr. George Allison Holland. He was not especially wealthy, famous, or powerful—society's three major yardsticks of success. Other pursuits and interests defined his life. Through my relationship with my grandfather I learned that success could be measured on many levels—it's about the goals we set, the dreams we pursue, and the lives we touch.

My grandfather and I had a very special bond; he was my teacher, playmate, mentor, and best friend. He taught me many things through lesson and example. His most important lesson was the way he lived a successful life by following his heart and his dreams.

He was a well-educated man, having completed formal studies in finance, theology, and medicine. He became a highly respected surgeon, ran a clinic from his home at the foot of a ski slope, and later, after professional retirement, signed on as a medical missionary with the World Health Organization. With my grandmother, he traveled the South Sea islands from one makeshift medical clinic to another, helping the islanders regain their health. He enjoyed a long and full life and passed away in his 100th year. Although many admired his longevity, Grandpa would shrug it off: "It's really quite simple—all you have to do is stay alive."

Although it's been two full years since his passing, Grandpa's spirit is very much alive. I'm still surrounded by his influence—his teachings, philosophies, jokes, and sayings. I habitually find myself using Grandpa's cussword of choice, "Cripes!" As I think back on the essence of him, I can identify five fundamental passions and foundations of his life: enrichment, imagination, contentment, words, and love of family. This was his true legacy and my blueprint for living a successful life of my own.

The first of his five passions was *enrichment*. My grandfather stressed enrichment over riches and fancied himself a student of the world. He dreamed of living a life full of experience. He lived his dream by pursuing many diverse interests, and in his leisure, he was a philosopher, humanitarian, world traveler, poet, published author, sportsman, painter, pianist, skilled game-player, teacher, club member, cook, and, indeed, a lifelong student. He felt his varied interests helped him to be a better doctor as well as a better person. At the very least, it made him a fascinating individual who could hold the attention of visitors of any age. It also made him a fantastic grandfather.

His second passion was *imagination*. Imagination was one of Grandpa's all-time favorite philosophical subjects. He believed imagination was what distinguished man from other species. For my grandfather, imagination was of paramount importance. He wrote much on the topic:

> *Imagination is the beginning of knowledge. First comes the vision.*
>
> *Imagination makes the ordinary extraordinary—under its light nothing is ordinary—like a garbage dump under moonlight. How to describe the ordinary with precision and with wonder—to realize that nothing is ordinary. There is a world of words in which everything comes to life.*

He frequently marveled at the wonder of a child's imagination. In my wedding toast, his wish for me touched my heart:

> *I trust that in the woman there remains the child whose imagination is so fresh and clean, who brings a sense of wonder from the womb. We recall the story of Jesus presenting a little child as a symbol of what is most important for the fullest life—simplicity, imagination, tolerance, and a sense of wonder.*

Grandpa himself never lost his own childlike wonder. He was colorful and imaginative throughout his life. He appeared buoyed by life in an ever-changing world. His imagination kept him fresh, young at heart, and content.

With a passion for enrichment and imagination, it follows that his third foundation of life was *contentment*. Grandpa's life defined contentment. He wrote, "The best that I could wish for us is the grace to be content—no matter what." And he was. He could sit alone for hours, with only his imagination to keep him company, and be at complete peace with himself. He was never bored; as he saw it, "There is always something to think about—in even the most humdrum day."

I truly admired his ability to be content and the way he enjoyed life for life's sake. Perhaps his own words best explain his gift for contentment and longevity:

> *Let's celebrate each day the fact of life, and, if you will, each hour and every moment.*
>
> *I have learned to believe that, indeed, each day I wake up alive is a day to celebrate.*

Words—Grandpa's fourth passion—are the common thread flowing through the first three: enrichment, imagination, and contentment. Through his love of words my grandfather preserved his own memory, leaving behind his musings, thoughts, imaginings, and philosophies in journals, scrapbooks, letters, toasts, poems, and two published volumes. He is truly alive in his writings. Many years ago I gave my grandfather a blank journal and challenged him to fill it. He accepted my challenge, and a tradition evolved. Over the years he filled five of those journals and entitled them *Words of a Grandfather*. Here is part of the dedication he wrote to me in the first volume, which captures his wonder of words:

> *The seed is the word. What I would hope to do is to encourage you into a love affair with words. Store up good words in your mind. They have magic. They will grow and make you rich all your life.*

His belief in words was so powerful that he often said, "Reading makes for a full mind but writing makes for an exact mind." Being of entirely sound mind right up to his passing, Grandpa brought life to his own words. His words were the symbols by which he lived his life.

Grandpa's fifth and final passion was *love of family*. As a true romantic and proud family man, there was nothing more important to him. "Let love be your greatest aim," he would tell us time and again. My grandfather was married for 66 years (my grandmother passed a year and a half after he did) and is survived by his five children, ten grandchildren and three great-grandchildren. He reveled in the tight bonds of family. When delivering the special toasts for which he became known, he regularly included his famous line, "Better a crust of bread where love is than a standing rib roast and hatred therewith." Family was his key to immortality. Many of his written works were dedicated to "my children and my children's children and to generations unborn, you who are my hope of everlasting life."

My grandfather's influence is manifest in his own offspring—his children and grandchildren are a living example of an enriched and successful family that includes Olympic athletes, tennis pros, physicians, business entrepreneurs, a computer animator, talented artists, a doctoral student, national-level coaches, an America's Cup champion, and many, many students of life. With his memory alive and well, his legacy shall continue with his great-grandchildren and those yet to come.

I look to Grandpa's memory as inspiration for how I want to live my own life and, more important, for how I wish to influence and inspire my own children. My grandfather lived his life based on the passions and foundations of enrichment, imagination, contentment, words, and love and family. With passion as his guide, he lived the life he wanted, and this made him a success. To quote an anonymous source: "There's only one success—to be able to spend your life in your own way."

Success is about your goals, your dreams, and the lives you influence. Grandpa knew the significance of dreams. He once told my aunt, "Dreams are precious; never, never let your dreams die." My grandfather had many dreams, including the one below, written in a love letter to my grandmother on April 12, 1935:

> *I trust that our happiness will be an always increasing one, and that our old age together will be the best of all (though I hope it will end at about 80).*

It didn't end at 80, but just shy of 100 years of age. That dream surely came true, and so did many more.

Most of what has gone before is about success as a destination. But perhaps this is misleading. Many have said, about other things, "Half the fun is getting there." Can it be that getting there is all *the fun? Michael Gerber, author of* The E-Myth Manager *and other popular business books, writes about success, spirituality, philosophy, and personal growth.*

THE FAILURE OF SUCCESS

MICHAEL E. GERBER

I've met many, many Successful people in my life. People at the top of their game. People in every imaginable endeavor: business, the arts, medicine, science, politics, education. People from every country in the world. People of every age, from their 20s to their 80s. Married people, single people, gay people, heterosexual people, men, women, divorced people, committed-to-marriage people. People of every race, every ethnicity, every political leaning, from the most lividly left to the most righteously right. There's no limit to the games these people have played or envisioned playing.

Success, I've found, fits no definable portrait or any preconceived model we might wish it to. Successful people are made up just like the rest of us—nothing different at all, other than the fact of their Success.

But, at the risk of generalization, there is something more I would like to say about the Successful people I've met:

That while on the face of it they all radiated a profound enthusiasm for what they had become Successful doing, every single one of them, without exception, given a little time and attention and interest on my part, revealed to me, without ever wishing to or, on the other hand, really, really needing to, their profound fear of losing their Success, and their profound lack of certainty that they could hold on to it.

That this thing called Success, this accomplishment of theirs—this singularly stunning thing that so markedly differentiated them from their Less Successful or Never Successful neighbors, colleagues, friends, peers, children, fathers, mothers, brothers, sisters—this very concrete thing that others could easily point to and say, "Ah, Success!": the money they made; the fame they projected; the achievements in sports, or theatre, or business, or academia, or publishing; the house they lived in; the car they drove; the fashions they surrounded themselves with, or self-consciously didn't—that this Success, to every single one of them, while satisfying in a temporal way, was never, not ever, enough.

In short, that the Successful among us can never get enough.

The money isn't plentiful enough. The joy isn't deep enough. The book isn't big enough. The applause isn't sustained enough. The relationship isn't rich enough. The ecstasy isn't long enough. The permanence isn't permanent enough. The landscape isn't imaginative enough. The garden isn't fragrant enough. And so it goes, as Kurt Vonnegut said. Life goes on, and everything ends. And along with it, the satisfaction derived from Success.

Of course, every one of you reading this knows that nothing I'm saying here is new, nor very original. I apologize for that. With this caveat: Though nothing I've just said is new or original, it's a stunning fact that no one I have ever met, Successful or not, has learned to deal with this phenomenon in a way that alters it one iota!

Oh, there are many personal development formulas and interventions—life models—out there in the world-of-the-rest-of-us, which suggests that a new model of Success is needed (and, thank God, available). The Mind-Body-Spirit Model. The Living in Balance Model. The Quality vs. Quantity Model. The Chi Gung Model. The Hatha Yoga Model. The Advaita Model. The Born-Again Christian Model. The Shiite Model. The Wrap Yourself in a Bomb Model. The Multiple Streams of Income Model. The Millionaire Next Door Model. The Rich Dad/Poor Dad Model. The E-Myth Model. The Seven Habits Model. Ad infinitum.

When you get right down to it, each and every single one of them is devoted to delivering to us this ineffable thing called Success. And yet, none of them, ever, not one of them other than the Wrap Yourself in a Bomb Model, which avoids the consequences entirely, has ever provided any of its subscribers with anything more—should Success happen, which it most often doesn't—with enough Success.

Success is never enough.

Which is why, in a book devoted to Masters of Success, I suggest that it is critical for anyone determined to become Successful, anyone who is starting out on the Road to Success, that you understand, from the very first step, that the road is endless.

That you will never, ever, ever be satisfied with where you find your-self on that road.

That the Road to Success has no end. There's only farther, beyond where you were yesterday, with no end to the walking, the eating, the questioning, the doubting, the frustration of getting a pebble in your shoe, of running out of water, of looking for your next meal, of having your next altercation with someone who is really, really pissed off at being caught unawares on the Road to Success, discovering much to his or her unenlightened distaste that he or she was duped, that Success isn't everything it's cracked up to be, having known it all the same, but having ignored what he or she knew, hoping that somehow it would be different.

You get my point?

Success isn't anything. You can't get there. You can't own it. It doesn't exist. And nothing that's nothing can give anyone anything, other than a longing for something more substantial.

———•·•———

This is the Failure of Success.
Which brings you and me to this moment.
We have arrived here successfully.
Bon voyage!

———•·•———

Conclusion

A friend of ours, Tom Harvey, once said that people today live in a "31 flavors world"—a world that is sweet and rich, colorful, exciting, tempting, and available in many flavors. It's a world that no one living 100 years ago, in a flavorless, meat-and-potatoes, day-to-day existence, could have imagined.

In the past, your choices of how to make a living were limited. You could be a farmer or a fisherman; you could move to the city and work in a factory; you could open a shop and sell goods to others; you could be a teacher or a clerk in an office; you could, if you were very ambitious or born right, be a doctor, a lawyer, a clergyman, or a banker. The world did not welcome people who thought outside the box. By comparison, today's career choices are far too numerous and varied to begin to list here.

The same holds true for opportunity of any kind. Although the means are still not always available to everybody, more people than ever have access to the resources needed to bring ideas to fruition. Want to start a new kind of business? Get on the Web, do some digging, put together that invention, round up some venture capital, and change the world. See a good way to solve a social problem? You've got a direct line to anybody on the planet whose experience and insight might help you achieve your goal.

Does this make today's world any easier to live in? Of course. People live longer, healthier, more interesting lives. But with so much choice, is it easier to choose a way to achieve success? Not necessarily. In a 31-flavors world, choice can become a roadblock.

If your options are limited, you are more likely to know exactly what you must to do make a success of your life. Is farming your only choice? Don't worry about the organic foods market; everything you grow is organic, if it survives the pests and diseases. Learn what to plant, when to cultivate, how to harvest, where to market. That's it. Mess up any of these steps, and you're no longer a farmer, you're a beggar. Are you lucky enough to inherit your father's medical practice? Forget plastic surgery, gynecology, arthroscopic laparotomy, immunology, and all the other -ologies. Just grab your small black bag, head into the night, deliver that baby, and give the fainting father a dose of salts. You do it all, to the extent that you can. No choices, no doubts, no time to dither about the direction your life has taken.

But what do you do when your universal education reveals the millions of paths available to you, the myriads of fascinating cultures, products, services, practices, treasures, and lifestyles within your reach? If you aren't a terribly decisive person, you can waste your whole life standing at the ice cream counter, trying to decide which flavor to pick, getting hungrier and growing older.

Some of the people you have read about in this book are people who have their choices made for them. Disease or serious injury can severely constrain your life choices and focus your attention on your drive to success, whether that is learning to walk again or climbing the highest mountain. Others featured in these stories, driven by something inside, have had no trouble finding their way through the mazes that baffle their fellow wanderers. Still others, tempted at first by the lure of the possible, have chosen to devote their lives to improbable goals.

All the successful people whose stories make up this book demonstrate one thing in common: they have chosen to do things other people do but to do these things in a way that nobody else does them. Whatever their objectives, they bring to their efforts passion, system, vision, leverage, and the determination to meet and overcome adversity. They know that success in all things comes from the _uncommon application of common knowledge_. This is what makes them masters of their own goals. And this is the secret that can make you a master of success. It's the one choice, before and above all others, that you and only you, must make. And so, in the end, success depends on many things, but mostly it depends on _you_.

About the Authors

IVAN R. MISNER, PH.D.

Dr. Ivan Misner is the founder and CEO of BNI (Business Network International), the largest business networking organization in the world. Founded in 1985, BNI now has thousands of chapters throughout North America, Europe, Australia, Asia, and Africa. Each year, BNI generates millions of referrals resulting in billions of dollars worth of business for its members.

Dr. Misner's Ph.D. is from the University of Southern California. He has written seven books, including his *New York Times* bestseller, *Masters of Networking*. He is a monthly contributor to the Expert Section of Entrepreneur.com and serves on the faculty of business at Cal Poly University, Pomona, as well as the board of directors for the Colorado School of Professional Psychology.

Called the "Networking Guru" by *Entrepreneur* magazine, Dr. Misner is a keynote speaker for major corporations and associations throughout the world. He has been featured in the *Wall Street Journal, Los Angeles Times, New York Times, CEO Magazine,* and numerous TV and radio shows, including appearances on CNBC and the BBC in London. In addition, Dr. Misner has twice been nominated for *Inc.* magazine's "Entrepreneur of the Year Award."

Dr. Misner is on the board of directors for the Haynes Children Center and is the founder of the BNI-Misner Charitable Foundation. He is married and lives with his wife, Elisabeth, and their three children in Claremont, CA. *In his spare time!* . . . he is also an amateur magician and a black belt in karate.

Dr. Misner can be reached at misner@bni.com.

DON MORGAN, M.A.

Don Morgan, M.A., has a professional career spanning almost four decades. Don's experience is varied and well rounded and includes positions as a psychotherapist, organizational consultant, educator, entrepreneur, and author. After helping many others establish their own businesses in health care, retail, and service industries, he expanded his own entrepreneurial reach with his marine dealership, a consulting and direct marketing

company, and—more recently—BNI Canada and BNI Northern Illinois.

As a community leader, Morgan received honorary recognition from the Ontario Ministry of Health (Canada) for his contribution to health-care planning. He received a masters degree in community mental health and taught at the University of Western Ontario and several colleges in Ontario, Canada. Part of his unique perspective comes from living and working in the United States, Canada, and Europe.

Morgan's many writing projects are well respected, including *Masters of Networking*, which is an international bestselling book.

Within eight years, Don and his wife, Nancy Holland Morgan, a past Olympic skier, developed a network of more than 300 business referral marketing groups across Canada and the United States, coordinated through their offices in Toronto, Vancouver, and Chicago. Don and Nancy have four grown children and live in Vancouver, British Columbia, and Telluride, Colorado, where they enjoy both sailing and mountain sports.

Don Morgan may be contacted through e-mail: Morgan@bnicanada.ca

ABOUT BNI

Business Network International (BNI) was founded by Dr. Ivan Misner in 1985 as a way for businesspeople to generate referrals in a structured, professional environment. The organization, now the world's largest referral network, has tens of thousands of members on almost every continent of the world. Since its inception, members of BNI have passed millions of referrals, generating billions of dollars for the participants.

The primary purpose of the organization is to pass qualified business referrals to the members. The philosophy of BNI may be summed up in two simple words: "Givers gain." If you give business to people, you will get

business from them. BNI allows only one person per profession to join a chapter. The program is designed for businesspeople to develop long-term relationships, thereby creating a basis for trust and, inevitably, referrals. The mission of the organization is to teach business professionals that the word-of-mouth process is more about farming than hunting: it's about the cultivation of professional relationships in a structured business environment for the mutual benefit of all.

You can contact BNI on the Internet at bni@bni.com or visit its Web sites at www.bni.com and www.MastersofSuccess.biz.

Index